W9-DIB-201

MADRID

THE MINI ROUGH GUIDE

There are more than one hundred Rough
Guide travel, phrasebook, and music titles,
covering destinations from Amsterdam to
Zimbabwe, languages from Czech to Thai,
and musics from World to Opera and Jazz

Forthcoming titles include

Bangkok • Barbados • Japan
Jordan • Syria • Music USA
Country Music

Rough Guides on the Internet

http://www.roughguides.com

Rough Guide Credits

Text editor: Jo Mead. Series editor: Mark Ellingham
Typesetting: Andy Hilliard, Link Hall, Helen Ostick
Cartography: Maxine Burke, Sam Kirby

Publishing Information

This first edition published February 1998 by
Rough Guides Ltd, 1 Mercer St, London WC2H 9QJ.

Distributed by the Penguin Group:
Penguin Books Ltd, 27 Wrights Lane, London W8 5TZ
Penguin Books USA Inc., 375 Hudson Street, New York 10014, USA
Penguin Books Australia Ltd, 487 Maroondah Highway,
PO Box 257, Ringwood, Victoria 3134, Australia
Penguin Books Canada Ltd, 10 Alcorn Avenue,
Toronto, Ontario, Canada M4V 1E4
Penguin Books (NZ) Ltd, 182–190 Wairau Road,
Auckland 10, New Zealand

Typeset in Bembo and Helvetica to an original design by Henry Iles.
Printed in Spain by Graphy Cems.

© Simon Baskett. 304pp, includes index
A catalogue record for this book is available from the British Library.
ISBN 1-85828-353-1

MADRID

THE MINI ROUGH GUIDE

by Simon Baskett

We set out to do something different when the first Rough Guide was published in 1982. Mark Ellingham, just out of university, was travelling in Greece. He brought along the popular guides of the day, but found they were all lacking in some way. They were either strong on ruins and museums but went on for pages without mentioning a beach or taverna. Or they were so conscious of the need to save money that they lost sight of Greece's cultural and historical significance. Also, none of the books told him anything about Greece's contemporary life – its politics, its culture, its people, and how they lived.

So with no job in prospect, Mark decided to write his own guidebook, one which aimed to provide practical information that was second to none, detailing the best beaches and the hottest clubs and restaurants, while also giving hard-hitting accounts of every sight, both famous and obscure, and providing up-to-the-minute information on contemporary culture. It was a guide that encouraged independent travellers to find the best of Greece, and was a great success, getting shortlisted for the Thomas Cook travel guide award, and encouraging Mark, along with three friends, to expand the series.

The Rough Guide list grew rapidly and the letters flooded in, indicating a much broader readership than had been anticipated, but one which uniformly appreciated the Rough Guide mix of practical detail and humour, irreverence and enthusiasm. Things haven't changed. The same four friends who began the series are still the caretakers of the Rough Guide mission today: to provide the most reliable, up-to-date and entertaining information to independent-minded travellers of all ages, on all budgets.

We now publish more than 100 titles and have offices in London and New York. The travel guides are written and researched by a dedicated team of more than 100 authors, based in Britain, Europe, the USA and Australia. We have also created a unique series of phrasebooks to accompany the travel series, along with an acclaimed series of music guides, and a best-selling pocket guide to the Internet and World Wide Web. We also publish comprehensive travel information on our web site: **http://www.roughguides.com**

Help Us Update

We've gone to a lot of effort to ensure that this first edition of *The Rough Guide to Madrid* is as up to date and accurate as possible. However, if you feel there are places we've under-rated or over-praised, or find we've missed something good or covered something which has now gone, then please write: suggestions, comments or corrections are much appreciated.

We'll credit all contributions, and send a copy of the next edition (or any other Rough Guide if you prefer) for the best letters. Please mark letters: "Rough Guide Madrid Update" and send to:

Rough Guides, 1 Mercer St, London WC2H 9QJ, or
Rough Guides, 375 Hudson St, 9th floor, New York NY 10014.
Or send email to: mail@roughguides.co.uk

Online updates about this book can be found on
Rough Guides' Web site (see opposite)

The Author

Simon Baskett lives and works in Madrid and is married to a *Madrileña*, Trini. He is a long-suffering Atlético Madrid fan and is currently busy conducting in-depth research into how to win the Spanish Fantasy Football League – the Liga Fantástica. His ambition is to win El Gordo (the huge Christmas lottery) and retire to a local bar.

Acknowledgements

Special thanks to Trini for all her hard work and patience. Thanks, too, go to James, Penny, Santiago, Rocio, Virginia, Fernando, Mairi, Conchi, Roger, Bibi, Arturo and Adam. Thanks also to Jo and Jonathan for all their hard work and expert advice (thank goodness for emails).

CONTENTS

CONTENTS

INTRODUCTION

Madrid became Spain's capital city at the whim of one man, **Felipe II**. Its site possesses few natural advantages – a fierce climate, no harbour and a pretty poor excuse for a river – but it lies exactly in the centre of Spain. In 1561, Felipe decided to base the formerly itinerant court here to avoid giving too much power and status to any one region in the recently unified Spain. In Madrid he created a symbol of the unification and centralization of the country, and a capital from which he could receive the fastest post and communications from each corner of the nation. However, it was only the determination of successive rulers to promote a strong central capital that ensured the city's survival and development.

Today Madrid is a large, predominantly modern city, with a population of some four million and a highly schizophrenic character. There are, in effect, two cities: "Madrid by day" and "Madrid by night"; the capital is freezing in winter, burning in summer; outwardly flamboyant, yet inwardly conservative; seemingly affluent, yet concealing serious levels of poverty. The highest, sunniest and greenest capital city in Europe – despite being choked with traffic and people – its inhabitants, the **Madrileños** modestly declare, "*Desde Madrid al Cielo*": that after Madrid there is only one destination left – Heaven.

Largely a city of immigrants, it is difficult to find a person whose real roots are in Madrid, apart from the *castizos* who proudly exhibit their *Madrileño* heritage during the *San Isidro* festival and the summer *verbenas* (street fairs). As a consequence, the city is a mosaic of traditions, cultures and cuisines. As you get to grips with the place you soon realize that it is the *Madrileños* themselves that are the capital's key attraction: hanging out in the cafés or the summer *terrazas*, packing the lanes of the Rastro flea market, or playing hard and very, very late in a thousand bars, clubs and discos.

Madrileños consider the **nightlife** of other European cities positively dull by comparison; for them enjoying themselves is a right not a luxury. Much of their everyday life is acted out in the streets of Madrid outside their rather small houses or apartments. They dress up whenever possible, never wanting to be seen at anything but their best. They are noisy – horns blare, TVs are set at full blast and conversations are conducted at top volume. Whatever Barcelona might claim, the Madrid scene, immortalized in the movies of Pedro Almodóvar, remains the most vibrant in the country.

Despite its recent rapid growth, Madrid still seems small for a capital city. It is strikingly compact, yet each *barrio* still manages to retain its own individual identity. However, the city can no longer be accused of provincialism, for it has changed immeasurably in the two decades since Franco died, guided by a poet-mayor, the late and much-lamented **Tierno Galván**. His efforts, including the creation of parks and the renovation of public spaces and public life, have left an enduring legacy, and were a vital ingredient of the **movida Madrileña**, the "happening Madrid", with which the city made its mark in the 1980s. The *movida* may have gone but Madrid has survived as a stylish city highly conscious of its image and in better shape than for many years, after an $800m refurbishment for its role as 1992

European Capital of Culture and the continuing urban regeneration programmes by the active local authority.

As a tourist destination, Madrid has been greatly underrated. By comparison with the historic cities of Spain – Toledo, Salamanca, Sevilla, Granada – there may be few sites of outstanding architectural interest, but the monarchs did acquire superlative picture collections, which form the basis of the **Prado** museum. This has long ensured Madrid a place on the European art-tour, and the more so since the 1990s' arrival – literally down the street – of the **Reina Sofía** and **Thyssen-Bornemisza** galleries, state-of-the-art homes to fabulous arrays of modern Spanish painting (including Picasso's *Guernica*) and European and American masters.

When to visit

Traditionally Madrid has experienced a typical continental climate, cold and dry in winter and hot and dry in summer. There are usually two rainy periods, in November and March/April. With soaring temperatures in July and August, the best times to visit are often spring and autumn, when the city is pleasantly warm. In recent years, however, the weather has become more unpredictable and there have been hot periods in spring and autumn while summer temperatures have dropped.

Madrid virtually shuts down in the **summer**; from around July 20 you'll suddenly find half the bars, restaurants and offices closed, and their inhabitants gone to the coast and countryside. Not until September does the city properly open for business again.

Luckily for visitors, and those *Madrileños* who choose to remain, sights and museums stay open and summer nightlife takes on a momentum of its own. In addition, the city council has initiated a major programme of summer entertainment. All in all, it's not a bad time to be in town, as long as you're not trying to get anything done.

Madrid's climate

	°F Average daily		°C Average daily		Rainfall Average monthly	
	max	min	max	min	in	mm
Jan	47	35	9	2	1.5	39
Feb	52	36	11	2	1.3	34
March	59	41	15	5	1.7	43
April	65	45	18	7	1.9	48
May	70	50	21	10	1.9	47
June	80	58	27	15	1.0	27
July	87	63	31	17	0.4	11
Aug	85	63	30	17	0.6	15
Sept	77	57	25	14	1.3	32
Oct	65	49	19	10	2.1	53
Nov	55	42	13	5	1.9	47
Dec	48	36	9	2	1.9	48

THE GUIDE

INTRODUCING THE CITY

T he city's layout is pretty straightforward. At the heart of Madrid is the **Puerta del Sol** and around it lie the oldest parts of Madrid, neatly bordered to the west by the **Río Manzanares**, to the east by the park of **El Retiro**, and to the north by the city's great thoroughfare, the **Gran Vía**.

Within this very compact area, you're likely to spend most of your time. The city's three big museums – the **Prado**, **Thyssen-Bornemisza** and **Reina Sofía** – lie in a "golden triangle" just west of El Retiro along the **Paseo del Prado**, while over towards the river are the oldest, Habsburg parts of town, centred on the beautiful arcaded **Plaza Mayor**. After Gran Vía, the most important streets (*calles* – abbreviated as c/) are **c/de Alcalá** and its continuation, **c/Mayor** – which cut right through the centre from the main post office at **Plaza de la Cibeles** to the Bourbon **Palacio Real** – and the long south–north boulevard beginning as the elegant Paseo del Prado and finishing up as the multi-lane **Paseo de la Castellana**. Although there is plenty of nightlife in the city centre, especially around **Plaza de Santa Ana** and **Huertas**, you may well find yourself venturing further north to the *barrios* of **Chueca** and **Malasaña** for the hippest bars and clubs.

Beyond the city centre, within a radius of 100km – and within an hour's travel by train or bus – are some of the greatest cities of Spain. Above all there is **Toledo**, immortalized by El Greco, which preceded Madrid as the Spanish capital, but other excellent day-trips include: **Segovia**, with its stunning Roman aqueduct; Felipe II's vast palace-mausoleum of **El Escorial**; **Aranjuez**, an oasis in the parched Castilian plain famed for its strawberries and lavish Baroque palace; and the beautiful walled city of **Ávila**, birthplace of Santa Teresa.

....

The telephone code for Madrid is ☎91.

....

Arrival

International **air**, **train** and **bus** arrival points are all some way from the centre. Transport into the city, however, is relatively easy and efficient. If you are **driving**, be prepared for a long trawl around the streets to find parking, or – a lot safer – put your car in one of the many signposted *parkings*. If you're staying more than a couple of weeks, you can get long-term parking rates if you ask at neighbourhood garages.

By air

The **Aeropuerto de Barajas** is 16km east of the city, at the end of Avenida de América; it has two terminals, one for *vuelos internacionales*, the other for *nacionales* (domestic services). The journey time into central Madrid is highly variable, depending on rush-hour traffic, and can take anything from twenty minutes to an hour.

A shuttle bus leaves from outside the arrivals terminal every ten to fifteen minutes (daily 5.15am–2am; 370ptas) and drops you at an underground terminal in the central Plaza de Colón (pedestrian entrance from the c/de Goya). If your plane arrives outside these times, there should be additional connecting bus services. **Taxis** are always available and cost around 2300ptas into the centre, assuming you don't get stuck in traffic. Supplements are charged for baggage, for going outside the city limits (which includes the airport) and for night-trips (11pm–6am).

Half a dozen or so **car rental** companies have stands at the airport, and there's also a 24-hour currency exchange, a post office, a RENFE office for booking train tickets (daily 8am–9pm), a tourist office and hotel reservations desk.

By train

Trains from France and north/northeast Spain arrive at the **Estación de Chamartín**, a modern terminal isolated in the north of the city. It has all the usual big station facilities, including currency exchange. A metro line connects Chamartín with the centre, and there are regular connections on the commuter train line *(cercanías)* with the much more central Estación de Atocha.

The **Estación de Atocha**, recently expanded and imaginatively remodelled, has two separate terminals: one for Toledo and other local services, the other for all points in southern and eastern Spain, including the high-speed AVE trains.

If you're coming from local towns around Madrid, you may arrive at the **Estación del Norte** (aka Príncipe Pío), fairly close to the centre near the Palacio Real.

ARRIVAL: BY TRAIN

By bus

Bus terminals are scattered throughout the city, but the largest – used by all of the international bus services – is the **Estación Sur de Autobuses**, recently relocated on c/Méndez Alvaro at the corner of c/Retama (Metro Méndez Alvaro), south of Atocha train station. For details of others, see *Directory* (p.233).

By car

All the main roads into Madrid bring you right into the city centre, although eccentric signposting and even more eccentric driving can be very unnerving. The inner ring road, the M30, and the Castellana are notorious bottle-necks, although virtually the whole city centre can be close to gridlock during the peak rush-hour periods (Mon–Fri 7.30–9.30am & 6–8.30pm).

It's advisable to find a hotel with a car park and keep it there during your stay in the city. Your own transport is really only of use for out-of-town excursions.

Information and maps

There are year-round **Turismo** offices at the following loca-tions: Barajas International Airport (Mon–Fri 8am–8pm, Sat 9am–1pm; ☎305 86 56); Estación de Chamartín (Mon–Fri 8am–8pm, Sat 9am–1pm; ☎315 99 76); Plaza Mayor 3 (Mon–Fri 10am–8pm, Sat 10am–2pm; ☎588 16 36); Mercado Puerta de Toledo, Ronda de Toledo 1 (Mon–Fri 9am–7pm, Sat 9.30am–1.30pm; ☎364 18 76); and c/Duque de Medinaceli 2 (Mon–Fri 9am–7pm, Sat 9am–1pm; ☎429 49 51).

In **summer**, Turismo posts operate at popular tourist spots such as the Puerta del Sol and the Prado, and there are

guides (in blue and yellow uniforms) on call outside the Palacio Real, Ayuntamiento and the Prado, and in the Plaza Mayor and Puerta del Sol. Estacíon de Atocha also has an information kiosk with a hotel reservations service. You can **phone for information** on ℂ001 300 600 and ℂ010 (English spoken).

Listings information is in plentiful supply in Madrid. The newspapers *El País* and *El Mundo* have excellent daily listings, and on Friday both publish sections devoted to events, bars and restaurants in the capital. If your time in Madrid doesn't coincide with the Friday supplements, or you want a full rundown, pick up the weekly listings magazine *Guía del Ocio* (125ptas) at any kiosk. The Ayuntamiento also publishes a monthly "What's On" pamphlet, *En Madrid*, free from any of the tourist offices. In addition, there's a telephone listings service in English on ℂ481 12 48. Finally, *In Madrid* is a free monthly magazine available in many bars, which bills itself as "Madrid's English monthly for the Hip, Cool and Transient" and features useful reviews of clubs and bars.

One word that might perplex first-timers in Madrid – and which crops up in all the listings magazines – is **madrugada**. This refers to the hours between midnight and dawn and, in this supremely late-night/early-morning city, is a necessary adjunct to announcements of important events. "*Tres de la madrugada*" means an event is due to start at 3am.

Free **map**s of Madrid are available from any of the Turismos detailed above. However, if you intend to do more than just a day's sightseeing, you would be well advised to invest in the *Almax Madrid Centro* map (300ptas), available from just about any kiosk in the city. This is very clear, 1:10,000 in scale, fully street-indexed, and has a colour plan of the metro on the reverse.

INFORMATION AND MAPS

MADRID ON THE INTERNET

The Useful Guide to Madrid
http://malika.iem.csic.es/~grant/modi.html
The best index of Madrid-related sites from museums,
tourist attractions and fiestas to sport and education.

Ole !
http://www.ole.es/
Popular search engine, giving access to most Spanish sites.

Spanish Tourist Office
http://www.spaintour.com/madrid/htm
Straightforward tourist information on the city.

The Madrid City Council
http://www.munimadrid.es/
The city council's official site is available in English, and
appears promising, but as yet the information is limited.

The British Council
http://www.britcoun.org/spain/spnbsic.htm
Useful information if you're thinking of teaching English,
and for more on the council's activities in Madrid.

The Pink 'Un
http://ourworld.compuserve.com/homepages/robraabe/
Homepage for the English five-a-side league in Madrid
and a good introduction to the British pub scene.

Atlético Madrid
http://www.aulatec.es/atletico/index2.html
Spanish-language official site for *Los Colchoneros*.
Everything from history and fixtures to the club song
and videos.

City transport

Madrid is a pretty easy city to get around. The central areas are walkable, the metro is modern and efficient, buses serve out-of-the-way districts, and taxis are always available.

If you're using public transport extensively and staying long-term, monthly **passes** or *abonos* (which cover metro, train and bus) are worthwhile. They must be ordered before the calendar month in question and put into service before the tenth of that month. If you have an InterRail or Eurail pass, you can use the RENFE urban and suburban trains (*cercanías*) free of charge – they're an alternative to the metro for some longer city journeys.

SIGHTSEEING TOURS

Several companies offer daily bus tours of the main sights in Madrid, which are worthwhile if your time is limited. Full details from the Municipal Tourist Board, c/Mayor 69 (✆588 29 06).

Madrid Vision, c/San Bernardo 23 (Metro Noviciado; ✆541 63 20 or 302 45 26). Bus tours of all the major city sights. Tickets cost 2000ptas and you can get on and off as many times as you like.

Juliá Tours, Gran Vía 68 (Metro Santo Domingo; ✆559 96 05). Day-trips to the cities surrounding Madrid. Prices start from 3000ptas.

Pullmantur, Plaza de Oriente 8 (Metro Opera; ✆541 18 05). Guided tours of Toledo, Segovia and Aranjuez.

CITY TRANSPORT & SIGHTSEEING TOURS

The metro

The **metro** is by far the quickest way of getting around Madrid and the system serves most places you're likely to want to get to. It runs daily from 6am until 1.30am and the flat fare is 130ptas for any journey, or 670ptas for a ten-trip ticket (*bono de diez viajes*). Lines are colour-coded and the direction of travel is indicated by the name of the terminus station. Extension of the existing network is at present underway and some alterations to routes and station closures may occur up to the end of 1999.

See colour map 10 for a plan of the metro.

Buses

The urban **bus network** is comprehensive but fairly complicated. Bus stops show the numbers of the buses that stop there along with details of the other stops on the route. There are information booths in the Plaza de la Cibeles, Plaza de Callao and Puerta del Sol, which dispense a huge route map (*plano de los transportes de Madrid*) and, along with other outlets, sell bus passes. Fares are the same as for the metro, at 130ptas a journey, payable on the bus, or 670ptas for a ten-trip ticket. It's also worth checking to see if the planned combined metro and bus ten-trip ticket is in operation yet. When you get on the bus, you punch your ticket in the machine by the driver.

Buses run daily from 6am to midnight. In addition, there are several **all-night** lines around the central area and out to the suburbs departing from Plaza de la Cibeles and Puerta del Sol: departures are half-hourly 12.30am–2am, hourly 2–6am.

THE METRO & BUSES

USEFUL BUS ROUTES

#2 From west to east across town: Argüelles metro station along c/de la Princesa, past Plaza de España, along Gran Vía, past Cibeles and out past the Retiro.

#3 From south to north: Puerta de Toledo, through Sol, up towards Gran Vía and then Alonso Martínez and northwards.

#5 From Sol via Cibeles, Colón and the Paseo de la Castellana to Chamartín.

#27 From Embajadores, via Atocha, up the length of the Castellana to Plaza de Castilla.

#33 From Príncipe Pío out via the Puente de Segovia to the Parque de Atracciones and Zoo in Casa de Campo.

#C The Circular bus route takes a broad circuit round the city from Atocha, via Puerta de Toledo, Plaza de España, Moncloa, Cuatro Caminos, Avenida de América and Goya.

Taxis

One of the best things about Madrid is that there are thousands of **taxis** – white cars with a diagonal red stripe on the side – and they're reasonably cheap; 700ptas will get you to most places within the centre and, although it's common to round up the fare, you're not expected to tip. In any area in the centre, day and night, you should be able to wave down a taxi (available ones have a green light on top of the cab) in a couple of minutes. To phone for a taxi, call ©547 82 00, ©447 51 80, ©405 12 13 or ©445 90 08.

USEFUL BUS ROUTES & TAXIS

11

PLAZA MAYOR
AND LA LATINA

Madrid under the Habsburgs was a mix of formal planning – at its most impressive in the expansive and theatrical **Plaza Mayor** – and areas of shanty-town development, knocked up in the sixteenth century as the new capital gained an urban population. The central area of old Madrid still reflects both characteristics, with its Flemish-inspired architecture of red brick and grey stone, slate-tiled towers and Renaissance doorways set in a twisting grid of streets, alleyways and steps. In fact, the layout of this area has changed little since the Middle Ages, and although there are few traces of the original buildings, you can still spend an enjoyable day exploring the remains of the old city. Most tourists head straight for the Plaza Mayor and leave it at that, but there are other appealing sights scattered throughout the area especially in the characterful *barrio* of **La Latina** which stretches south of the square. The delightful **Plaza de la Villa**, with its amalgam of architectural styles, the Baroque excesses of the **Basílica de San Miguel** and the **Capilla de San Isidro** and the decayed splendour of **San Francisco el Grande** are all worth seeking out, as are the culinary delights of the *mesones* (taverns) and tapas bars in and around **Cava Baja**.

....

**The area covered by this chapter is shown
in detail on colour map 4.**

....

PLAZA MAYOR AND AROUND

Map 4, G2. Metro Sol.

The grand **Plaza Mayor** was originally the brainchild of Felipe II, who wanted to construct a more prestigious focus for his new capital of Madrid. The **Casa de la Panadería**, on the north side of the square, is the oldest building, begun in 1590. Once housing the city bakers and bakers' guild, it later became a palace. The original building has been almost completely rebuilt as it and much of the rest of the square was damaged by the many fires that occurred in the plaza in the seventeenth and eighteenth centuries. Its main facade features a balcony from which the royals could watch proceedings below and is decorated with recently repainted frescoes. The real work on the plaza did not get off the ground until the reign of Felipe III, but the city architect, **Juan Gómez de Mora**, made light work of it and finished it in just two years in 1619. Capable of holding up to fifty thousand people, the square was used for state occasions, autos-da-fé, executions, jousts, plays and bullfights. The Italian-designed **bronze equestrian statue** in the middle of the plaza is of Felipe III. Dated 1616, it was originally sited in the Casa de Campo (see p.108) and only moved to its present position in 1847.

Today, Plaza Mayor is primarily a tourist haunt, full of outdoor cafés and restaurants that advertise themselves as "typical Spanish" – best stick to a drink here. However, an air of grandeur clings to the place and the plaza still performs public functions. In the summer months it becomes an outdoor theatre and music stage; in the autumn there's a book fair; and in the winter, around Christmas, it becomes a bazaar for festive decorations, site of one of the largest *belenes* (cribs) and home to stalls selling all kinds of practical joke material for Spain's equivalent of April Fool's day, *El Día de Los Santos Inocentes* on December 28. Every Sunday, too, stamp and coin collectors convene here to talk philately and rummage through boxes of rare coins in the open-air market. On the whole, though, unless you're a fan of tacky souvenir shops and caricature artists, you'll find more of real interest in the areas surrounding the square.

Around Plaza Mayor

Just to the east on **Plaza Provincia**, the design of the **Palacio de Santa Cruz** echoes that of the Plaza Mayor and may also be the work of Juan Gómez de Mora. It was built between 1629 and 1639, was once the city prison and now houses the Ministry of Foreign Affairs.

Calle Postas, a fascinating street linking the northeastern corner of Plaza Mayor with Puerta del Sol, has a selection of good-value bars and weird shops selling all manner of religious articles, from models of the baby Jesus, rosary beads and icons to dog collars and habits.

Over on the west side of the square, **Cava San Miguel** used to be the ditch of the twelfth-century city wall and still retains an ancient feel, lined by towering seventeenth-century houses, whose facades have recently been restored. To the southwest of Plaza Mayor, down the steps by the bar *El Pulpito*, you'll find one of Madrid's more famous institutions, **Botín** at c/Cuchilleros 17, serving classic Castilian fare in traditional surroundings. Mentioned in Galdós' novel, *Fortunata y Jacinta*, and in the *Guinness Book of Records* as the oldest restaurant in Europe, its other claim to fame is that the 19-year-old Goya worked here washing dishes. In typically understated fashion Hemingway merely described it as the "best restaurant in the world".

....
For more on Botín see p.140.
....

In this and the other *mesones* you'll no doubt be serenaded by passing **tunas** – musicians and singers dressed in knickerbockers and waistcoats who wander around town playing and passing the hat. These men-only troupes are attached to various faculties of the university and are a means for students of supplementing their grants.

Finally, leading south from the square down to San Isidro (see p.22), **c/de Toledo** has a host of idiosyncratic little shops, specializing in fortress-like corsetry and hairpins. Casa Hernanz, at no. 81, is a must if you're a fan of espadrilles. The king reputedly buys his here and you can purchase models of every description with prices ranging from 900 to 3000ptas.

CALLE MAYOR

North of Plaza Mayor, **c/Mayor** is one of the most ancient thoroughfares in the city, along which religious processions from the Palacio Real to the Monasterio de Los Jerónimos have passed for centuries. The street is home to a whole host of intriguing little shops and bars and is flanked by the facades of some of the most beautiful and evocative buildings in the city whose grimy exteriors conceal an array of treasures. Heading west from the entrance to Plaza Mayor, you'll soon pass the decorative ironwork of the **Mercado de San Miguel**, built in 1916. Magnificent

CALLE MAYOR

turn-of-the-century apartment blocks are swathed in wrought-iron balconies, their brooding facades lightened by splashes of colour from flowering geraniums. Further along, it's worth pausing at the gloriously antiquated **Farmacia de La Reina Madre**, at no. 59 where, according to legend, Isabel de Farnese, second wife of Felipe V, preferred to purchase her medicines rather than in the royal pharmacy in the palace because she feared being poisoned by her stepson Fernando VI. The decoration dates from 1914 and inside are over three hundred sixteenth- and seventeenth-century ceramic and glass jars. The highlight of this section of the street is the **Plaza de la Villa**, but it's worth stopping off at no. 84, the **Casa Ciriaco**, for a wine or a coffee. A favourite meeting place for the intelligentsia, politicians and bullfighters, there's plenty of memorabilia inside, detailing the colourful history of the building, in particular the notorious attack on the royal wedding procession of Alfonso XIII and his English bride, Victoria Eugenie, in 1906. A bomb secreted in a bunch of flowers was thrown from one of the second-floor balconies, killing 23 onlookers, but leaving the royal couple unscathed. The assassin, Mateo Morral, was executed a few days later and a bronze angel commemorating the victims can be seen on the opposite side of the street in front of the Iglesia Arzobispal Castrense. To the north, up c/San Nicolás, stands the oldest surviving church in Madrid, **San Nicolás de los Servitas** (Mon 8.30am–1.30pm & 5.30–8.30pm), with its twelfth-century Mudéjar tower featuring Arabic horseshoe arches. The rest of the church was rebuilt between the fifteenth and seventeenth centuries and houses a very small, but interesting display on the history of Muslim Madrid. Continuing on along c/Mayor you'll pass the **Italian Institute of Culture** on the right. It stands on the site of the house of the Princess of Eboli where Juan de

Escobedo, John of Austria's Secretary, was murdered by three assassins in March 1578, a murder in which King Felipe II himself was implicated. Opposite is the grand **Palacio de Uceda**, originally built by one of the favourites of Felipe III in the early seventeenth century and now home to the Capitanía General (Military Headquarters), while on the corner of the busy c/Bailén, the wonderful music shop crammed full of ancient musical instruments and accessories is worth a look.

PLAZA DE LA VILLA AND AROUND

Map 4, E2. Metro Sol.

Plaza de la Villa is the oldest square in the city and is a perfect example of three centuries of Spanish architectural development. Originally the old market square of Muslim and medieval Madrid, today the centre is marked by a statue of the Marquis of Santa Cruz, an admiral under Felipe II and hero of the great naval battle of Lepanto in 1571. The battle involved over 100,000 men with the Spanish navy vanquishing the Turks off the coast of Greece much to the relief and joy of Christendom. Ironically it only served to spur the Turks into building an even mightier fleet soon afterwards.

The oldest ensemble of surviving buildings is the simple but eye-catching fifteenth-century **Torre y Casa de Los Lujanes**, where Francis I is said to have been imprisoned in 1525 after his capture at the Battle of Pavia. Although substantially restored, you can see the fine Mudéjar tower, the characteristic arched doorway and the original coat of arms of its owners, the powerful Lujanes family. On the southern side of the square is the **Casa de Cisneros**, constructed for the nephew of the celebrated Cardinal (Inquisitor-General 1507–1517 and Regent of Spain after Fernando's death in 1516) in the sixteenth-century Plateresque style, a style of architecture and sculpture that incorporated the intricate techniques of silversmiths or *plateros*. The building was acquired by the Ayuntamiento (Council) of Madrid in 1909 and was extensively remodelled by Luis Bellido. It now houses the Mayor of Madrid's offices.

The Casa de la Villa

The west side of the square is taken up by the **Casa de la Villa** (tours at 5pm every Mon), one of the most important, emblematic buildings of Habsburg Madrid. It was constructed in fits and starts from the mid-seventeenth century in order to house the offices and records of the council which had outgrown their previous home in the church of San Salvador. The initial design was by **Juan Gómez de Mora**, but the construction wasn't completed until 1693, 45 years after his death, and has been mellowed by the addition of Baroque details in the late eighteenth century.

The weekly tour is well worth it if you're here during one of the quieter periods, but if there are more than fifty people in the group, you'll see very little as you're herded through the the lavish municipal interior. The **Salón de Goya** contains a copy of Goya's *Allegory of Madrid* – the original being in the Museo Municipal (see p.93) – a testament to the turbulent political history Madrid experienced in the nineteenth century. The painting underwent no less than seven alterations in order to satisfy the sensibilities of the various rulers of Madrid during this period and the final version shows the story of "*Dos de Mayo*" commemorating the heroic resistance of the city against the French in 1808 (see *Contexts*, p.272). Also here is the monumental canvas by Palmorli, *The Morning of May 3rd*, in which you can see the dawn panorama of Madrid featuring the Palacio Real and the dome of San Francisco El Grande. The **Patio** de Los Cristales contains a stunning stained-glass roof depicting some of the most celebrated city sights and houses busts of famous *Madrileño* writers, painters and playwrights including Tirso de Molina, Lope de Vega, Claudio Coello and Quevedo. The highlight of the tour is the **Salón de Plenos** or Assembly Room, where meetings of the council still take place. The chamber is lavishly decorated, dripping with gold leaf and burgundy velvet curtains, red leather benches and frescoes by Antonio Palomino.

The Convento de Las Carboneras and the Basílica de San Miguel

Next to the Torre de los Lujanes a small alleyway, c/del Codo (Elbow Street), leads out of the square down to c/Sacramento. On the right as you walk down, an unassuming wooden door hides the **Convento de Las Carboneras**. The convent was founded in the early seventeenth century and belongs to the closed Hieronymite Order. The name itself originates from a painting of the virgin found in a coal bunker and donated to the convent. The convent also makes and sells its own cakes – a tradition that has existed in Spanish convents since the time of St Teresa of Avila who gave out sweetened egg yolks to the poor of her city. The cakes can be purchased every day 9.30am–1pm and 4–6pm. Ring the bell and you will be let in; the business takes place by means of a revolving drum so that the closed nature of the order is not violated.

At the end of the alleyway you reach the **Basílica de San Miguel** on **c/Sacramento**, a beautiful, well-preserved and quiet street crowded with municipal buildings. The church itself was designed at the end of the seventeenth century for Don Luis, the precocious five-year-old Archbishop of Toledo and youngest son of Felipe V. It's one of the few examples of a fully blown Baroque church in Madrid, showing the unbridled imagination of Italian architect, Santiago Bonaviá. It features an unconventional convex facade with four recesses each containing a statue, variously representing Charity, Strength, Faith and Hope.

LA LATINA

Immediately to the south of c/Sacramento is the **Plaza de la Cruz Verde**, one of the sites of the notorious autos-da-fé and executions organized by the Inquisition. From here the Costanilla de San Andrés leads up into the old Muslim quarter, **La Morería**. Keep an eye out on your left for the Mudéjar tower of the second oldest church in Madrid, **San Pedro El Viejo** (daily 6–8pm), said to have been founded in the fourteenth century by Alfonso XI on the site occupied by the old mosque, although the rest of the church was largely rebuilt in the seventeenth century. At the end of the Costanilla you'll reach one of the real gems of old Madrid, the **Plaza de La Paja**. This sloping acacia-shaded fountain square was the commercial and civil hub of the city before the construction of the Plaza Mayor and has recently been superbly remodelled, with the newly restored frontages of the houses beaming down on the former market square. There's a fine selection of bars and restaurants in and around the square and in the summer you'll usually find a *terraza* here. This is one of the few areas in the city where you can get a break from the interminable Madrid traffic.

La Iglesia de San Andrés, Capilla del Obispo and Capilla de San Isidro

On the southern side of Plaza de la Paja stands the **Iglesia de San Andrés**. Badly damaged by an anarchist attack in 1936, the church is bandaged in protective netting and has been closed since 1991. However, the two adjoining chapels, Capilla del Obispo and Capilla de San Isidro, are open to visitors. The **Capilla del Obispo** (Mon–Sat 8.00–9.30am & 5.30–7.30pm, Sun 9am–2pm) is in Gothic style and contains some finely carved tombs of local aristocrats and bishops, Plateresque doors and a retablo behind the altar. The Baroque **Capilla de San Isidro** (same hours), reached by walking round the building into the courtyard, was built in the mid-seventeenth century to house the remains of the saint which were later transferred to the Catedral de San Isidro in c/de Toledo (see p.22). The chapel's interior is richly decorated with a beautifully sculpted dome in greens and yellows depicting angels laden with fruit. The lower level, inspired by the pantheon in El Escorial, features red and black columns embroidered with gold leaf and sculptures of saints.

La Morería

To the west of Plaza de la Paja you can explore the narrow, labyrinthine streets of **La Morería** still clearly laid out on the old Moorish lines; it is said that c/de la Morería 3 is the oldest house in Madrid. On **Plaza Gabriel Miró** *El Ventorrillo* is a good place to stop for refreshment. This *terraza* is also known as *Las Vistillas* (Little Views) and here you can sample a reasonably priced menu and assorted tapas accompanied by unrivalled views of the Almudena Cathedral, Casa de Campo and the Sierra Guadarrama. North, towards the cathedral, you'll reach the **Cuesta de la Vega**, the former site of one of the main entrances to Muslim Madrid. In the adjoining Parque Emir Mohammed I, a rather scruffy patch of sandy open land, are some of the few remaining fragments of the **city walls** dating back to the ninth and twelfth centuries.

Cava Baja and Cava Alta

Map 4, E5. Metro La Latina.

Continuing south from the San Andrés complex you'll come to a series of plazas, variously named Plaza San Andrés, Plaza Puerta de Moros, Plaza de Los Carros and Plaza Humilladero, which now effectively merge into one. They form an excellent site for summer *terrazas* and tapas bars which are always crowded with locals at the weekends. The web of streets running northeast out of the square back towards Plaza Mayor – c/del Almendro, **Cava Baja** and **Cava Alta** – are also well worth investigating. Here you'll find some of the best places to eat and drink in all of Madrid. Cava Baja used to be full of workshops, but is now famous for its *mesones,* serving traditional Castilian and *Madrileño* fare, and its wide selection of bars (see *Eating* and *Drinking* for more details).

San Isidro

Map 4, G4. Mon–Sat 7.30am–1pm & 6.30–8.30pm; Sun & public holidays 9am–2pm & 5.30–8.30pm. Metro La Latina.

North of La Latina metro station along c/de Toledo, is the massive church of **San Isidro**, built in 1622–33 as part of the Colegio Imperial – the centre of the Jesuit Order in Spain – according to the express wishes of Felipe IV's wife, Mariana de Austria, who left a very large legacy to the Jesuits. The illustrious alumni include the writers Lope de Vega, Calderón de la Barca, Quevedo and Góngora. After Carlos III fell out with the Jesuits in 1767, the church was dedicated to San Isidro, the patron saint of Madrid. His remains and those of his wife were brought here in 1769 from the Capilla de San Isidro just down the road. The church became the city's provisional cathedral from 1886, when Madrid was given its own diocese, until 1993 when the new Catedral de la Almudena was finally completed. It contains a single nave with large, ornate lateral chapels and an impressive altarpiece.

San Francisco El Grande

Map 4, B7. Tues–Sat: June–Sept 11am–1pm & 5–8pm; Oct–May 11am–1pm & 4–7pm; 50ptas with guided tour. Metro Puerta de Toledo/La Latina.

From Plaza Puerta de Moros there's a splendid view of the Neoclassical exterior of the huge domed church, **San Francisco El Grande**. Tradition has it that St Francis of Assisi came to Spain in 1214, on a pilgrimage to the tomb of St James in Santiago and built a humble home next to a monastery on this site. The monastery was enlarged and enriched over the years, but was demolished in 1760 in order to build a still more beautiful one. Plans were ambitious and included a great dome with radial chapels crowned by a cupola modelled on the Pantheon in Rome. The building was finally completed in 1784, its magnificent dome exceeding that of St Paul's in London by a metre in diameter. In 1837 the church was converted into a national mausoleum reverting to the control of the Franciscan friars in 1926. Inside, it's difficult to appreciate the size of the church as it's filled with a forest of yellow scaffolding, in place for a painfully slow restoration scheduled to be completed in 2012. The paintings are the greatest treasures and include an early Goya, *The Sermon of San Bernadino of Siena*, as well as works by José de Ribera and Contreras.

THE PALACIO REAL AND OPERA

The compact area around Opera metro station, bounded by c/Mayor and c/de Segovia to the south, Cuesta de San Vicente to the north, Paseo Virgen del Puerto to the west and Puerta del Sol to the east, contains a rich array of architectural and artistic treasures. The main sites date from the sixteenth to the eighteenth centuries, although the area itself only became really fashionable from the mid-nineteenth century onwards. The imposing **Palacio Real** dominates the area, bordered by the rather disappointing **Catedral de la Almudena** to the south and the tranquil gardens of the **Campo del Moro** to the west. The newly renovated **Teatro Real** and **Plaza de Oriente** are restoring some of the original nineteenth-century sophistication to the area while the two monastery complexes, **La Encarnación** and **Las Descalzas Reales**, conceal an astounding selection of artistic delights behind their modest exteriors. You will have to plan your itinerary carefully to dovetail the opening times of the sights as the hours of the monasteries are restricted.

The area covered by this chapter is shown
in detail on colour map 3.

THE PALACIO REAL

Map 3, B4. April–Sept Mon–Sat 9am–6pm, Sun & holidays
9am–3pm; Oct–March Mon–Sat 9.30am–5pm, Sun 9am–2pm; closed
occasionally for state visits; guided tours 950ptas, unguided 850ptas,
concessions 350ptas, Wed free for EU citizens. Metro Opera.

The **Palacio Real** (Royal Palace) scores high on statistics. It
claims more rooms than any other European palace; a library
with one of the biggest collections of books, manuscripts,
maps and musical scores in the world; and an armoury with
an unrivalled collection of weapons dating back to the fifteenth century. It is no longer compulsory to follow a guided
tour and this has the distinct advantage that you don't have to
be herded around at high speed listening to the guide rattle
off lists of figures. Much better to wander through the rooms
on the fixed route yourself, although bear in mind that the
visitor's guide books while beautifully illustrated are very
poorly translated. A number of rooms are in the process of
being restored which has made the tour more manageable,
but there have also been some important losses – it is, for
example, at present not possible to visit the King's Library.

The palace stands on the site of the old Alcázar erected by
the Arabs in the ninth century to defend the route to Toledo.
This became the royal residence of Felipe II when he moved
his court to Madrid in 1561. However, on Christmas Eve
1734, the Alcázar burned down after some curtains caught
fire, destroying, in the process, some of the great works of
Velázquez and Rubens. Felipe V, a Bourbon who had been
brought up in the considerably more luxurious surroundings
of Versailles, took the opportunity to order the construction

THE PALACIO REAL

of an altogether grander palace. However, he did not live to see the completion of his project; the palace only became habitable in 1764 during the reign of Carlos III.

Inside the palace

To enter the palace, you first cross the vast shadeless **Plaza de la Armería** used for state parades. From here there are superb views of the vast colonnaded southern facade, the Cathedral, Casa de Campo and the Sierra. As you enter the building you are directed up the magnificent main staircase, light pouring in from the portholes in the vaulted ceiling, reflecting off the golden stucco work and illuminating the epic frescoes of Corrado Giaquinto. In the **Salón de los Halbardiers** (Halbardiers' Room), Tiepolo's masterpiece fresco *Venus commanding Vulcan to forge arms for Aeneas* features billowing clouds, heroic military figures and majestic gods, while the **Salón de las Columnas** (Hall of Columns) contains several excellent Flemish tapestries woven with wool, gold, silver and silk. One of the highlights is the **Salón del Trono** (Throne Room) with its magnificent celestial fresco by Tiepolo depicting *The Grandeur and Power of the Spanish Monarchy*. The walls are decorated in red velvet, with ornamental framed mirrors exaggerating the size of the room, while gold drips from the furniture, the stucco work and the bronze lions guarding the thrones; an ostentatious display of wealth and power rather at odds with Spain's true condition at the time. There is also a selection of splendid clocks, two rock crystal and silver chandeliers and assorted candelabras. Carlos III's **Conversation Room** (Antécamara de Gasparini) contains two pairs of Goya masterpieces: one pair portraying Carlos IV and his wife Queen María Luisa of Parma in formal style with the king wearing the uniform of a Royal Guard colonel and the queen dressed in court clothes;

the other, more casual, with the king in hunting attire and the queen dressed as a *maja* with a black skirt and mantilla. The exotic fancy of the **Salón de Gasparini**, decorated in an incredible oriental style by Carlos III's court painter, features a swirling marble floor, gold and silver embroidered wall hangings and beautiful stucco work of plants, animals and fruits. There are yet more fantastic frescoes, rococo furniture and lavish decoration in Carlos III's bedroom.

One of the real treats is the marvellous **Sala de Porcelana** (Porcelain Room), decorated with one thousand gold, green, and white pieces – made in the Buen Retiro porcelain factory in the eighteenth century – depicting cherubs, garlands and urns. The **Comedor de Gala** (State Dining Room) is a truly massive affair again blessed with a selection of superb frescoes, this time by Antonio González Velázquez and Francisco Bayeu, and adorned with golden French candelabras and sixteenth-century tapestries. The table seats 145 and is still used for official banquets. Other rooms display royal silverwear from the nineteenth century (Joseph Bonaparte ordered the original silver dinner service to be melted down to meet war needs), crockery and a very impressive collection of musical instruments including a number of Stradivarius' creations and a fantastic jewelled guitar by José Frias. The tour of the main building is completed with the **Capilla Real** (Royal Chapel) and Queen María Cristina's official apartments which are more modest in scale.

The Armería Real, Farmacia and Jardines de Sabatini

The palace outbuildings and annexes include the **Armería Real** (Royal Armoury; currently closed for refurbishment), a huge room full of guns, swords and armour, with such

curiosities as El Cid's sword and the suit of armour worn by
Carlos V in his equestrian portrait by Titian in the Prado.
Especially fascinating are the complete sets of armour, with
all the original spare parts and gadgets for making adjust-
ments, and the suits designed for children, horses and dogs.
Also open to visitors is the eighteenth-century **Farmacia**,
which served the Royal Family and employees at the
palace; a curious mixture of alchemist's den and laboratory,
whose walls are lined with jars labelled for various reme-
dies. Immediately north of the palace the disappointing
Jardines de Sabatini contain some well-manicured trees
and bushes and give a pleasant view of the northeast facade
of the palace, but the ornamental lake is often dry and
many of the benches have been spoiled by graffiti.

THE CATHEDRAL

Map 3, B6. Mon–Sat 10am–1.30pm & 6–8.30pm, Sun
10am–2.30pm & 6–8.30pm. Metro Opera.

Facing the Palacio Real to the south is Madrid's cathedral,
Nuestra Señora de la Almudena, its bulky Neoclassical
facade designed to match the palace. Planned centuries ago,
the building has been plagued by lack of funds, bombed out
in the civil war, worked upon at intervals since, and was
eventually opened for business in 1993 by Pope John Paul
II. Its cold Gothic pastel-coloured interior is uninspiring,
though the boutique-like Capilla Opus Dei is worth a look
amid an array of largely unfilled chapel alcoves.

   Outside, nestling on the wall behind the cathedral, facing
the Parque Emir Mohammed I, is a figure of the **Virgin of
the Almudena** marking the site of the first recorded miracle in Madrid. The figure was said to have been brought to
Spain by Saint James and was concealed in the wall of the
old castle here by early Christians to protect it during the

conquest of the city by the Muslims. When the city was reconquered by Alfonso VI at the end of the eleventh century, he was anxious to unearth the virgin to re-establish the city's Christian credentials. He organized a huge procession appealing for divine help and when the faithful arrived at the appointed spot a woman offered her life in return for the statue's reappearance. The wall crumbled away to reveal the virgin in all her splendour and the woman dropped dead immediately.

EL CAMPO DEL MORO AND THE PUENTE DE SEGOVIA

Map 2, A5. Metro Principe Pío.

North of the Jardines de Sabatini, the Cuesta San Vicente leads past the partly restored **Estación del Norte** and the modern replica of the eighteenth-century Puerta de San Vicente to the **Campo del Moro** (entrance on Paseo de la Virgen del Puerto). One of the most underused and most beautiful of Madrid's parks, it was the site of the Moors encampment from where, in 1109, they mounted their unsuccessful attempt to reconquer Madrid and the Alcázar. It later became a venue for medieval tournaments and celebrations. After the building of the Palacio Real plenty of plans to landscape the area were put forward, but it wasn't until 1842 that Pascual y Colomer got things underway. Based around two monumental fountains, *Las Conchas* and *Los Tritones,* the grassy gardens are very English in style, featuring shady paths and ornamental pools, and provide a splendid view of the palace. They were first opened to the public during the Second Republic in 1931, but closed under Franco and not reopened until 1983.

A short walk south along Paseo de la Virgen del Puerto is the early eighteenth-century **Ermita de la Virgen del Puerto**, Pedro de Ribera's Baroque-style fairytale chapel with its original octagonal slate cupola. Set in grounds right beside the River Manzanares, the Ermita stands alongside the oldest bridge in Madrid, the **Puente de Segovia**, designed by Juan de Herrera and completed in 1584. The bridge is an imposing structure but the river below doesn't really match up. A French aristocrat once remarked, "with such a fine bridge, they really ought to get a river", while the German ambassador Rhebines called it the best river in Europe because it had the advantage of being "navigable by horse and carriage".

PLAZA DE ORIENTE AND BEYOND

Map 3, D4. Metro Opera.

With the completion of a major pedestrianization project, entailing the diversion of the busy c/Bailén beneath the square, the aristocratic **Plaza de Oriente** has become one of the most pleasant open spaces in Madrid. Narciso Pascual y Colomer designed the showpiece **fountain** in the centre and transferred the bronze equestrian statue of Felipe IV here from the garden of the Buen Retiro Palace near the Prado. It was based on designs by Velázquez, and Galileo is said to have helped with the calculations to make it balance. The square is full of other **statues** depicting Spanish kings and queens. These were originally designed to adorn the palace facade but were too heavy or, according to one version, were removed on the orders of Queen Isabel of Farnese, second wife of Felipe V, who dreamt they had fallen on her during an earthquake.

There is a very French feel to the buildings facing the palace, with their glass-fronted *terrazas* and decorated balconies, underlined by the elegant neo-Baroque **Café de Oriente** whose summer *terraza* is one of the stations of Madrid nightlife. The café looks as traditional as any in the city but was in fact opened in the 1980s, by a priest, Padre Lezama, who ploughs his profits into various charitable schemes.

The bulky, rather squat **Teatro Real** (Opera House) straddles the area between Plaza de Oriente and Plaza de Santa Isabel. Designed by Antonio López Aguado and opened in 1850 it was once the hub of fashionable Madrid staging highly successful operas by Verdi and Wagner. Plagued by municipal wrangling, unstable foundations, and pure incompetence, the opera house has only just been reopened after a ten-year refurbishment that should have lasted four and which ended up costing a mind-boggling $150 million.

For more information on seeing opera in Madrid see p.187.

Calle de Arenal

Map 3, F4–H5. Metro Opera/Sol.

C/de Arenal, stretching from the Teatro Real to Puerta del Sol, was once a stream which frequently dried up to leave a sandy channel (*arena* means sand). Today, it's lined with shops, but does contain a few, easily missed sights. The Palacio de Gaviria (no. 9) was originally an ornate palace constructed in 1851 by the Marquis of Gaviria, and now houses a disco, nightclub, dance school and cocktail bar all rolled into one. Further along, the *Joy Eslava* disco occupies the site of the Teatro Eslava, established in 1872 to provide popular light entertainment. Behind it, the **Chocolatería San Ginés**, a Madrid institution, which at one time catered for the early-rising worker now churns out *churros* and hot chocolate for the late nightclub crowd (see p.175). The ancient church of **San Ginés**, one of the original ten

PLAZA DE ORIENTE AND BEYOND

31

parishes included in the 1202 Madrid charter, stands nearby, and the neighbouring seventeenth-century **Capilla de Cristo** (entrance in c/Bordadores) contains an El Greco canvas showing the moneychangers being chased from the temple. It is open only during services.

CONVENTO DE LA ENCARNACIÓN

Map 3, D2. Compulsory tours (some in English) Wed & Sat 10.30am–12.45pm & 4–5.45pm, Sun 11am–1.45pm; 425ptas, concessions 225ptas, Wed free for EU citizens. Metro Opera.

North of Plaza de Oriente, the **Convento de la Encarnación** is worth a visit for its reliquary alone which is one of the most important in the Catholic world. Founded in 1611 by Felipe III and his wife Margarita de Austria, the convent was intended as a retreat for titled women. The solemn granite facade is the hallmark of architect Juan Gómez de Mora and was modelled on the Iglesia de San José de Avila, built by his uncle, Francisco de Mora. Much of the painting contained within is uninspiring artistically, but there are some interesting items including an extensive collection of royal portraits and a highly prized collection of sculptures of Christ, with an extremely gory post-crucifixion one by Gregorio Fernández. The library-like **reliquary** is lined with a cupboard full of more than 1500 (sixteenth- to eighteenth-century) saintly relics from around the world: skulls, arms encased in beautiful ornate hand-shaped containers, and bones from every conceivable part of the body. The most famous relic of all is a small glass bulb said to contain the blood of St Pantaleón, a four-teenth-century doctor martyr whose blood supposedly liquifies at midnight on the eve of his feast day (July 28). The tour ends with a visit to the Baroque-style church which features a beautifully frescoed ceiling by Bayeu and the González Velázquez brothers depicting scenes from the life of the monastery's patron, St Augustine, and a jasper and marble columned altarpiece.

MONASTERIO DE LAS DESCALZAS

Map 3, H3. Compulsory tours (some in English) Tues–Thurs & Sat 10.30am–12.45pm & 4–5.45pm, Fri 10.30am–12.45pm, Sun & holidays 11am–1.45pm; 650ptas, concessions 250ptas, Wed free for EU citizens. Metro Opera.

Just north of c/de Arenal in Plaza de las Descalzas, behind an unobtrusive wooden door, stands one of the hidden treasures of Madrid, the **Monasterio de las Descalzas Reales** (Monastery of the Barefoot Royal Ladies). Originally the site of a medieval palace, then the residence of Emperor Carlos V's royal treasurer, Alonso Gutiérrez, the building was transformed by Juana de Austria, born here in 1535, into a convent in 1564; the architect of El Escorial, Juan Bautista de Toledo, being entrusted with its design. Juana was daughter of the Emperor Carlos V, sister of Felipe II, and already, at the age of 19, the widow of Prince Don Juan of Portugal. The original nuns were from Gandía, near Valencia, but were later joined by a succession of titled ladies who, not wanting to leave behind all evidence of earthly delights, brought with them a whole array of artistic treasures. As a result, the monastery has accumulated a fabulous collection of paintings, sculptures and tapestries. The place is unbelievably rich, though beautiful and tranquil, too, and is still in use as a monastery housing 26 shoeless nuns of the Franciscan order.

The **main staircase**, connecting a two-levelled cloister lined with small but richly embellished chapels, is truly magnificent with floor-to-ceiling frescoes painted at the end of the seventeenth century by José Ximénez Donoso

MONASTERIO DE LAS DESCALZAS

and Claudio Coello. Felipe IV and his family are pictured gazing down at visitors from a balcony at the very top.

The **Coro** (Choir) contains the tomb of Empress María of Austria, sister of Felipe II, who had fifteen children and later died in the convent. Juana de Austria is also buried here. Look out for the moving sculpture of the *Doloroso* that actually appears to be crying with its incredibly realistic tears and cloudy eyes. There is also a small waist-high chapel especially for the children of the ladies. One of the most outstanding features of the monastery is the **Tapestry Room**, containing a magnificent collection of early seventeenth-century Flemish tapestries based on designs by Rubens, now in the Prado and representing the Triumph of the Eucharist. A mass of royal portraits, and beautiful painted wooden sculptures, most of which are of unknown origin, decorate other rooms. Keep an eye out for the little spiked slippers worn by the nuns to mutilate their feet, and for a marvellous Bosch school *Ship of Salvation* full of devilish mutant figures. As you make your way out you pass screened windows which hide the orchard and gardens still tended by the nuns.

THE RASTRO, LAVAPIÉS AND EMBAJADORES

The areas south of Plaza Mayor have traditionally been tough, working-class districts, with tenement buildings thrown up to accommodate the huge expansion of the population in the eighteenth and nineteenth centuries. In many places these old houses survive, huddled together in narrow streets, but the character of the area is beginning to change as their inhabitants, and the districts themselves, become younger and more fashionable. Built on land that sloped down towards the River Manzanares, **Lavapiés** and **Embajadores** were traditionally known as the *barrios bajos* (lower districts) and developed their own identity separate from the rest of Madrid. The city's early industrial and commercial centre, now the **Rastro**, was concentrated here and it became home to the **castizos** – authentic *Madrileños* – renowned for their sharp native wit and fierce pride.

The area covered by this chapter is shown
in detail on colour map 5.

Castizo

The word **castizo** is used to signify anything authentically
Madrileño and the inhabitants of the *barrios* of Lavapiés and
La Latina as well as Chamberí all lay claim to the label. In
many ways similar to the Cockney tradition in London, but
without their own form of slang, the *castizos* came into their
own in the nineteenth century with the development of
Madrid's working-class districts. Quick-witted, sarcastic,
sharp-dresssed and very proud, they were immortalized in
many of Goya's paintings and are celebrated in *zarzuelas*,
Madrid's own form of operetta (see box, p.40). Today, their traditional dress of black-and-white-checked caps and waistcoats and black trousers for the men, embroidered dresses,
petticoats, shawls and headscarfs plus red carnation for the
women, is most likely to be seen during the festivals of San
Isidro, the summer *verbenas* of San Cayetano, San Lorenzo
and La Paloma or at the *zarzuela*. Here too you are most likely
to hear the traditional *chotis*, a sort of upbeat wild west saloon
type of music played on a barrel organ and supposed to have
descended from the Scottish jig.

THE RASTRO

Map 5, C5. Metro La Latina/Puerta de Toledo.
The best starting point for an exploration of the **Rastro**
is the church of San Isidro on c/de Toledo (see p.22).
From here take the signposted route down c/Estudios to
Plaza de Cascorro where the main thoroughfare **Ribera**

de Curtidores begins. This area was formerly the site of two large slaughterhouses and the resulting blood that flowed down the hill gave the area its name (*rastro* means stain). The establishment of the slaughterhouses acted as a magnet to other traders and craftsmen; the tanners after which Ribera de Curtidores is named, leather workers and food sellers all soon set up in the area. These days Ribera de Curtidores is lined with furniture shops, antique dealers (some extremely upmarket) and outdoor pursuits equipment suppliers, but the best day to visit is Sunday when it's taken over by Madrid's most famous market, **El Rastro**.

At the southern end of Ribera de Curtidores you'll see a large arch, the **Puerta de Toledo** on your right. The arch is an eloquent testament to the political vicissitudes that Madrid endured in the nineteenth century. Originally commissioned by José Bonaparte to commemorate his accession to the Spanish throne, it ended up celebrating his defeat when it was completed in 1827.

Just in front of the arch, the **Mercado Puerta de Toledo**, once the city's fish market, has pretentions to be a stylish arts and crafts centre, but in reality it stands practically empty, apart from the under-used tourist office that lies within. Below, past the lines of anonymous apartment blocks lies the **Puente de Toledo**, a pedestrian bridge designed by Pedro de Ribera for Felipe V and built between 1718 and 1732. The arched construction spanning the rather sad-looking River Manzanares and the hopelessly congested M30 ring road can still be crossed to reach the summer *terraza* on the other side. As you cross on your right you'll see the M30 disappearing underneath the main stand of the huge red and white striped **Vicente Calderón** football stadium, home to Atlético Madrid.

The Flea Market

Madrid's flea market, **El Rastro**, is as much part of the city's weekend ritual as Mass or a *paseo*. This gargantuan, thriving, thieving shambles of a street market sprawls south from Metro La Latina to the Ronda de Toledo, especially along Ribera de Curtidores. Through it, crowds flood between 10am and 3pm every Sunday and increasingly on Friday, Saturday and public holidays too. On offer are secondhand and pseudo-designer clothes, military surplus items, T-shirts, sunshades, razor blades, Taiwanese radios, cutlery, canaries, and coke spoons – in fact just about anything you can imagine. The serious antique trade has now mostly moved off the streets and into the adjacent shops, while the real junk is found only on the fringes. The atmosphere is always enjoyable and the bars around these streets are as good as any in the city.

One **warning**, however: keep a tight grip on your bags, pockets, cameras (best left at the hotel) and jewellery. The Rastro rings up a fair percentage of Madrid's tourist thefts.

LAVAPIÉS AND EMBAJADORES

Lavapiés and **Embajadores** stretch south and east from Plaza Tirso de Molina (Metro Tirso de Molina). Just to the south of the plaza at c/de San Pedro Mártir 5 is the house where the young Pablo Picasso stayed during his visits to Madrid at the time he was painting *The Woman in Blue* (now hanging in the Reina Sofía). From here you can follow **c/Mesón de Paredes**, stopping for a drink at the darkly panelled *Taberna Antonio Sánchez* at no. 13, which dates back to 1830. Now owned by an ex-*torero,* it's decked out with two bull's heads and numerous taurine paintings. The street is buzzing, colourful and cosmopolitan, lined with ethnic shops, cafés, an Arab tea house and small plazas.

On c/Caravaca, a side street off c/Mesón de
Paredes, you can pop in to the *Pastelería Licorería El
Madroño* (closed July & Aug) to sample Madrid's
native liquor made from the berries of the
Madroño tree.

Halfway down on the right is **La Corrala**, built in 1839
and restored in the 1980s, one of many traditional *corrales*
(tenement blocks) in the quarter, built with balconied
apartments opening onto a central patio. The cramped
housing means that much of the drama of everyday life is
played out on the balconies or in the courtyard below –
neighbours conducting long-distance conversations with
each other, children crying, dogs barking, old men arguing
over the football. The ruined building alongside was a
church and religious school destroyed in the Civil War and
left as a monument. Plays, especially farces and **zarzuelas**,
used to be performed regularly in Spanish *corrales* and the
open space here usually hosts a number of performances in
the summer as part of the *Veranos de la Villa* (see *Festivals*,
p.201). Some of the audience come dressed up in traditional *castizo* costume and sit, eating, drinking and chatting at
the tables set up in the courtyard here.

Running parallel to the west of Mesón de Paredes is **c/de
Embajadores**, one of the oldest streets in Madrid, brim-
ming with traditional traders, shops and markets. The name
of the street originates in the fifteenth century when a
number of ambassadors fled to the area in order to escape
an outbreak of the plague in the city centre. The elaborately sculpted and ornamented church of **San Cayetano**,
patron of one the area's most important festivals in August,
dominates the upper part of the street. José de Churriguera
and Pedro de Ribera, renowned for their extravant designs,
were involved in the design of the facade constructed in

The Zarzuela

Madrid is the birthplace of the **zarzuela**, Spain's very own down-to-earth opera, incorporating features of classical opera as well as the more bawdy elements of music hall. The name originates from the royal palace and hunting lodge just to the north of Madrid where entertainments were laid on for Felipe IV. Today's version, however, developed in the early nineteenth century, when it reached the peak of its popularity, the most famous work being *La Revoltosa* by Ruperto Chapí. The *zarzuela* is usually centred on a local community with small-time protagonists, minor romances and soap-opera type plots. The season runs throughout the summer (June–Sept) and although it is no longer the mainstay of Madrid's entertainment scene, there are *zarzuela* perfomances at several venues in the city (see p.188 for details).

1761. Most of the rest of the church was destroyed in the Civil War and has since been reconstructed. The remainder of the street is a jumble of traditional shops, many with tiled frontages, and dilapidated dwellings, while at the bottom is the oldest **tobacco factory** in Europe. Originally built as a distillery but modified to produce tobacco in 1809, its austere, unornamented facade is a classic example of early nineteenth-century industrial architecture. Its workforce was overwhelmingly female and constituted, by the end of the century, about twenty percent of Madrid's working population. The flamboyant *cigarreras*, as they were called, were renowned for their independence, solidarity and strength. They bargained with the management to achieve the establishment of special schools, crèches and improvements in working conditions.

Just east of here, along c/Miguel Servet, you'll reach **Plaza Lavapiés**. This district was the core of the **Jewish**

quarter in medieval Madrid with the synagogue situated on the site now occupied by the Teatro Olimpia. In 1492 the Jews were given the choice of expulsion or conversion to Christianity by the fanatically Catholic Spanish monarchs; those that converted took Christian names, traditionally using Manuel for the eldest son, the area therefore being dubbed "*El Barrio de los Manolos*". Meanwhile, the converted Muslims (Moriscos) tended to congregate in the zone around c/del Ave María. With its Chinese, Arabic and African inhabitants Lavapiés remains a cosmopolitan place to this day. The plaza is a very pleasant spot with a variety of bars and cafés in various states of decay. There are *terrazas* and more bars along the cool tree-lined c/de Argumosa which leads out to Atocha and the Reina Sofía Art Gallery (see p.74).

Calle de Atocha

Map 5, E1–I4. Metro Tirso de Molina/Atocha.

Lavapiés is bounded to the northeast by **Calle de Atocha**, one of the old ceremonial routes from Plaza Mayor to the basílica at Atocha. At its southern end it's a mishmash of fast food and touristy restaurants, developing, as you move north up the hill, into a perverse mixture of cheap hostels, fading shops, bars, lottery kiosks and sex emporia. The huge sex shop, El Mundo Fantástica, at no. 80 with its brash neon lighting and shiny black facade, stands unashamedly opposite a convent and the site of an old printing house that produced the first edition of the first part of *Don Quixote*. Further up, just before you reach Plaza Antón Martín, you'll pass Pasaje Doré, a narrow alley on the left bordered by an indoor market crammed with miniature stores. At the end is the **Cine Doré**, the oldest cinema in Madrid, dating from 1922. It has been converted to house the Filmoteca Nacional, an art-film centre with bargain admission prices, and has a pleasant and inexpensive café/restaurant (Tues–Sun 1.30pm–12.30am).

**For more information on
Madrid's cinemas see p.198.**

Back on c/de Atocha, **Plaza Antón Martín** is named after the founder of a sixteenth-century hospital for the treatment of venereal diseases once situated here, and now the site of the Teatro Monumental where Prokofiev premiered his second violin concerto in 1935. Around the plaza are a variety of great-value bars, cafés and flamenco joints, including *Casa Patas* in c/de Cañizares (see p.189).

SOL, SANTA ANA AND HUERTAS

T he **Puerta del Sol** marks the western tip of the **Santa Ana/Huertas** area, a triangle bordered to the east by the Paseo del Prado, to the north by c/de Alcalá, and along the south by c/de Atocha. The city expanded into this area in the 1560s during the Spanish Golden Age and this *barrio de las letras* is steeped in **literary tradition**. It was home to many of the great Spanish authors and playwrights, including Lope de Vega, Cervantes and Góngora. Theatres, bookshops and literary cafés proliferate and the *barrio* also contains the **Ateneo** (literary guild), **Círculo de Bellas Artes** (Fine Arts Institute), **Teatro Nacional** and the **Cortes** (parliament). Just to the north, there is also an important museum, the **Real Academia de Bellas Artes de San Fernando**. For most visitors, though, the major attraction is that this district contains some of the best and most beautiful **bars** and *tascas* in the city. They are concentrated particularly around **Plaza de Santa Ana**, which, following a rather seedy period, has been smartened up by the council and is now one of the finest squares in the city.

The area covered by this chapter is shown
in detail on colour map 6.

PUERTA DEL SOL

Map 6, A3–B3. Metro Sol.

The best place to start exploring this part of Madrid (and many other areas of the centre) is the **Puerta del Sol**. This square marks the epicentre of the city - and, indeed, of Spain. It is from here that all distances are measured, and on the pavement outside the clock tower building on the south side of the square, a stone slab shows Kilometre Zero. In front of *El Corte Inglés* is a statue of the city's emblem, the bear and *madroño* (arbutus) tree, and an equestrian bronze of King Carlos III. For most *Madrileños*, however, the square's most renowned landmarks are the *Tío Pepe* sign perched above the buildings to the east and the sweet-smelling *Mallorquina* cake shop just outside the metro station entrance to the west.

The square's most important building, the **Casa de Correos**, was built in 1766 by Jaime Marquet and served as the city's post office until 1847, when it became home to the Ministry of Interior, the headquarters of the much-feared security police under Franco. It now houses the main offices of the Madrid regional government, the Comunidad de Madrid. The Neoclassical building is crowned by the nation's most famous **clock** which officially ushers in the New Year while *Madrileños* pack into the square below and attempt to scoff twelve grapes, one on each of the chimes of midnight to bring themselves good luck for the succeeding twelve months. There was a national outcry recently when the chimes were mistimed so that the majority of Spain was left still holding its grapes.

The square has been a popular meeting place since the mid-sixteenth century when the steps of the former monastery San Felipe (on the site now occupied by *McDonald's*) acted as one of the officially recognized *mentideros* or gossip mills. Citizens came here to catch up on all the latest news and scandals. Later the plaza was the site of the *Café Pombo*, scene of one of the most famous *tertulias* (see p.159) of the 1920s, and portrayed in José Gutiérrez Solana's painting now hanging in the Reina Sofía. It has also been witness to several events of national importance. On May 2, 1808, troops of Napoleon's marshal, Murat, aided by the infamous Egyptian cavalry (the "Mamelukes") cold-bloodedly slaughtered a rioting crowd, an event commemorated in Goya's canvas, now hanging in the Prado. Just off the square, in c/de Carretas, the liberal prime minister of Spain, José Canalejas, was assassinated in 1912 while browsing in a bookshop. The communist Julián Grimau met his end here in 1963 in even more sinister fashion after being thrown out of a window of the Casa de Correos, then occupied by the secret police, and later being finished off by firing squad. Just north of the plaza, is *Casa Labra* on c/Tetuán. Famous for its tapas of fried *bacalao*, this is where the Spanish Socialist Party, the PSOE, was founded in 1879.

The road leading out of the southeast corner of Puerta del Sol is carrera de **San Jerónimo**, a route laid out in 1538 to provide access to the San Jerónimo Monastery. Although now a rather anonymous street it does contain the marvellous **Lhardy** restaurant and shop founded by Frenchman Emilio Lhardy in 1839. Entering the shop you take a step back into the nineteenth century: shelves packed with ancient preserves, patés and soups; crystal decanters and glasses on silver salvers; impeccably mannered ancient staff dressed in aprons. Help yourself to the consommé from the giant silver urn, select a savoury cake or vol au vent from the octagonal glass display case and pay at the till on your way out. The restaurant upstairs is famous for its *cocido madrileño* but is only for those with large wallets.

PLAZA SANTA ANA

Map 6, C5. Metro Sol.

Plaza Santa Ana lies southeast of Puerta del Sol; head along c/San Jerónimo and take any of the streets off to the right. Recently renovated, **Plaza Santa Ana** was one of the series of squares created by Joseph Bonaparte, whose passion for open spaces led to a remarkable remodelling of Madrid in the six short years of his reign. The plaza is dominated by two distinguished buildings at either end; to the west, the *Reina Victoria*, a giant cream cake of a hotel which looks as though it would be more at home in Nice or Cannes, and to the east, the nineteenth-century Neoclassical **Teatro Español**. The theatre, whose facade is decorated with busts of famous Spanish playwrights, is the oldest in Madrid and there has been a playhouse on the site since 1583. The main reason for visiting the area, however, is to explore the mass of **bars**, **restaurants** and **cafés** on the square itself and in the nearby streets.

....

Places to eat and drink in Santa Ana are reviewed on pp.133–4 and 155–8.

....

HUERTAS

The **Huertas** area, east of Plaza Santa Ana, has a highly schizophrenic identity. By day it's rather dull and sleepy with doors closed, windows shuttered and the odd stray cat and dog roaming the empty streets, but at night, the buildings metamorphose into an astounding variety of **bars** – cocktail, jazz, karaoke, disco – the place a hive of activity, with people thronging the streets and car horns hooting until 2 or 3 am. North of c/Huertas, and parallel to it, are two streets named after the greatest figures of Spain's seven-teenth-century literary Golden Age, **Cervantes** and **Lope de Vega**. Bitter rivals in life, both are probably spinning in their graves now, since Cervantes is interred in the Convento de las Trinitarias on the street named after Lope de Vega, while the latter's house, the Casa de Lope de Vega, finds itself at c/de Cervantes 11.

Casa de Lope de Vega

Map 6, E5. Tues–Fri 9.30am–2pm, Sat 10am–1.30pm; 200ptas, concessions 100ptas, Wed free. Closed mid-July to mid-Aug. Metro Antón Martín.

The reconstructed home of the great Golden Age Spanish dramatist merits a visit if only for its reconstruction of life in seventeenth-century Madrid. **Lope de Vega** lived here for 25 years until his death in 1635 at the age of 48. These were the most prolific years of his literary life and also proved to be the most complex of his tangled private life; the house playing a central role in both spheres. His first wife died in childbirth, his second also died and he had five children with his actress mistress. He prepared for ordina-tion as a priest and lived out his final days caring for his blind, mad mistress. The house itself has been furnished in authentic fashion using the inventory left at the writer's death. Period furniture was collected from the Prado and other museums and the family possessions were preserved by his daughter who became a nun at the nearby Convento de las Trinitarias. The highlights include a chapel contain-ing some of Lope de Vega's original relics, the writer's study with a selection of contemporary books, an Arabic-style harem complete with silk cushions and a *brasero* (an open pan in which hot coals were placed to warm the room). The garden with its orange tree, vine, well and courtyard

HUERTAS

has been replanted and designed according to references found in the writer's correspondence.

Ateneo Artístico, Científico y Literario

Map 6, D4. Mon–Sat 9am–1pm, Sun & public holidays 9am–10pm. Metro Sevilla.

The **Ateneo**, c/del Prado 21, was founded after the 1820 Revolution and provided a home to some of the new liberal political ideas circulating at that time. It was accordingly closed down by Fernando VII on his return, although it eventually reopened on its present site in 1835 becoming one of the focuses of cultural and political life in nineteenth-century Madrid. The exterior is Neoplateresque in style while the inside features a neo-Greek lecture theatre and a splendid reading room with individual desks, lights and green leather writing boards. There's also a good value cafeteria inside; the atmosphere in the whole place being more of a student library rather than an elite club.

El Congreso de Los Diputados

Map 6, E4. Sat 10.30am–1pm. Closed Aug & public holidays. Metro Sevilla.

A short stroll down c/del Prado from the Ateneo to Plaza de las Cortes, takes you past an unprepossessing nineteenth-century building where **El Congreso de Los Diputados** (the lower house of the Spanish parliament) meets. Sessions can be visited by appointment only, though anyone can turn up (with a passport) and queue for a tour on Saturday mornings. During a high-speed tour you are shown several of the most important rooms and the chamber itself where the bullet holes left by mad Colonel Tejero and his Guardia Civil associates in the abortive coup attempt of 1981 are pointed out (see *Contexts*, p.275).

Círculo de Bellas Artes

Map 6, E2. Café daily 8am–2am; Exhibitions Tues–Fri 5–9pm, Sat 11am–2pm & 5–9pm, Sun 11am–2pm;100ptas. Metro Banco España.

Cutting across to c/de Alcalá from the Plaza de las Cortes you will emerge close to the **Círculo de Bellas Artes** at c/Marqués de Casa Riera 2, a strange-looking 1920s building crowned by a statue of Pallas Athene. This is Madrid's best arts centre, and includes a theatre, music hall, exhibition galleries, cinema and a very pleasant café - all marble and leather decor, with a nude statue reclining in the middle of the floor. For many years a stronghold of Spanish culture, it attracts the city's arts and media crowd but it's not in the least exclusive, nor expensive, and there's an adjoining *terraza*, too. The Círculo is theoretically a members-only club, but it issues day membership on the door, for which you get access to all areas. Pick up the centre's *Minerva* magazine to find out what's on or ask the helpful staff.

CALLE DE ALCALÁ AND PLAZA DE LA CIBELES

Calle de Alcalá, the original road to the Roman University town of Alcalá de Henares, runs west–east from Puerta del Sol to Plaza de la Cibeles at the junction with Paseo del Prado and on past the Retiro. Lined with gargantuan buildings, its architectural highlights include the colonnaded Neoclassical **Banco Central Hispano** designed by Antonio Palacios and Joaquín Otamendi in 1910, the more severe **Banco del Comercio** and the **Ministry of Education and Culture**. The pastel pink building at no. 25, down towards Puerta del Sol is the Baroque **Iglesia de las Calatravas**, a seventeenth-century church built for the nuns of the Calatrava, one of the four

Spanish military orders. Look out for the splendid early twentieth-century wedge-shaped **Banco Español de Crédito**, adorned with elephant heads and plaques listing all the branches of the bank in Spain; the **Banco de Bilbao Vizcaya**, with its Neoclassical concave facade complete with charioteers on top; and the classic Baroque **Ministerio de Hacienda**. Yet more delights await with the **Casino de Madrid**, constructed according to the design of Luis Esteve after an international competition in 1903 organized by the business and intellectual elite who wanted a more upmarked setting for their meetings. It has a suitably opulent central staircase and main salon – ask the doorman if you can have a look.

Museo de La Real Academia de Bellas Artes de San Fernando

Map 6, C2. Tues–Fri 9am–7pm; Mon ,Sat, Sun & public holidays 9am–2.30pm; 300ptas, concessions 150ptas, free Sat & Sun.
Free guided visits Mon–Fri 10am–2.30pm for organized groups.
Metro Sevilla.

Two hundred metres east of Puerta del Sol on c/de Alcalá, art buffs who have some appetite left after the Prado, Thyssen and Reina Sofia, should head for the **Real Academia de Bellas Artes de San Fernando**, c/de Alcalá 13. One of the most important art galleries in Spain, it has sections dealing with painting, sculpture, architecture and music. Its extraordinary collection of Spanish painting includes work by Velázquez, Murillo, Zurbarán, Goya, Sorolla and Picasso as well as interesting French and Italian work. The Real Academia was set up by Felipe V at the request of his state secretary and his court sculptor, with the present building being acquired in 1773. The Goya section includes, among other gems, two revealing self-portraits, the contemptuous depiction of the royal favourite *Don Manuel Godoy*, and the desolate representation of *The Madhouse*. There are some supremely ugly royal portraits such as De la Calleja's *Carlos III*, and a variety of sculptures including, scattered throughout the museum, a dismembered *Massacre of the Innocents* by sculptor José Ginés. Look out, too, for the penetrating, rather haunting, portrait of *Haile Selassie* by Delgado. The gallery is also home to the national chalcography collection which includes some Goya etchings.

Plaza de la Cibeles

Map 6, G1. Metro Banco de España.

Encircled by four of the most overstated monumental buildings in Madrid – the Palacio de Comunicaciones (the Post Office), Banco de España (the Central Bank), the Palacio de Buenavista (the Army HQ) and the Palacio de Linares (the Casa de América) – **Plaza de la Cibeles** must be the most glorified roundabout in the city. Awash in a sea of traffic, the centre is dominated by a **fountain** and statue of the goddess Cibeles riding in a chariot drawn by two lions. It was designed, as were the two other fountains gushing magnificently along the Paseo del Prado, by Ventura Rodríguez, who is honoured in modern Madrid by having a metro station and a street named after him. It survived the Civil War by being swaddled in sandbags but was recently damaged in celebrations after one of the victories of the national football team in the 1994 World Cup. Fully repaired, it still hosts celebrations for victorious Real Madrid fans (Atlético supporters bathe in the fountain of Neptune just down the road).

The wedding cake building on the eastern side of the square is Madrid's main post office, the aptly named

Palacio de Comunicaciones. Constructed between 1904 and 1917, it is vastly more imposing than the parliament and runs the Palacio Real pretty close. A fabulous place, flanked by polished brass postboxes for each province, it preserves a totally byzantine system within, with scores of counters each offering just one particular service, from telegrams to string, and until quite recently, scribes. The **Casa de América** (Tues–Sat 11am–7pm, Sun 11am–2pm) is used for concerts, films and exhibitions of Latin American art and has a good bookshop and fine café-restaurant.

THE MUSEO DEL PRADO

The **Museo del Prado** is Madrid's premier tourist attraction, and one of the oldest and greatest collections of art in the world. The Prado houses all the finest works collected by Spanish royalty – for the most part avid, discerning, and wealthy buyers – as well as Spanish paintings gathered from other sources over the past two centuries. The museum is desperately short of space with only about ten percent of its artistic holdings actually on permanent display (still a pretty daunting tally). A controversial plan to modernize and extend the museum, adding three nearby buildings, would enable the Prado to double the amount of works currently on show, but as yet nothing has been decided. Major reorganization, for the installation of air-conditioning, much-needed lighting improvement and the repair of the leaking roof, has, however, been going on for years. It is due to be completed in September 1998, and until then you may find some displays moved or temporarily closed.

> The Museo del Prado (Map 6, H6) is open
> Tuesday–Saturday 9am–7pm, Sunday & public
> holidays 9am–2pm; 500ptas, free on Saturday after
> 2.30pm & all day Sunday. Metro Banco de
> España/Atocha.

The museum's highlights are its Flemish collection – including almost all of **Bosch**'s best work – and its incomparable display of Spanish art, especially **Velázquez** (including *Las Meninas*), **Goya** (including the *Majas*) and **El Greco**. There's also a huge section of **Italian painters** (**Titian**, notably) collected by Carlos V and Felipe II, both great patrons of the Renaissance, and a strong showing of later Flemish pictures collected by Felipe IV. Even in a full day you couldn't hope to do justice to everything here, and it's perhaps best to make a couple of more focused visits. In summer the crowds can become oppressive with the incursions of large tour groups; hang back and let them sweep by on their whirlwind progress.

There are two main **entrances** to the museum: the **Puerta de Goya**, which has an upper and a lower entrance opposite the *Hotel Ritz* on c/Felipe IV, and the **Puerta de Murillo** on Plaza de Murillo, opposite the Botanical Gardens. The upper entrance of the Puerta de Goya takes you up to the first floor, with the Italian Renaissance giving way to the main Spanish collections, while the lower entrance is the one to take if you want to embark on a chronological tour. The Puerta de Murillo is a ground-floor entrance which steers you towards Bosch and the other Flemish galleries. Thankfully there is no prescribed or obvious route which does ease congestion, and rooms are numbered in Roman numerals above the doorways. A temporary exhibition space on the ground floor by the Puerta de Goya is used to show visiting exhibitions and selections from the museum holdings not on permanent view.

Illustrated **guides and catalogues** describing and explaining the paintings are on sale in the two museum shops (1000–2000ptas), one on each floor. Particularly helpful is the *Quick Visit Guide* which selects and explains the background to about fifty of the most important works. Useful **notes** (100ptas) on Velázquez, Goya and El Greco are also available in their respective galleries. The museum has a decent cafeteria and restaurant in the basement (closes at 1.30pm on Sun).

> If you plan to visit all three art museums on the Paseo del Prado during your stay, it's well worth buying the under-advertised Paseo del Arte ticket (1050ptas) which is valid for a year and allows one visit to each museum at a substantial saving.

SPANISH PAINTING

The Prado's collections of **Spanish painting**, not surprisingly the largest in the world, begin on the ground floor, where **Room 51c** houses cycles of twelfth-century **Romanesque frescoes**, reconstructed from a pair of churches from the Mozarabic (Muslim rule) era in Soria and Segovia. **Early panel paintings** – exclusively religious fourteenth- and fifteenth-century works – include a huge *retablo* by Nicolás Francés, the anonymous *Virgin of the Catholic Monarchs*, Bermejo's ornate portrayal of *Santo Domingo de Silos*, Pedro Berruguete's *Auto-de-Fé* and depictions of the lives and tortuous deaths of a variety of saints.

The Golden Age

Upstairs, to the left of the Puerta de Goya entrance, and beyond the Italian galleries (see below), are the Prado's collections from Spain's Golden Age: the late sixteenth and seventeenth centuries under Habsburg rule. They are prefigured, in **Rooms 9b and 10b**, by a collection of paintings by **El Greco** (Domenikos Theotocopulos, 1540–1614), the Cretan-born artist who worked in Toledo from the 1570s. You really have to go to Toledo to appreciate fully his extraordinary genius, but the portraits and religious works here are a good introduction. The development of his Mannerist style can be traced from the early richly coloured Italian-influenced *Trinity* in which there is little sign of the distortions and exaggerations that characterize his later work, to the visionary *Adoration of the Shepherds*, painted 35 years later for his own burial chapel, with its ghostly elongated bodies and sombre oily colouring. His skills as a portrait painter are amply demonstrated in *The Nobleman with his Hand on his Chest*, where the depiction of the Mayor of Toledo with his pointed beard, ruffed collar and sleeve, austere black dress and stern expression has become an archetypal image of the sixteenth-century Spanish nobleman.

See p.251 for details on visiting the city of Toledo.

With **Rooms 11–15**, you confront the greatest painter of Habsburg Spain, **Diego Velázquez** (1599–1660). Born in Seville, Velázquez became court painter to Felipe IV, whose family is represented in many of the works: "I have found my Titian," Felipe is said to have remarked of his appointment. Velázquez's masterpiece, **Las Meninas** (The Maids of Honour, 1656), is in **Room 12**, displayed alongside studies for the painting. Manet remarked of it, "After this I don't know why the rest of us paint", and the French poet Théophile Gautier asked, "But where is the picture?", because it seemed to him a continuation of the room. The work captures a moment in the artist's study featuring the artist himself, the Infanta Margarita, the court dwarves, ladies-in-waiting, a butler, the palace marshal watching from the stairs at the back, and Felipe IV and his wife Mariana of Austria standing in the viewer's footsteps and reflected in the mirror on the wall. Velázquez's superlative brushwork and his mastery of colour, light and perspective mark the painting out as one of the all-time great works of art.

Don't ignore the painter's other canvases, though. With the aid of light and loose brush strokes in *Las Hilanderas* Velázquez again plays with simultaneous action in the foreground and background, depicting the story of Minerva, the goddess of the arts, challenging Arachne to see who could weave the most beautiful tapestry. In the foreground yarns are being prepared for the weaving of the tapestries, while in the background Minerva is preparing to turn Arachne into a spider for producing a work of superior quality to her own. The portraits of Felipe IV are sympathetic and intimate representations of the monarch with his childlike features, and tired eyes, while that of the dwarf, *Don Sebastián de Morra* focuses on his morose, pensive expression. *Christ Crucified* with his bowed head and shimmering halo, *Los Borrachos* (The Drunkards), a clever corruption of which can be seen in the *Los Gabrieles* bar (see p.157), *Vulcan's Forge* and *The Surrender of Breda* are further magnificent works. In fact, almost all of the fifty works on display (around half of the artist's surviving output) warrant close attention. Don't overlook the two small panels of the *Villa Medici*, painted in Rome in 1650, in virtually Impressionist style.

In the adjacent rooms are examples of just about every significant Spanish painter of the seventeenth century, including many of the finest works of **Francisco Zurbarán** (1598–1664), **Bartolomé Esteban Murillo** (1618–82), **Alonso Cano** (1601–67), **Juan de Valdés**

Leal (1622–1660) and **Juan Carreño** (1641–85). Murillo's soft, vapourous, almost mystical, style is seen to best effect in *The Immaculate Conception of Soult* and *The Good Shepherd* (**Rooms 28** and **29**). Look out for Carreño's portrait of the last Habsburg monarch, the drastically inbred and mentally retarded *Carlos II*, rendered with terrible realism. Here too are the Prado's holdings of **José Ribera** (1591–1652), who worked mainly in Naples, and was influenced there by Caravaggio. His masterpieces are considered to be *The Martyrdom of St Philip* (**Room 22**), where he shows the preparation of Philip for his ordeal of being skinned alive using light to focus on the naked body of the saint, and the dark, realist portrait of *Archimedes*.

Goya

The final suite of Spanish rooms (**19–23**, **29**, **32** and **36–39**) provides an awesome and fabulously complete overview of the works of **Francisco de Goya** (1746–1828), the largest and most valuable collection of his works in the world with some 140 paintings and 500 drawings and engravings. Goya was the greatest painter of Bourbon Spain and a chronicler of Spain in his time, an artist whom many see as the inspiration and forerunner of Impressionism and modern art.

After an apprenticeship in Zaragoza, Goya studied in Italy in 1770–71, returning to Spain to draw cartoons for the Royal Tapestry Workshop and later, in 1789, becoming court painter to Carlos IV. Illness in 1792 made him deaf and from then on his painting became more intense, introverted and stylized. He left for France in 1824 and died there four years later.

Goya was an enormously versatile artist: contrast the voluptuous *Maja Vestida* and *Maja Desnuda* (The Clothed and Naked Belles) with the horrors depicted in *Dos de Mayo* and *Tres de Mayo* (on-the-spot portrayals of the rebellion against Napoleon in the streets of Madrid and the subsequent reprisals). Then again, there are the series of pastoral cartoons – designs for tapestries – and the extraordinary *Black Paintings*, a series of murals painted by the deaf and embittered painter in his old age. His many portraits of his patron, Carlos IV, are remarkable for their lack of any attempt at flattery while those of Queen María Luisa, whom he despised, are downright ugly.

The **tapestry cartoons** include a series dedicated to the seasons of the year; others feature toothless, starving peasants, dainty playful aristocrats, mischievous boys and a hunchback bridegroom. Most are produced in clearly separated pastel colours to help the weavers and are set against the Madrid landscape. The two **Majas** were painted at different times – the brushwork used on each of the paintings is quite contrasting – but may have formed part of a game whereby the clothed figure was placed over the naked one. *The Family of Carlos IV*, hanging in the octagonal **Room 32**, provides a rather sardonic commentary on Goya's patron: the domineering María Luisa is clearly in charge, while the well-fed Carlos is pictured staring into space. In a clear tribute to Velázquez, Goya places himself staring out at the viewer from the left-hand corner. The two canvases portraying the events of the **Second and Third of May, 1808**, and painted six years later, have immortalized the heroic resistance to the Napoleonic invasion of Spain, and also allowed Goya to reaffirm his somewhat compromised patriotic credentials having worked for Joseph Bonaparte. Both works are incredibly powerful condemnations of the violence. *The Colossus or Panic* is also said to refer to the upheavals inflicted by the Napoleonic invasion, some claiming that the giant figure represents Napoleon wreaking

SPANISH PAINTING

havoc on Spain, while others claim it symbolizes Spain rising against her oppressor. The disillusioned *Self Portrait* in **Room 39** bears a passing resemblance to that other famous deaf artist, Beethoven, with his deeply troubled demeanour and penetrating eyes seeking to make sense of the world around him.

The Black Paintings (1819–23) were originally painted straight on to the wall of Goya's house, known as "*Quinta del Sordo*" (The Deaf Man's Villa), beside the Manzanares. The works were transferred to canvas in 1873 and donated to the Prado in 1881, being given titles after Goya's death by people who had known him. The thoroughly disconcerting canvases are often hard to penetrate, but provide a vivid image of an isolated, bitter and seriously ill old man. *Saturn Devouring One of his Sons* symbolizes the destruction of everything by time; *The Cudgel Fight* illustrates a fight to the death by two men; others feature ghoulish skull-like faces, witches and devils and a half-submerged dog.

ITALIAN PAINTING

The Prado's early **Italian galleries (Rooms 2–10** and **41–44)** are distinguished principally by **Fra Angelico's** (1387–1455) devout and mystical *Annunciation* (c.1445) which originally hung in the Monasterio de Las Descalzas (see p.33) and by a trio of panels by **Botticelli** (1444–1510). The latter illustrate a deeply unpleasant story from the *Decameron* about the strange vision experienced by a young man who sees a woman hunted by hounds and caught by a nobleman who tears her heart out and feeds it to his dogs; the fourth panel (in a private collection in the US) shows a happier conclusion.

With the sixteenth-century Renaissance, and especially its Venetian exponents, the collection really comes into its own. The Prado is said to have the most complete collection of Titian and painters from the Venice school in any single museum. There are major works by **Raphael** (1483–1520), including a fabulous *Portrait of a Cardinal*, and masterpieces from the Venetians **Tintoretto** (1518–94), including the beautifully composed *Lavatorio*, bought by Felipe IV when Charles I of England was beheaded and his art collection was auctioned off, and **Veronese** (1528–88), as well as **Caravaggio** (1573–1610). The most important group of works, however, are by **Titian** (1487–1576). These include portraits of the Spanish emperors, *Carlos V* and *Felipe II*. The magnificent equestrian portrait, *The Emperor Carlos V at Mühlberg*, depicts his triumph in 1547 over the Protestant armies of Germany with Carlos resplendent in his armour (the suit is preserved in the Palacio Real) astride a huge black charger. It is rather ironic, then, that by the time Titian painted his subject he could hardly sit on a horse because of his gout. The collection also features a famous, and much-reproduced piece of erotica, *Venus, Cupid and the Organist* (two versions are displayed here), a painting originally owned by a bishop.

FLEMISH AND GERMAN PAINTING

The biggest name in the extremely rich **Flemish collection** (**Rooms 54–63**) is **Hieronymus Bosch** (1450–1516), known in Spain as "El Bosco". The Prado has several of his greatest triptychs. The early-period *Hay Wain* features fish-headed monsters devouring humans. The middle-period *Garden of Earthly Delights*, begins on the left with the Creation of Man, then, in the centre the worldly pleasures and sins and finally Hell on the right; fantasy animals, sexual imagery and satanic visions abound. These and the late *Adoration of the Magi* are all familiar from countless reproductions but infinitely more chilling in the original. Bosch's hallucinatory genius for the macabre is at its most extreme in these triptychs, but is reflected here in many more of his works, including three versions of *The Temptations of Saint Anthony* (though only the smallest of these is definitely an original). Don't miss the amazing table-top of *The Seven Deadly Sins*, displayed in the centre of the room, showing devils, roasting, spanking and tormenting peasants, while ghostly skeletons creep around in the background.

Bosch's visions find an echo in the works of **Pieter Brueghel the Elder** (1525–69), whose *Triumph of Death* must be one of the most frightening canvases ever painted. Death is pictured triumphing over all earthly things: riding on a wizened horse hauling cartloads of skulls, driving humanity against an army of skeletons shielded with coffin lids, dragging bloated bodies from the water, and preparing to slice off the head of a wretched figure on a hill. The grim unrelenting image is emphasized by the use of dark shades of brown and black and by the burning smoke in the background.

Another elusive painter, **Joachim Patinir** (1480–1524), precursor of landscape painting, is represented by four of his finest works, including the dream-like blue-green toned *Crossing the Styx Lake*. From an earlier generation, **Rogier van der Weyden**'s (1400–1464) *Deposition* is outstanding, its monumental forms make a fascinating contrast with his miniature-like *Pietà*. There are also important works by Memling, Bouts, Gerard David and Massys.

Among later Flemish painters, the outstanding portraiture work of **Mor**, or "**Antonio Moro**" (1519–1567) as he was known when he worked in the Spanish court, is shown in his fine representation of the haughty gaze of *Mary Tudor*. **Rubens** (1577–1640) is extensively represented, though he supervised rather than executed the most interesting works – a series of eighteen mythological subjects designed for

Felipe IV's hunting lodge in El Pardo. The gruesome horror of his version of *Saturn Devouring a Child* clearly influenced Goya. Typically, there is plenty of pearly white female flesh set amongst sensual landscapes in works such as *Nymphs and Satyrs* and *The Three Graces*.

There are, too, a fine collection of works by his contemporaries **Van Dyck**, **Jan Brueghel** and **David Teniers**, whose scenes of lowlife get a whole room to themselves. For political reasons, Spanish monarchs collected very few works painted in seventeenth-century Protestant Holland; the only important exception is an early Rembrandt, *Artimisia*.

The **German rooms** are dominated by **Dürer** (1471–1528) and **Lucas Cranach the Elder** (1472–1553). Dürer's magnificent *Adam and Eve* was saved from destruction at the hands of the prudish Carlos III only by the intervention of his court painter, Mengs. The most interesting of Cranach's works are a pair of paintings depicting Carlos V hunting with Ferdinand I of Austria.

FRENCH PAINTING

Most of the French work held by the Prado is from the seventeenth and eighteenth centuries (**Rooms 15a, 16a, 40 and 41**). Royal marriages and the establishment of the Bourbon royal house helped establish closer links between the two countries, although a large part of the collection was lost in the Peninsular War. The outstanding painters represented are **Nicolas Poussin** (1594–1665) with his classical Baroque style and intense colours shown to best effect in *Triumph of David*, *Bacchanal*, *Landscape with St Jerome* and *Parnassus*; while the romantic landscapes and sunsets of **Claude Lorraine** (1600–82) are well represented by *The Port of Ostia with the Embarcation of Santa Paula Romana* and *Landscape with Tobias and the Archangel Raphael*.

FRENCH PAINTING

SCULPTURE AND THE DAUPHIN'S TREASURE

Various pieces of **sculpture**, from the classical era to the nineteenth century, are grouped around the entrance halls and scattered throughout the museum. There's an interesting selection of busts of Carlos V and Felipe II by **Leone Leoni** and his son **Pompeo Leoni** and an impressive figure by them both of *The Emperor Carlos V Subduing Rage* on which the emperor's armour can be removed to reveal his nude figure.

The basement houses a display of part of the **collection of jewels** that belonged to the Grand Dauphin Louis, son of Louis XIV and father of Felipe V, Spain's first Bourbon king. The collection includes goblets, cups, trays, glasses and other pieces richly decorated with rubies, emeralds, diamonds, lapis lazuli and other precious stones. The collection was taken back to France during the Napoleonic invasion but returned to Spain in 1815. One of the highlights is the onyx saltcellar with a gold mermaid, adorned with rubies.

CASÓN DEL BUEN RETIRO

Just east of the Prado is the **Casón del Buen Retiro** (entrance on c/de Alfonso XII, admission on the same ticket as the Prado), which used to be a dance hall for the palace of Felipe IV, but is now devoted to **nineteenth-century Spanish art**. It is at present in the process of being restored, but you can still look around the collection in which Neoclassical, romantic and historical themes dominate. The Realist work of **Eduardo Rosales** in the melodramatic deathbed scene of *Queen Isabella's Will* and **Francisco Pradilla** in *Doña Juana la Loca*, where he captures a scene from the long march from Burgos to Granada of Joanna the Mad with her dead husband's coffin, are perfect representatives of this style. **José de Madrazo Agudo's** (1781–1859) *The Death of Viriato* is a characteristic epic piece; **Vicente López's** portrait of the ageing *Goya* is certainly worth a look as is the luminescent Impressionist work *Children at the Beach* by **Joaquín Sorolla** (1863–1923; see p.98 for the Museo Sorolla).

CASÓN DEL BUEN RETIRO

MUSEO THYSSEN-BORNEMISZA

Only a step away from the Prado is another exceptional museum, the **Museo Thyssen-Bornemisza**, an ideal complement to the former establishment as the strong points of the Thyssen collection are precisely those in which the Prado is weak. It houses an important selection of German Renaissance works, seventeenth-century Dutch painting, Impressionism, German Expressionism, Russian Constructivism, Abstract and Pop Art. Although both museums are essentially personal – the Prado reflecting the tastes of the Spanish monarchy and the Thyssen those of the present baron and his father – the Thyssen also provides an unprecedented excursion through the history of Western art from the fourteenth to the late-twentieth century.

The Museo Thyssen-Bornemisza (Map 6, F4) is open
Tuesday–Sunday 10am–7pm; 600ptas, concessions
350ptas, under-12s free. Metro Banco de España.

The Thyssen collection – whose 800-odd paintings many would argue is the world's greatest private art trove after that of the British royals – was begun in the 1920s by German-Hungarian industrial magnate **Baron Heinrich Thyssen-Bornemisza**. However, on his death in 1947, the works were distributed amongst his heirs. The present baron, Hans Heinrich, tried to reunite the collection by buying back the paintings and later expanding it with the purchase of additional old masters and modern art. As his own Villa Favorita in Lugano in Switzerland could only accommodate about 300 pictures the baron sought a new home for his collection. Despite stiff competition from other suitors including Prince Charles, the Swiss and German governments, and the Getty foundation, Spain managed to secure the display of the collection for a knock-down $350m (£230m) in June 1993. The museum itself operates as a private institution, administered by the Thyssen Foundation, and proceeds from the entrance fees of the 700,000 visitors each year are ploughed back into the running of the museum.

The museum occupies the mid-eighteenth-century Neoclassical **Palacio de Villahermosa**, diagonally opposite the Prado, at the end of the Carrera de San Jerónimo. The building was brilliantly remodelled by architect Rafael Moneo who redistributed the rooms and changed the ceilings in order to make the most of the natural light available. Without a doubt the availability of this prestigious site played a large part in Spain's acquisition. Another trump card was Baron Thyssen's current (fifth) wife, "Tita" Cervera, a former Miss Spain, once married to Tarzan actor Lex Barker, who steered the works towards Spain. Tita's portrait – a kitsch (and dangerously anorexic) stunner of her in fairy-like winged dress – hangs in the great hall of the museum, alongside her husband and King Juan Carlos and Queen Sofía.

The basement houses a handy, good-value **cafeteria** and **restaurant** which can be entered separately from the museum and there's also a temporary exhibition space down here which has staged a number of interesting and highly successful shows. The museum **shop** sells an informative and well-illustrated guide (1800ptas) as well as the first instalments of the fifteen-volume catalogue of the baron's collection. Re-entry to the museum is allowed as long as you get your hand stamped at the exit desk.

EUROPEAN OLD MASTERS: SECOND FLOOR

Cross to the far side of the building and take a lift or the stairs to the second floor and you'll find yourself at the chronological beginning of the museum's collections: European painting (and some sculpture) from the fourteenth to eighteenth century. The core of these collections was accumulated in the 1920s and 1930s by the present baron's father, Heinrich, who was a friend of the art critics Bernard Berenson and Max Friedländer.

He was clearly well advised. The early paintings include incredibly good (and rare) devotional panels by the Sienese painter **Duccio di Buoninsegna**, and the Flemish artists **Jan van Eyck** and **Rogier van der Weyden**. In **Rooms 1** and **2** the pilgrimage through the history of Western art begins with a fine exhibition of the evolving styles that prefigured the Renaissance: the development of spatial depth, inclusion of gestures and the increasing repertoire of artistic skills can be seen in the differences between the Master of Magdalen's *Madonna and Child* and Duccio's *Christ and the Samaritan Woman* (both painted in the first half of the fourteenth century). The International Gothic style is well represented by Johann Koerbecke's expressive and emotional *Assumption of the Virgin* (1457) and the eight panels dedicated to the four evangelists by Gabriel Maelesskircher (1478). In **Room 3** Jan van Eyck's highly original and remarkable *Annunciation Diptych* (c.1434–1441) in which he depicts the Angel, Virgin and Holy Spirit is conspicuous, as is Petrus Christus' *Our Lady of the Tree* (c.1450) where the Virgin is shown as a flowering shoot bringing life to the dry tree. Look out for the haunting, translucent *Ressurrected Christ* by **Bramintino** (c.1465–1530) in the room dedicated to the Italian Quattrocento.

You then move into a fabulous array of Early Renaissance portraits, marking a change from the portrayal of the supernatural to more worldy matters. **Ghirlandaio**'s *Portrait of Giovanna Tornabuoni* (1488) captures the serene beauty of the subject, the Latin epigram within stating, "If the artist had been able to portray the character and moral qualities there would not be a more beautiful painting in the world." **Hans Holbein**'s portrait of the self-confident *Henry VIII* (the only one of many variants in existence which is definitely genuine), is accompanied by the austere melancholy *Spanish Infanta* by **Juan de Flandes**, which may represent the first of Henry VIII's wives, Catherine of Aragón. Among the sixteenth-century Italian paintings, **Raphael**'s subtly coloured *Portrait of a Young Man* and Titian's *Portrait of the Doge Francesco Vernier* stand out, while the *Young Knight* by **Carpaccio** is one of the earliest known full-length portraits. Beyond these a collection of **Dürers** and **Cranachs** rivals that in the Prado, and includes Dürer's *Jesus Among the Doctors* showing an effeminate-looking Christ hounded by decrepit old men. As you progress through this extraordinary panoply, display cases along the corridor contain scarcely less spectacular works of sculpture, ceramics and gold-and silverwork.

Next in line is **Titian**, ushering in a stylistic revolution with his greater range of tones and almost Impressionistic brush-work as evidenced in his masterpiece *St Jerome in the*

Wilderness. The influence of Titian can be seen in the work of **Tintoretto** – his massive canvas of *Paradise* is exhibited in the central gallery on the ground floor – and in *The Annunciation* by **El Greco** in which Mannerist influence is also patent.

The Early Baroque fascination with light and shade is brilliantly demonstrated by **Caravaggio**'s *St Catherine of Alexandria* and by **José Ribera**'s *Lamentation over the Body of Christ* in which the ghostly white body of Christ and the grieving faces are highlighted. The **Bernini** sculpture of *St Sebastian* heralds the more exuberant later Baroque work exemplified by **Murillo**'s *Madonna and Child with St Rosalina of Palermo*. **Claude Lorrain**'s *Pastoral Landscape with the flight into Egypt* encapsulates his characteristic romantic twilight landscape and nostalgia for the classical world while **Tiepolo**'s *Death of Hyacinthus* uses monumental figures and rich colours to capture the drama of the moment. The eighteenth-century interest in architectural scenes and the demand for souvenirs of the Grand Tour of Italy is represented by three flawless views of Venice by **Canaletto**, the most accomplished creator of such work. The floor is completed with still more classics, this time Flemish and Dutch. The richly coloured small oil of *Christ in the Storm on the Sea of Galilee* by **Jan Brueghel the Elder**, **Van Dyck**'s marvellous portrait of the disdainful *Jacques Le Roy* and **Ruben**'s luxurious *Toilet of Venus* are amongst the highlights.

AMERICANS, IMPRESSIONISTS AND EXPRESSIONISTS: FIRST FLOOR

The present baron, Hans Heinrich Thyssen, began collecting, according to his own account, to fill the gaps in his late father's collection, after it was split among his siblings. He, too, began with old masters, but in the 1960s started on

German Expressionists, closely followed by Cubists, Futurists, Vorticists and De Stijl, and also American art of the nineteenth century. The first floor, then, is largely down to him.

The floor begins with a comprehensive round of seventeenth-century Dutch painting of various genres: still lifes, scenes from everyday life, landscapes and seascapes. The supreme technical skill and minute observation is demonstrated in still lifes such as **Willem Claesz Heda**'s *Rummer, Silver Tazza, Pie and Other Objects*, while Frans Hals introduces more lively subjects with his *Family Group in a Landscape* and his laughing *Fisherman Playing a Violin*. The characteristic Dutch landscape plays a major role in a number of pictures including *View of Naarden* by **Jacob Isaacksz van Ruisdael** where alternating patches of sunlight and shade are used to give the sensation of depth. The British eighteenth-century painters **Thomas Gainsborough** and **Sir Joshua Reynolds** also get a look in with their contrasting portraits of English aristocrats.

In **Rooms 29** and **30** is displayed one of the largest and best collections of American painting outside the US. The theme of landscape seen to good effect in **Thomas Cole**'s *Expulsion, Moon and Firelight* predominates, reflecting the nineteenth-century vision of America as an idyllic virgin land awaiting the settlement of the pioneers. The native population only feature as nostalgic stereotypes in the later paintings such as Frederick Remington's *Apache Fire Signal*. Works by James Whistler, Winslow Homer and John Singer Sargent are displayed as is James Goodwyn Clonney's wonderful *Fishing Party on Long Island Sound*.

This is followed by a group of European **Romantics and Realists**, including Constable's *The Lock*, bought not so long ago for $14m, **Goya**'s *Asensio Julia* and his *El Tío Paquete* from his *Black Paintings* (see *The Prado*, p.60).

Impressionism and **post–Impressionism** are also strong points of the collection, with works by **Manet**, **Monet** and **Renoir** in the former style and **Gauguin**, **Degas**, **Lautrec** and **Cézanne** in the latter (**Room 33**). Monet and Pisarro indulge in some marvellous experimentation with light and reflections in their respective works, *The Thaw at Vétheruil* and *Saint-Honoré Street in the Afternoon. Effect of Rain*. The shimmering green dress of the *Swaying Dancer* and the pastel shades of the jockey's colours in *Race Horses – The Training*, both by Degas, are a real treat. The pioneering *Portrait of a Farmer* by Paul Cézanne foreshadows the cubism of Braque and Picasso seen on the ground floor and marks him out as one of the most influential of this group of painters. The collection is especially strong in the choice of paintings by **Vincent van Gogh**, which includes the fiery *Stevedores at Arles* and one of his last and most gorgeous works, *Les Vessenots*. The influence of van Gogh is apparent in the work of the Fauvists, particularly *Waterloo Bridge* by André Derain and *Olive Trees* by Maurice Vlaminck.

The broad-ranging **Expressionist movement** with its enunciation of powerful emotions and use of equally powerful colours is fully represented. The stunningly vivid paintings of **Ernst Ludwig Kirchner**, **Wassily Kandinsky** and **Franz Marc** are fascinating, as is the apocalyptic work, *Metropolis,* by **George Grosz**.

AVANT-GARDES: GROUND FLOOR

Works on the ground floor run from the beginning of the twentieth century through to around 1970. The good baron doesn't, apparently, like contemporary art: "If they can throw colours, I can be free to duck," he explained, following the gallery's opening. The most interesting work in his "experimental avant-garde" sections is from the **Cubists**.

There is an inspired, side-by-side hanging of parallel studies by **Picasso** (*Man with a Clarinet*), **Braque** (*Woman with a Mandolin*) and **Mondrian** (*Grey-Blue Composition*).

The **Synthesis of Modernity** section includes the minimalist work *Catalan Peasant with a Guitar*, by **Joan Miró**, the chaotic *Brown and Silver* by **Jackson Pollock**, and the explosive *Picture with Three Spots* by **Wassily Kandinsky**. Surrealism is, not surprisingly, represented by **Salvador Dalí** with his *Dream caused by the Flight of a Bee Around a Pomegranate a Second before Awakening* in which the artist's wife is depicted sleeping naked in the centre of a fantastic landscape populated by dream images of elephants on stilts and fish-eating tigers. Following on in the surrealist tradition is **Francis Bacon**'s distorted image *Portrait of George Dyer in a Mirror*. More down to earth are the stark *Hotel Room* by **Edward Hopper** and the cartoon iconography of **Roy Lichtenstein**'s *A Woman in A Bath*. Sharing the same room is a fascinating **Lucian Freud**, *Portrait of Baron Thyssen*, posed in front of the Watteau Pierrot hanging upstairs. To finish there is a clever play on light and reflections in Richard Lester's *Telephone Booths*, while downstairs by the café is the series of five extensive flowing, colourful canvases that make up *The Blinding Exile* cycle by Roberto Matta.

CENTRO DE ARTE REINA SOFÍA

T he final essential stop on the Madrid art circuit (or *Paseo del Arte*) is the **Centro de Arte Reina Sofía**, an immense exhibition space covering some 12,505 square metres and providing a permanent home for the Spanish collection of contemporary art, acquisitions of modern art made by the Reina Sofía, the twentieth-century collections from the Prado, and Miró and Picasso legacies including the jewel in the crown of the museum's collection – **Guernica**.

....

The Centro de Arte Reina Sofía (Map 5, I5) is
open Monday & Wednesday–Saturday 10am–9pm,
Sunday 10am–2.30pm; 400ptas, concessions
200ptas, free on Saturday after 2.30pm
& all day Sunday. Metro Atocha.

....

The museum is housed in a vast building that was once the Hospital General de San Carlos. Constructed on the initiative of Carlos III and designed by Francesco Sabatini, the initial scheme for the hospital envisaged a gargantuan complex of seven quadrangles of which this was the only one ever actually completed. It ceased functioning as a hospital in 1965 and twelve years later was declared a monument of historical and artistic interest with work beginning on transforming it into a museum of modern art. The initial conversion took until 1986 when Queen Sofía opened the space for staging temporary exhibitions. It was not until 1990 that the final renovation work was completed and it was opened as a museum with a permanent collection, and in July 1992, *Guernica* was brought here from the Casón del Buen Retiro.

Although rather sombre-looking from the outside, inside the light from the central courtyard, the white walls, vast galleries and high ceilings creates a sensation of spaciousness ideally suited to the display of so many large-scale works. Transparent lifts designed by British architect, Ian Ritchie, shuttle visitors up the outside of the building, whose levels feature a **cinema**, excellent art book and design **shops**, a print, music and photographic **library**, a **restaurant**, **bar** and **café** in the basement and a peaceful inner courtyard garden, as well as temporary exhibition halls and the collection of twentieth-century art (second and fourth floors). There are audio-guide headphones in English giving a good introduction to Spanish art, by the second-floor entrance.

....

The museum keeps different opening hours and days to its neighbours and is one of the few museums open on Monday, so don't make the mistake of trying to cram in a visit after a Prado-Thyssen overdose.

....

THE SECOND FLOOR

The permanent collection begins on the second floor with
a selection of work entitled "A Change of Century" exam-
ining the origins of modern Spanish art mainly through the
two artistic nucleii that developed in Cataluña and the
Basque Country at the end of the nineteenth century.

Picasso's *Mujer en Azul* (1901), a study of a bourgeois
woman in all her finery, piercing eyes and over-the-top
make up, is one of the early highlights, painted during one
of the artist's brief stays in Madrid at the turn of the century
and given an honorary mention at the National Exhibiton
of Fine Arts in 1901. Picasso failed to reclaim it and it was
mislaid for a number of years before being rescued. Look
out too for the luscious *Retrato de Sonia de Klamery* (1913) by
Anglada Camarasa and the vivid Expressionist work *La
Comulgante* (1914) by María Blanchard. The Madrid painter,
José Gutiérrez Solana, has a room dedicated to his highly
original indiosyncratic work which includes the solemn *La
Visita del Obispo* (1926), the melancholic *La Procesión de la
Muerte* (1930) and his famous portrayal of *La Tertulia del Café
de Pombo* (1920) which features a range of artistic and liter-
ary figures including Solana himself on the far right.
Sculpture is well represented with the Cubist-influenced
iron work of Julio González and the innovative studies by
Pablo Gargallo such as the mysterious *Máscara de Greta Garbo
con Mechón* (1930), the semi-religious semi-dictatorial figure
of *El Gran Profeta* (1933), and the plump-faced head of
Picasso (1913). This is followed by strong sections on
Cubism, including fine work by **Juan Gris** and Picasso, as
well as the Paris School featuring the early Cezanne-influ-
enced *Paisaje de Cadaqués* (1923) by Salvador Dalí.

Midway round the collection is the main reason that
most come to the Reina Sofía – **Picasso's Guernica**.

Superbly displayed and now without its former bullet-proof glass and steel girders to protect it, this icon of twentieth-century Spanish art and politics carries a shock that defies all familiarity. The sheer size of the monumental work at 3.5m high and over 7.5m long is the first thing that impresses and it's certainly worth jockeying for position among the crowds to get a good view. The preliminary studies, displayed around the room, show how Picasso developed its symbols – the dying horse, the fallen soldier, the mother and dead child, the bulls, the blacked-out dove, the grief-stricken woman, the sun, the flower, the burning figure plummeting to its death – making their incorporation into the painting all the more marvellous. Picasso's notorious reluctance to talk about the painting has led to decades of debate by art historians about its exact meaning. Common interpretations view the screaming horse as symbolizing the suffering of the people and the bull the overthrow of reason and the rise of animal passion. Whatever the arguments, this disturbing monumental work certainly lives up to expectations.

The post-*Guernica* halls feature rooms devoted to the heavyweights **Dalí** and **Miró** as well as a host of lesser known Spanish artists representing the main currents in Spanish art in the years immediately following World War II. The development in Dali's work is clearly displayed from the classic portrait of his sister gazing out of the window, *Muchacha en la Ventana* (1925), to the Cubist-influenced *Arlequín* (1925), and onto his more famous Surrealist work such as *El Gran Masturbador* and *El Enigma de Hitler* with their dream landscapes, sexual imagery, insects and symbols of putrefaction. A large range of Miró's rather impenetrable but pleasing canvases and sculptures are exhibited with their characteristic images of dots, spots and crescents symbolizing the stars, sun, moon, birds and people.

THE SECOND FLOOR

The story of Guernica

When the **Spanish Civil War** broke out in July 1936 Picasso was living in France, continuing his rather hedonistic lifestyle detached from politics and public life, although he did accept the honorary post of Director of the Prado in support of the Popular Front government. Then in January 1937 he accepted a commission to paint a mural for the Spanish Republic's pavilion at the **World Fair** in Paris on a subject and title of his own choice. By April he had still not started the work, but on April 26, 1937, the German Condor Legion, acting in concert with Franco's Nationalist forces, bombed and machine-gunned the Basque town of **Guernica**, celebrated home of Basque "liberties" and cultural traditions. Defenceless and without obvious military significance, the three-hour bombardment by wave upon wave of German planes almost completely destroyed the town, although the famous oak before which the Spanish monarchs had sworn to observe local Basque rights was miraculously preserved. Despite initial denials, the Nationalists later admitted responsibility for the atrocity and Göring, head of the German Luftwaffe, admitted in a chilling statement made shortly before his suicide that Germany had regarded Guernica as a testing ground for **aerial bombing**. Photo journalists captured the horror of the atrocity which sent shock waves around Europe. The war had forced many intellectuals, especially in France, to take sides on the issue of Fascism versus Democracy and the time for sitting on the fence for Picasso was over. He began working on the commission and amid rumours that he was pro-Franco issued the following statement: "The Spanish struggle is the fight of reaction against the people, against freedom. My whole life as an artist has been nothing more than a continuous struggle against reaction and the death of art. How could anyone think for a moment that I could be in agreement with reaction and death. In the panel on which I am working and which I shall call *Guernica* and in all my recent works of art I clearly express my abhorrence of the military caste which has sunk Spain in an ocean of pain and death."

The resulting canvas produced in little over a month relied on allegory and metaphor, combined with the legacy of Cubism to produce a general commentary on the barbarity and terror of war itself. The Right criticized the painting as the degenerate work of a madman while many on the Left were disappointed because of its inaccessibility and its failure to make an explicit rallying call for the forces opposed to Fascism. After the Paris Expo the work was "loaned" to the **Museum of Modern Art in New York**, until such time, as Picasso put it, Spain had regained its democratic liberty. The artist never lived to see that time, dying as he did two years before Franco in 1973, but in 1981, following the restoration of democracy, the painting was, amid much controversy, moved to Madrid to hang (as Picasso had stipulated) in the **Prado**. Its transfer to the Reina Sofía in 1992 again prompted much soul-searching and protest, though for anyone who saw it in the old Prado annexe, it looks truly liberated in its present setting.

THE FOURTH FLOOR

The permanent collection continues on the fourth floor, covering Spain's postwar years up to the present day including work from the abstract and avant-garde movements, to **Pop Art**, **Constructivism**, and **minimalism**. Interesting Spanish work from **Antoni Tàpies** and **Eduardo Chillida** is set in the context of international avant-garde work by **Francis Bacon**, **Graham Sutherland** and **Henry Moore**. The collection ends with galleries dedicated to contemporary art using manufactured products and industrial materials and range from the dizzying experience of Jesús Rafael Soto's *Extensión amarilla y blanca* to the blinding display of fluorescent strip lighting by Dan Flavin.

THE FOURTH FLOOR

THE RETIRO AND AROUND

I n addition to the heavyweight sites of the Prado,
Thyssen-Bornemisza and Reina Sofía galleries, the area
around the Paseo del Prado, is home to a host of other
minor attractions. These include the recently renovated
Estación de Atocha itself, the fascinating **Real Fábrica
de Tapices**, a number of the city's smaller museums, the
startlingly peaceful **Jardines Botánicos** and the **Parque
del Retiro**, a delightful mix of formal gardens and wider
open spaces – the perfect place to escape for a few hours.

The area covered by this chapter is shown
in detail on colour map 8.

PARQUE DEL RETIRO

Map 8. Metro Retiro/Atocha.

The origins of the park lie in the early seventeenth century
when Felipe IV's royal adviser, the Conde Duque de

Olivares, produced a plan for a new palace and playground for the court, the Buen Retiro (Good Retreat). Work began in 1630 and the architects Crescenzi, Gómez de Mora and Carbonell built a huge complex of which only the ballroom (**Casón del Buen Retiro**, see p.64) and the Hall of Realms (**Museo del Ejército**, see p.83) survive to this day. Gardens were laid out at the same time and included a zoo for the exhibition of savage animals, an aviary for exotic birds and a large lake where mock battles and waterborne dramas could be staged. Other elements were added over the years, such as a French-style parterre during the reign of Felipe V (1700–1746), a royal porcelain factory constructed by Carlos III (1759–1788) and an astronomical observatory by Carlos IV (1788–1808). During the Peninsular War, the gardens, used by the French as a fortified barracks, were badly damaged but restored under Fernando VII who opened most of the park to the public. After the 1868 Revolution, the park became municipal property.

Although *Madrileños* jog, rollerblade, cycle, picnic and row on the lake (you can rent boats by the Monumento a Alfonso XII) in the park, their main activity here is to promenade. The busiest day is Sunday, when half of Madrid turns out for the **paseo**. Dressed for show, families stroll around nodding at neighbours and building up an appetite for a long Sunday lunch. Strolling aside, there's almost always something going on in the park, including a good programme of concerts and *ferias* organized by the city council. The most popular of the fairs is the **Feria del Libro** (Book Fair), held from the end of May into early June, when every publisher and half the country's bookshops set up stalls and offer a 25 percent discount on their wares. In the summer months, **free films** are shown in the evenings in the area known as La Chopera, in the southwest corner of the park, while on Saturday and Sunday there are **puppet shows** by

PARQUE DEL RETIRO

the Puerta de Alcalá entrance (1pm, 7pm & 8pm). On Sunday, you can often watch groups of Peruvian musicians or Catalans performing their counting dance, the *sardana*.

In addition, travelling art exhibitions are frequently housed in the beautiful **Palacio de Velázquez** (June–Sept Mon & Wed–Sat 11am–8pm, Sun 11am–6pm; Oct–May Mon & Wed–Sat 10am–6pm, Sun 10am–4pm), the nearby **Palacio de Cristal** and **Casa de Vacas** (daily 10.30am–2.30pm & 4–8pm; closed Aug except for puppet shows). Look out, too, for *El Angel Caído* (Fallen Angel), the world's only public statue to Lucifer, in the south of the park. Alongside is the very fine **rose garden** designed by municipal head gardener Cecilio Rodríguez who died in 1953. His service spanning 75 years is commemorated by the well-groomed formal gardens that bear his name on the east side of the park (daily 8.00am–3pm). In the northeast corner, remains of Fernando VII's private recreational zone can be clearly seen around the pink folly, **La Casita del Pescador**, in the middle of an ornamental lake.

Although El Retiro has a very safe reputation by day, it's best not to wander alone in the late evening. Note also that the area east of La Chopera is known as a cruising ground for gay prostitutes.

PUERTA DE ALCALÁ TO LOS JARDINES BOTÁNICOS

Leaving the park at the northwest corner takes you into Plaza de la Independencia, in the centre of which is one of the two remaining gates of the old city walls. Built in the late eighteenth century by Francesco Sabatini to commemorate Carlos III's first twenty years on the throne, the **Puerta de Alcalá** was the biggest city gate in Europe at that time and, like the bear and bush, has become one of the city's monumental emblems.

South from here, you pass the **Museo de Artes Decorativas** (Tues–Fri 9.30am–3pm, Sat & Sun 10am–2pm; 400ptas, concessions 200ptas, free on Sun) which has its entrance at c/Montalbán 12. The aristrocratic residence houses an interesting but unspectacular collection of furniture, reconstructed sixteenth- and seventeenth-century rooms and *objets d'art* from all over Spain. The *azulejos* and other decorative ceramics are, without doubt, the highlight.

A couple of blocks west, in a corner of the Naval Ministry at Paseo del Prado 5 is the **Museo Naval** (Tues–Sun 10.30am–1.30pm; free). Beyond the impeccably turned out saluting guards you'll find a well-presented array of models, maps and charts, paintings, weapons and navigational instruments grouped into periods of Spanish naval history. Highlights include the first map to show the territories of the New World drawn by Juan de la Costa in 1500, canons from the Spanish Armada, part of Cortés' standard used during the Conquest of Mexico and the giant globes made by Coronelli in the late seventeenth century.

The military theme continues with the **Museo del Ejército** (Tues–Sun 10am–2pm; 100ptas, free on Sat. Metro Retiro) just to the south at c/Méndez Núñez 1. A gloomily eccentric timewarp of a museum, it's crammed full of military memorabilia, often chaotically displayed, and, seemingly unaware of the changes over the past twenty years, preserving a distinctly pro-Franco stance. The morbid, motley collection includes a piece of the shirt worn by Pizarro when he was assassinated, a death mask of Napoleon and part of the bomb thrown by anarchist Mateo Morral at the wedding procession of Alfonso XIII and Victoria Eugenie, all accompanied by curious piped music ranging from *Doctor Zhivago* to the theme from *Shaft*. Of

PUERTA DE ALCALÁ TO LOS JARDINES BOTÁNICOS |

more interest perhaps are the beautiful ceilings of the building itself, fragments of Don Juan's Flag used at Lepanto (1571), mementos of Cervantes from the same battle and the tent used by Carlos I on his Tunis Campaign in 1535.

South again, past the Prado's Casón del Buen Retiro annex, is **San Jerónimo el Real** (July–Sept Mon–Fri 8am–1.30pm & 6–8pm, Sat & Sun 9am–1.30pm & 6.30–8pm; Oct–June Mon–Fri 8am–1.30pm & 5–8pm, Sat & Sun 9am–1.30pm & 5.30–8pm). A monastery was founded on this site in the early sixteenth century by the Catholic monarchs, Fernando and Isabel, becoming an important destination for religious processions from the city, site of the swearing in of the heirs to the throne (the Princes of Asturias) and stage for royal marriages and coronations (including that of King Juan Carlos in 1975). Despite significant remodelling with a restored interior and the addition of two Gothic towers in the mid-nineteenth century, the old form of the church is still clearly visible.

Opposite is the Neoclassical **Real Academia Española de la Lengua** (Royal Language Academy) established in 1714 by Felipe V to "cultivate and establish the purity and elegance of the Castilian language", whose job nowadays is to make sure that the Spanish language is not corrupted by foreign or otherwise unsuitable words. The results are entrusted to their official dictionary – a work that bears virtually no relation to the Spanish you'll hear spoken on the streets.

Los Jardines Botánicos

Map 8, A6. Daily: March & Oct 10am–7pm; April & Sept 10am–8pm; May–Aug 10am–9pm; Nov–Feb 10am–6pm; 200ptas. Metro Atocha.

Just below the Plaza de Murillo entrance to the Prado are the delightful, shaded **Jardines Botánicos**. Opened in 1781 by Carlos III, the gardens and buildings were developed by Juan de Villanueva and botanist Casimiro Gómez Ortega. The aim was to collect and grow species from all over the Spanish Empire, develop a research centre and supply medicinal herbs and plants to Madrid's hospitals. The gardens were abandoned after the Peninsular War and although they were renovated later in the nineteenth century with a zoo installed, they soon fell into disrepair once more. The nineteenth-century writer and traveller, Richard Ford, reported that they became so neglected they were inhabited by a pair of escaped boa constrictors who survived on a diet of stray cats and dogs. The gardens were eventually restored in the 1980s using the original eighteenth-century plans and are now home to some thirty thousand species from around the globe. Make a point of visiting the state of the art hothouse with its collection of tropical plants and amazing cacti.

On the southern side of the botanical gardens is the sloping **Cuesta de Claudio Moyano**, lined with little wooden bookstalls. You can buy anything here, new or old, from secondhand copies of Captain Marvel to Cervantes or Jackie Collins. There's always something of interest, such as old prints of Madrid and relics from the Franco era. Although it's at its busiest on Sundays some of the stalls are open every day.

ESTACIÓN DE ATOCHA AND BEYOND

Map 7, B9. Metro Atocha.

At the bottom of the Paseo del Prado stands the impressive **Estación de Atocha**, worth a look even if you're not travelling out of Madrid. It's actually two stations, old and new; the former, a glorious 1880s glasshouse, revamped as a kind of tropical garden by Rafael Moneo in 1992. It's a wonderful sight from the walkways above, while on the platforms beyond sit the gleaming white high-speed AVE trains, built to ferry passengers to the 1992 Expo in Sevilla in two and a half hours.

Also in this area is the **Museo Nacional de Etnología** (Tues–Sat 10am–7.30pm, Sun 10am–2pm; 400ptas, free Sat after 2.30pm & all day Sun), founded by the eccentric Dr. Pedro González Velasco to house his collection. The unimaginatively displayed exhibits are designed to give an overview of different cultures of the world, in particular those intertwined with Spanish history; the ground floor focuses on the Philippines and Asian religions, the first floor Africa and the second the Americas. The most interesting exhibits from the good doctor's original collection are to be found in a side room on the ground floor – a macabre collection of deformed skulls, a Guanche (the original inhabitants of the Canary Islands) mummy, shrivelled embryos and the skeleton of a circus giant (2m 35cm tall). It is said the old doctor embalmed his own daughter when she died and was regularly seen taking her out for meals and rides in his carriage.

On the hill opposite at the edge of the Retiro, the **Observatorio Astronómico** (Mon–Fri 9am–2pm) was another ingredient of Carlos III's academic complex, although not actually finished until 1845. It's a beautiful Neoclassical building housing a poorly displayed collection of telescopes, chronometers, sundials and sextants.

Real Fábrica de Tapices

Map 8, F9. Mon–Fri 9am–12.30pm; 250ptas. Metro Atocha.

Ten minutes' walk southeast of the station, the fascinating **Real Fábrica de Tapices** (Royal Tapestry Workshop) on c/Fuentarrabia is well worth a visit. The original factory, situated in Plaza Santa Bárbara, was founded in 1721 by Felipe V, who wanted to emulate the Gobelins factory in

Paris. The young Goya was employed to paint the cartoons that now hang in the Prado for a series of tapestries depicting everyday *Madrileño* life. The factory was moved to its present site at the end of the nineteenth century but the processes have not changed for hundreds of years, and the eighteenth-century vertical looms are still in use. The workers (now numbering only 42 compared to 400 fifty years ago) can be seen coolly looping handfuls of bobbins around a myriad of strings, sewing up worn out masterpieces with exactly matching silk, and weaving together hundreds of different threads to produce different shades for a new tapestry. The intricacy of the work, the patience of the weavers and their artistic skill is astonishing. With progress being painfully slow – a square metre of tapestry every two months – the astronomical price of two million pesetas per square metre soon becomes believable. One of the giant sixteenth-century Flemish tapestries on display, produced before the era of the electric light, took more than two generations to complete.

GRAN VÍA, CHUECA AND MALASAÑA

The **Gran Vía**, Madrid's great thoroughfare, runs from just above Plaza de la Cibeles to Plaza de España, effectively dividing the old city to the south from the newer northern parts. Permanently jammed with traffic and crowded with shoppers and sightseers, it's the commercial heart of the city and, if you spare the time to look up, quite a monument in its own right, with its turn-of-the-century, palace-like shops, offices and hotels.

C/de Fuencarral heads north of the Gran Vía to the Glorieta de Bilbao, site of the *Café Comercial*, scene of many *tertulias* after the Civil War and still one of the most popular meeting places in Madrid. To either side of c/de Fuencarral are two of Madrid's most characterful *barrios*: **Chueca** to the east, and **Malasaña** to the west. Their chief appeal lies in their amazing concentration of bars, restaurants and, especially, nightlife. However, the **Museo Municipal**, **Museo Romántico** and a number of beautiful **churches** provide a more than adequate excuse to look around here by day. Further to the east is the elegant area of **Las Salesas**, while north lies the former working-class suburb of **Chamberí** with its strong sense of identity, plentiful supply of bars, pleasant plazas and an excellent market.

....

**The area covered by this chapter is shown
in detail on colour map 7.**

....

GRAN VÍA

The **Gran Vía** (Great Way) was constructed in three stages over nearly half a century in order to link the two new districts of Argüelles and Salamanca. Its construction involved the destruction of fourteen other streets, the alteration of fourteen more, and the road itself became a symbol of the nations's arrival into the twentieth century. Financed on the back of the boom due to Spain's neutrality in World War I, the Gran Vía is a showcase for a whole gamut of architectural styles, from Modernist and Art Deco to neo-Rococo and Rationalist.

The finest section of the Gran Vía is the earliest, constructed between 1910 and 1924, stretching from c/de Alcalá to the Telefónica building. Two buildings at the junction with c/de Alcalá really stand out. The **Edificio Metropolis**, built between 1905 and 1911 by the French architects Jules and Raymond Fevrier, with its cylindrical facade, paired columns, white-stone sculptures, zinc-tiled roof decorated with gold garlands and topped by a winged statue, is suitably over the top, while the **Grassy building** (1916–17) just above it is equally overblown featuring curved balconies, colonnades and a dome. Look out for the Art Deco **Museo Chicote** at no. 12 where you can sample a rather overpriced cocktail in the bar founded back in 1931 by Perico Chicote in order to "mix drinks, lives and opinions" (see p.163 for more on this bar).

This section of Gran Vía was known as "Shell Alley" during the Civil War as the monumental **Telefónica building** was used as a reference point by Franco's Nationalist forces to bomb the Gran Vía from their trenches in Casa de Campo. The vast 81-metre slab of a building with its plain beige facade decorated with touches of Spanish Baroque was Spain's first skyscraper and prompted King Alfonso XIII to declare that Spain had finally entered the modern world.

The next stretch of the street down to Plaza de Callao is dominated by shops, cafés and cinemas, the latter with their massive old-fashioned hand-painted posters. The neon-lit Plaza de Callao is now the gateway to the shoppers' paradise of **c/de Preciados**, home to the new French store *FNAC* and to the ubiquitous department store *El Corte Inglés*. Don't miss the classic Art Deco **Capitol** building (1930–33) on the corner just before the street begins to slope down towards Plaza de España, its curved facade embellished with lurid neon signs.

CHUECA AND LAS SALESAS

The smaller streets immediately to the north of Gran Vía are shady hinterland areas home to all manner of vice-related activities and are notorious for petty crime, but this only becomes a problem at night. In the *barrio* of **Chueca**, east of c/de Fuencarral, there's a strong neighbourhood feel, with kids and grannies on the streets during the day, and a lively gay scene springing into action around **Plaza de Chueca** at night. The plaza (Metro Chueca) is fronted by one of the best old-style *vermut* bars in the city, *Bodega*

Angel Sierra on c/Gravina at the northwest corner. To the south at c/de Augusto Figueroa 35 is *La Tienda de Vinos* or "*El Comunista*", which gets its nickname because it acted as a meeting place of left-wing critics of the old Franco regime.

For details of the bars and nightlife venues in Chueca, see pp.161–5, pp.170–2 and pp.175–7.

From Plaza de Chueca **east to Paseo de Recoletos** (the beginning of the long Paseo de la Castellana) are some of the city's most enticing streets. Offbeat restaurants, small private art galleries and odd corner shops are to be found here in abundance and **c/Almirante** has some of the city's most fashionable clothes shops, too. Head south down c/del Barquillo to the **Plaza del Rey** for a look at the **Casa de las Siete Chimeneas** (House of Seven Chimneys), which is supposedly haunted by a mistress of Felipe II who disappeared in mysterious circumstances. The sixteenth-century house has been heavily restored but is still recognizable as the work of the two architects of El Escorial, Juan Bautista de Toledo and Juan de Herrera. Charles I stayed here when he came to Madrid to press his unsuccessful suit for marriage to the Infanta María.

To the north up c/del Barquillo is the stately **Plaza de las Salesas** dominated by the church and convent of Las Salesas Reales, founded in 1747 by Barbara of Braganza, Portuguese wife of Fernando VI, as a retreat and escape from her mother-in-law, Isabella Farnese in case her husband died before she did. It was never used by Barbara as she was outlived by her husband. The church, with its impressive white granite Baroque facade decorated with marble statues, is set behind a very fine forecourt containing a rose garden, palm trees and magnolias. Inside there's a grotto-like chapel, impressive frescoes and stained-glass windows, an extravagant pulpit and striking green marble altar decoration. The elaborate tombs of Fernando VI and Barbara of Braganza lie in a side chapel, as does that of the military hero General O'Donnell. The convent behind the church now houses the Palacio de Justicia, the City's Law Courts, facing the elegant Plaza de la Villa de París.

West along c/Fernando VI past the marvellous grocers and fishmongers are the Gaudiesque flowing lines of the cream-coloured **Sociedad de Autores** (Society of Authors), its dripping decoration of flowers, faces and balconies giving the appearance of a melting candle. The only really significant *modernista* building in Madrid, it was designed in 1902 by the Catalan José Grasés Riera. Just beyond is Plaza de Santa Bárbara and Alonso Martínez, one of the main centres of student nightlife in Madrid, with the nearby streets packed with trendy bars and nightclubs.

Museo Romántico

Map 7, H4. Tues–Sat 9am–3pm, Sun & public holidays 10am–2pm; 400ptas, concessions 200ptas, free on Sun. Metro Tribunal.

Nearby at c/San Mateo 13, the **Museo Romántico** aims to show the lifestyle and outlook of the late-Romantic era through the recreation of a typical residence of the period. It's a successful attempt with its musty atmosphere, creaking floorboards, cracking walls crowded with canvases and rooms overflowing with kitsch memorabilia and period furniture. Contributing to the pleasant aura of nostalgia are a series of idealized folk portraits of bullfighters, flamenco dancers and gypsies and some fine old engravings of Madrid at the end of the eighteenth century. The air of Romanticism is maintained by a pair of small paintings by Leonardo Alcázar satirizing the romantic idea of suicide, and a case displaying the pistols Mariano José de Larra used to shoot himself in 1837. The more serious artistic element is limited to Goya's *St Gregory* hanging in the chapel, portraits by Federico de Madrazo and other work by Zurbarán, Murillo and Sorolla.

Museo Municipal

Map 7, G4. Tues–Fri 9.30am–8pm, Sat & Sun 10am–2pm; 300ptas, free Wed & Sun. Metro Tribunal.

Just around the corner is the **Museo Municipal**, c/de Fuencarral 78, opened on this site in 1929 in the former city almshouse built in the early eighteenth century by Pedro de Ribera. True to form he created a fantastically decorated elaborate Baroque doorway placed on an otherwise plain red-brick facade. Inside, the museum contains a chronological collection including paintings, photos, models, sculptures and porcelain all related to the history and urban development of Madrid, although some sections are likely to be closed because of renovation.

The lower ground floor houses archeological finds from the banks of the Manzanares, and from nearby Roman villas. The ground floor contains displays related to Habsburg Madrid, including Pedro Texeira's fascinating plan of Madrid dated 1656, and Pedro Berruguete's outstanding *Virgin and Child*, paintings of Plaza Mayor, Casa de Campo, the Retiro and other famous Madrid landmarks. Bourbon Madrid is the focus of the first floor with some huge Bayeu canvases portraying *Madrileño* life, Goya's *Allegory of the City of Madrid* (see p.18), a great display of crude cartoons satirizing Napoleon and a supremely accurate model of Madrid in 1830 by León Gil de Palacio. A good selection of reasonably priced prints, posters and books is available in the museum shop.

CHUECA AND LAS SALESAS

MALASAÑA

To the west of c/de Fuencarral is **Malasaña**, named after the young orphan and seamstress, Manuela Malasaña, who became a heroine of the 1808 Rebellion. One version of the story states that French troops searched her on her way home from work and found the scissors she used for cutting cloth. Since they had forbidden the carrying of any weapons she was summarily executed. The area, also known as the Barrio de Maravillas, became extremely poor and dishevelled after the Civil War and there were even plans to bulldoze it. However, the availability of cheap accommodation brought an injection of life with the arrival of students and young people in the 1960s. More recently, the quarter was the focus of the *movida Madrileña*, the "happening scene" of the late 1970s and early 1980s. As the country relaxed after the death of Franco and the city developed into a thoroughly modern capital under the leadership of the late lamented mayor, Tierno Galván, Malasaña became the mecca of the young. Bars appeared behind every doorway, drugs were sold openly in the streets, and there was an extraordinary atmosphere of new-found freedom. Today, the threatened takeover by drug addicts has been largely halted and the area immediately around **Plaza Dos de Mayo** has been redeveloped with a fantastic selection of **bars**, **restaurants**, **clubs** and **cafés** springing up, many of which have a very particular eccentric identity. The maze of dark and narrow streets to the south of the square, however, is best avoided at night.

Bars and restaurants aside, the streets have an interest of their own and there are some wonderful old shop signs and architectural details. Best of all is the old pharmacy on the corner of c/San Andrés and c/San Vicente Ferrer with its irresistible 1920s *azulejo* scenes depicting cures for diarrhoea, headaches and suchlike. Finally, two churches are

worth a visit. The **Convento de San Plácido** (Mon–Fri
10am–noon & 4–6pm, Sat 4–6pm) on c/de San Roque was
founded in the early seventeenth century although the present building dates from 1661. It features a magnificent
high-altar canvas of the *Annunciation* by Claudio Coello and
frescoes by Francisco Rizzi. Scandal plagued the convent
with rumours that the nuns had become possessed by devils, and of the sexual misdemeanours perpetrated by their
confessor. **San Antonio de los Alemanes** (daily
9am–1pm & 6pm–8pm) on Corredera de San Pablo was
designed in 1624 by the Jesuit architect Pedro Sánchez and
Juan Gómez de Mora, although it was renovated in the late
nineteenth century. The interior is covered with dizzying
floor-to-ceiling fresco decorations painted by Luca
Giordano featuring scenes from the life of St Anthony.

MALASAÑA

SALAMANCA

The elegant tree-lined Paseo del Prado continues beyond Plaza de la Cibeles as the aristocratic and palatial Paseo de Recoletos, finally metamorphosing into the Manhattan-style urban landscape of the **Paseo de la Castellana**. Bus 27 will take you the full distance – an architectural odyssey spanning the eigtheenth to the late twentieth centuries. Spreading out to the east of the Castellana is the exclusive **Barrio de Salamanca**, Madrid's designer shopping district. There are also a scattering of other sights, museums and galleries that might tempt you up here, in particular the **Museo de Lázaro Galdiano** and the **Museo Sorolla**, the pick of Madrid's smaller museums.

....

The area covered by this chapter is shown in detail on colour map 9.

....

The grid-like *barrio* of **Salamanca** was developed in the second half of the nineteenth century as a new upmarket residential zone under the patronage of the Marquis of Salamanca. This flamboyant larger-than-life arch-capitalist became Minister of Finance at the age of 32, went on to establish the forerunner to the Bank of Spain, developed Madrid's first rail and tram lines and was the proud owner of the first flush toilets in Madrid. A generous patron of the arts, renowned party host and master of insider dealing and speculation, he made and lost a fortune on three separate occasions, the last time as a result of his massive investment in the Barrio de Salamanca. Today the area is still a smart address for apartments and even more so for shops. The streets are populated by the furcoat and sunglasses brigade decked out in Gucci and plenty of gold. The *barrio* is also the haunt of *pijos* - universally denigrated rich kids - and the grid of streets between c/de Goya and c/de José Ortega y Gasset contains most of the city's **designer emporiums**. Unsurprisingly the bars and restaurants in this area tend to be rather pricey, although the quality is high (see pp.138, pp.150–2 and p.167).

For a full rundown of Salamanca's best shops see p.214.

Along the Paseo de la Castellana several modern buildings stand out, including the green-capped Torres Heron completed in 1976, La Pirámide at no. 31, the shiny black La Unión y el Fénix (no. 33) and further north the Catalana Occidente with its impressive opaque glass finish. Look out, too, for the **Museo de Escultura al Aire Libre** (Metro Rubén Darío; free), an innovative use for the space underneath the Juan Bravo flyover, with its haphazard collection of sculptures including a huge six-tonne suspended block –*The Meeting* by Eduardo Chillida, *Mere Ubo* by Miró, and assorted cubes, walls, fountains and optical trickery. The Salamanca area is also home to a number of excellent **exhibition spaces** sponsored by a variety of companies and foundations (see box overleaf).

SALAMANCA

Exhibition spaces

A number of financial institutions have **exhibition spaces** scattered across the city - mainly around the Castellana and Salamanca - and they stage a variety of high-quality exhibitions and cultural events during the year. See press and the *Guía del Ocio* for details.

Fundación Banco Central Hispano, c/Marqués de Villamagna 3 (Metro Rubén Darío; Tues–Sat 11am–2pm & 5–9pm, Sun 11am–2.30pm; free). A permanent collection spanning the sixteenth to twentieth centuries along with temporary exhibitions.

Fundación La Caixa, c/de Serrano 60 (Metro Serrano; Mon & Wed–Sat 11am–8pm, Sun 11am–2pm; free). Hosts a variety of prestigious exhibitions which recently included a very popular display of photography on life in Spain under Franco.

Fundación Caja de Madrid, Sala de las Alhajas, Plaza de San Martín 1 (Metro Sol; Tues–Sat 11am–2.30pm & 5–8pm, Sun 11am–2.30pm; free). Presents a number of major exhbitions each year featuring artists from Spain and abroad.

Fundación Juan March, c/de Castelló 77 (Metro Núñez de Balboa; Jan–June & Sept–Dec Mon–Fri 10am–2pm & 5.30–9pm, Sat & Sun 10am–2pm; free). Situated in a garden full of modern sculptures, this outstanding cultural centre houses a collection of over 1300 works and is a venue for major art exhibitions. Founded in 1955 by a Catalan businessman seeking to make amends after spending time in prison for embezzlement.

MUSEO SOROLLA

Map 9, A2. Tues–Sat 10am–3pm, Sun 10am–2pm; 400ptas, concessions 200ptas, free Sun. Metro Iglesia-Ruben Darío.

To the west of the Glorieta de Emilio Castelar on the Paseo de la Castellana, Paseo del General Martínez Campos leads to one of the hidden treasures of Madrid. Part museum and part art gallery, the Museo Sorolla gets little of the publicity of the mammoth collections to be found in the Prado and the Thyssen-Bornemisza, but this tribute to a single artist's life and work is in many ways just as rewarding. The museum is situated in Joaquín Sorolla's former home built in 1910 and donated to the nation by his widow after his death in 1923. It's a delight to stumble upon this oasis of peace and tranquillity, its cool and shady Andalusian-style courtyard and gardens decked with statues, fountains, assorted plants and fruit trees.

Sorolla himself was born in Valencia in 1863 and studied in Rome and Paris. Enormously successful during his lifetime and famous throughout Europe and the USA, he was dubbed the "Spanish Impressionist" and received countless prizes for his paintings, including first prize at the Paris Universal Exhibition of 1900. However, his work experienced a decline in popularity after his death and soon went out of fashion, and it's only more recently that it has experienced a revival.

A video on the artist's life and work is shown Tuesday–Friday at 11am and noon. The ground floor has been kept largely intact re-creating the authentic atmosphere of the artist's living and working areas. These rooms contain his **collection of popular jewellery**, including religious icons and charms, hair combs and earrings, gathered during his travels around the Iberian peninsula. The **studio** itself is bathed in the powerful Madrid sunlight from massive skylights and, amongst the artist's clutter, you'll see the *cama a la turca*, a small bed lined on three sides by cases of books, where Sorolla used to take his afternoon siesta.

Upstairs, originally the sleeping quarters of the house, has been turned into a **gallery**, with works arranged chronologically from the far end. The development from his first darker, more sombre paintings such as *Trata de Blanca* (1894)

MUSEO SOROLLA

and *An Investigation* (1897) to brighter, more optimistic works such as the lush green dreamlike *Siesta* (1911) and the vivid red *Puerto de Valencia* (1907) is striking. Powerful sunlight, sea, intense colours, women and children dominate his rather romantic paintings. On your way out, there's a small, tastefully displayed collection of his sketches and gouaches in the patio Andaluz.

MUSEO LÁZARO GALDIANO

Map 9, E1. Tues–Sun 10am–2pm; 300ptas, concessions 150ptas. Metro Rubén Darío.

Just east of the Glorieta de Emilio Castelar at c/de Serrano 122 is the **Museo Lázaro Galdiano**. This former private collection of publisher and businessman José Lázaro Galdiano was given to the state after his death in 1947 and spreads over the four floors and 37 rooms of his former home. It's a vast treasure trove of paintings and *objets d'art*, with some very dodgy attributions, but includes some really exquisite and valuable pieces. The scope of the collections is enormous, comprising paintings, sculptures, ivories, enamels, jewellery, ceramics, arms, armour and furniture, ranging from the seventh century BC to the twentieth century. The museum provides informative leaflets in both Spanish and English.

The **ground-floor collection** contains some outstanding archeological pieces, beautifully decorated thirteenth-century Limoges enamels and a magnificent late sixteenth-century rock crystal and bejewelled drinking cup belonging to Emperor Rudolf II, the mad cousin of Felipe II. In the room on Renaissance sculpture is a superb little picture of *The Saviour* from the late fifteenth-century Lombard School, formerly claimed by the museum to be by Leonardo da Vinci.

The other floors contain an excellent collection of European paintings from the fifteenth to nineteenth centuries. Among the painters represented are Bosch, Dürer, Rembrandt, Lucas Cranach, Gainsborough, Reynolds, Turner and Constable. Unsurprisingly, there's a host of Spanish artists, including Berruguete, Murillo, Zurbarán, Velázquez, José de Ribera, El Greco and Goya.

MUSEO LÁZARO GALDIANO

PLAZA DE ESPAÑA AND BEYOND

The northwest corner of the city, beyond Plaza de España, is a mixture of aristocratic suburbia, university campus and parkland, distinguished by the green swathes of **Parque del Oeste** and **Casa de Campo**. Sights include the downbeat **Museo Cerralbo**, the fascinating **Museo de América**, the **Ermita de San Antonio de la Florida**, with its stunning Goya frescoes and, further out, the pleasant royal residence of **El Pardo**, while the spacious **terrazas** along Paseo del Pintor Rosales provide ample opportunity for refreshment.

PLAZA DE ESPAÑA

Map 7, B5. Metro Plaza de España.

The **Plaza de España** at the west end of Gran Vía, is marked by two of the city's former tallest buildings (their status has recently been usurped by the flurry of corporate construction along the Paseo de la Castellana). The grandiose apartment complex of the **Edificio de España** which heads the square, looking as though it has been transplanted from 1920s New York, was in fact completed in 1953. Four years later, the neighbouring **Torre de Madrid** took over as the tallest building in Spain. Together they tower over an elaborate monument to Cervantes in the middle of the square, which overlooks the bewildered bronze figures of Don Quixote and Sancho Panza. The plaza itself is a rather seedy place, although it does play host to an interesting **craft fair** during the fiesta of San Isidro (on or around May 15), and behind the Edificio de España, on c/San Leonardo and c/San Bernardino, you'll find a host of multinational restaurants ranging from Mexican and Peruvian to Egyptian, Thai and Indian.

To the northwest, **c/Martín de los Heros** is a lively place, day and night, with three of the city's best original-version cinemas, and behind them the **Centro Princesa** with shops, clubs, bars and a 24-hour branch of the ubiquitous *VIPS* supermarket – just the place to have your film developed at 4am or get a bite to eat before heading onto a late club.

Museo Cerralbo

Map 7, A5. Tues–Sat 9.30am–2.30pm (July till 2pm), Sun 10am–2pm, closed Aug; 400ptas, concessions 200ptas, free Wed & Sun. Metro Ventura Rodríguez.

Just to the west of Plaza de España is the **Museo Cerralbo**, c/Ventura Rodríguez 17, an elegant nineteenth-century mansion endowed by the seventeenth Marqués de Cerralbo, a reactionary politician, poet, traveller and archeologist, who still had time to build up a substantial collection of paintings, furniture, armour and artefacts. He bequeathed his home and its eclectic contents to the state, although it didn't open as a museum until 1962. The cluttered nature

PLAZA DE ESPAÑA

of the exhibits is partly explained by the fact that he stipulated in his will that the collection should be displayed exactly as he arranged it. Among the chaos of objects and ornaments is a dark and moody *Francis of Assisi* by El Greco, work by José de Ribera, Zurbarán, Van Dyck and Tintoretto, a fascinating collection of clocks, pocket watches and mini sundials and some outrageously gaudy icing-sugar chandeliers. The highlight is a fabulous over-the-top mirrored ballroom with a Tiepolo-inspired fresco, golden stucco work and marbled decoration.

ARGÜELLES AND MONCLOA

C/de la Princesa stretches northwest from Plaza de Espana into the *barrios* of Argüelles and Moncloa, the former home to some elegant apartment blocks, the latter a centre of student life. Up the steps opposite the Centro Princesa is **c/del Conde Duque**, dominated by the massive former barracks of the royal guard constructed in the early eighteenth century by Pedro de Ribera. The barracks have been turned into a dynamic **cultural centre** which stages concerts, plays and dance as part of the *Veranos de la Villa* season and also hosts a variety of temporary exhibitions. Just to the east of this, the **Plaza de las Comendadoras**, a tranquil space bordered by a variety of interesting craft shops, bars and cafés, is named after the convent that occupies one side of the square. The nuns are from the military order of Santiago and the attached church is decked out with banners celebrating the victories of the knights. A large painting of their patron, St James the Moor-slayer, by Luca Giordano, hangs over the high altar.

About 400m from Plaza de España along c/de la Princesa, obscured by trees, stands the **Palacio de Liria**, the residence of one of the wealthiest and most important aristocratic families in Spain, the dukes of Alba. Housed within is a vast private collection of artistic treasures, but visitors are only allowed entry once a week, after a written request and the current waiting list is well over a year. The far end of the Princesa is dominated by the Ministerio del Aire (Air Ministry) and the neighbouring **Arco de la Victoria** built by Franco in 1956 to commemorate the Nationalist military triumph in the Civil War. During term time the stretch of parkland by the arch often becomes the scene of one big student party, with huddles of picknickers and singing groups under the trees.

The **Mirador del Faro** (Tues–Sun: June–Aug 11am–1.45pm & 5.30–8.45pm; Sept–May 10.30am–2pm & 5.30–8pm; 200ptas; metro Moncloa), the futuristic 92-metre-high tower just past the Arco de la Victoria was opened in 1992 and provides stunning views over the city and to the mountains beyond. Alongside, with its main entrance at Avenida de los Reyes Católicos 6, is the **Museo de América** (Tues–Sat 10am–3pm, Sun 10am–2.30pm; 400ptas, concessions 200ptas, free on Sat after 2pm and all day Sun). This fabulous collection of pre-Columbian American art and artefacts includes objects brought back at the time of the Spanish conquest as well as more recent acquisitions and donations. The museum was subject to one of Madrid's most protracted renovation sagas and was closed for twelve years up until 1994. The new layout is thematic with sections on ideas and myths about America, geography and history, social organization, religion and communication. The Aztec, Mayan and Inca civilizations are all well represented and exhibits include the Madrid Codex (one of only three surviving hieroglyphic manuscripts depicting scenes from everyday Mayan life), the Tudela Codex, describing the events of the Spanish conquest, and the Quimbayas Treasure, a fabulous breathtaking collection of

ARGÜELLES AND MONCLOA

gold objects and figures from the Quimbaya culture of Colombia.

Beyond the museum lies the campus of the **Ciudad Universitaria**, rebuilt after the Civil War when it was completely devastated in some of the fiercest fighting, lying as it did along the front line between the defending Republican forces and the besieging Nationalists. Alongside the campus, by the side of the road, is the **Palacio de la Moncloa**, the official residence of the Spanish prime minister since 1977.

THE PARQUE DEL OESTE

Map 2, B3. Metro Argüelles.

To the west of Plaza de España, the **Parque del Oeste** follows the railway tracks up to the suburbs of Moncloa and Ciudad Universitaria. Originally laid out by municipal gardener, Cecilio Rodríguez, at the beginning of the twentieth century, the park was devastated by the Civil War and had to be completely redesigned. It features a pleasant stream, assorted statues and shady walks, and in summer there are numerous *terrazas* overlooking the park on Paseo del Pintor Rosales. Also here is the **Teleférico** (April–Sept daily 11am–2.30pm & 4.30–dusk; Oct–March Sat, Sun & public holidays noon–2.30pm & 4.30–8pm; 355ptas one-way, 505ptas return) which shuttles its passengers high over the river with great views of the Palacio Real, the Almudena Cathedral and the city skyline, to the middle of Casa de Campo (see p.108). Below the Teleférico is the beautiful **Rosaleda**, a vast rose garden at its best and most sweet smelling in May and June. On its south side is the **Templo de Debod** (Tues–Fri 10am–1pm & 5–7pm, Sat & Sun 10am–1pm; free) a fourth-century BC Egyptian temple given to Spain in 1968 in recognition of the work done by

Spanish engineers on the Aswan High Dam. Reconstructed here stone by stone, it seems comically incongruous.

The Ermita de San Antonio de la Florida

Tues–Fri 10am–2pm & 4–8pm, Sat & Sun 10am–2pm; 300ptas, free Wed & Sun. Metro Príncipe Pío.

Rail lines from commuter towns to the north of Madrid terminate at the recently renovated **Estación del Norte**, a quietly spectacular construction of white enamel, steel and glass which enjoyed a starring role in Warren Beaty's film *Reds*. About 500m from the station along the Paseo de la Florida stands the **Ermita de San Antonio de la Florida** at Glorieta de la Florida 5. This little church on a Greek cross plan was built by an Italian, Felipe Fontana, between 1792 and 1798 and decorated by **Goya**, whose **frescoes**, which took him only 120 days to complete, provided Carlos IV with enough evidence to appoint him court painter. The frescoes in the dome depict a miracle performed by Saint Anthony of Padua, while around it, heavenly bodies of angels and cherubs hold back curtains to reveal the main scene – the saint resurrecting a dead man. Beyond this central group, Goya created a gallery of highly realistic characters modelled on court and society figures, while for a lesser fresco of the angels adorning the Trinity in the apse, he took prostitutes as his models. The church also houses the artist's remains. The mirror-image chapel on the other side of the Glorieta was built in 1925 for parish services so that the original could become a museum. On St Anthony's Day (June 13) girls queue up at the chapel to ask the saint to bring them a boyfriend; if the pins dropped into the holy water in the font stick to their hands, their wish will be granted.

THE ERMITA DE SAN ANTONIO DE LA FLORIDA

107

CASA DE CAMPO

Metro Batán/Lago. Bus #33 from Príncipe Pío goes to the zoo and Parque de Atracciones or you can get here by cable car from Paseo del Pintor Rosales (see p.106) or on foot from the Estación del Norte via the Puente del Rey.

The **Casa de Campo**, an enormous expanse of heath and scrub, is in parts surprisingly wild for a place so easily accessible from the city. Founded by Felipe II in the mid-sixteenth century as a royal hunting estate it was only opened to the public in 1931 and it later acted as a base for Franco's forces from which they shelled much of the city. Large sections have been tamed for conventional pastimes and there are picnic tables and café-bars throughout the park, the ones by the lake providing fine views of the Palacio Real, Cathedral, Plaza de España and San Francisco el Grande. There are also mountain bike trails, a jogging track, open-air swimming pool (mid-June to Sept 11am–9.30pm; 300ptas; metro Lago), tennis courts, and rowing boats for rent on the lake (again near metro Lago). During the summer, concerts are held at the lakeside Rockodromo. Other attractions include a popular, well-laid-out **Zoo** and a sprawling **Parque de Atracciones** (see *Kids' Madrid*, p.227 for information on both). Be warned that many of the main access roads through the park have been taken over by prostitutes, both day and night (the council has banished them from the streets of the city) and can become crowded with kerb-crawlers; not particularly pleasant for picnics or excursions with the kids.

EL PARDO

Map 1, E5. April–Sept Mon–Sat 10.30am–6pm, Sun 9.30am–1.30pm; Oct–March Mon–Sat 10.30am–5pm, Sun

9.30am–1.30pm; 650ptas, free Wed. Bus from Moncloa (services daily every 10–15min, 6.30am–midnight; 25min).

Nine kilometres northwest of central Madrid is Franco's former principal residence at **El Pardo**. A garrison still remains at the town, where most of the Generalísimo's staff were based, but the stigma has lessened over the years, and this is now a popular excursion for *Madrileños*, who come here for long lunches in the *terraza* restaurants along Avenida de la Guardia, or to play tennis and swim at one of the nearby country clubs. The tourist focus is the **Palacio del Pardo**, rebuilt by the Bourbons on the site of the hunting lodge of Carlos V. The present building is largely the work of Francesco Sabatini although traces of the old palace by Juan Gómez de Mora are still evident. The interior is pleasant enough and houses the chapel, where Franco prayed, and the theatre, built for Carlos IV's wife María Luisa, where the Caudillo and his cronies used to censor films. On display are a number of mementos of Franco including his desk, a portrait of Isabel la Católica by her court painter, Juan de Flandes, and an excellent collection of tapestries, many after Goya's cartoons in the Prado. Tickets to the palace are valid also for the neighbouring pavilion, the **Casita del Príncipe**, though this cannot be entered from the palace gardens and you must return to the main road. Like the *casitas* at El Escorial, this was built by Juan de Villanueva and is highly ornate.

EL PARDO

LISTINGS

ACCOMMODATION

Madrid has lots of **accommodation**, and most of it is pretty central. It is, on the whole, pretty functional, though. Few places, in any price range, have great character, and you're basically paying for location and facilities. At the lower end of the range, there are bargains to be had, with double rooms for as little as 3000ptas a night – and less if you're looking for an extended stay. Move upmarket a little and you can find plenty of places at 6000–8000ptas a night, offering comfortable rooms with a private bath or (more often) shower. The upper-range hotels often provide special deals, so it's well worth checking these out even if your budget is limited.

Although it is advisable to make **reservations** at all times of year, especially during Spanish fiestas (see p.201), you will always be able to find something if you are prepared to spend time looking around. If you prefer to use an **accommodation service**, you'll find them at the airport, the Estación Sur de Autobuses and the train stations. *Brújula* (©559 97 05) is particularly helpful, with offices at Atocha and Charmartín train stations, Colón bus terminal and on the sixth floor of the Torre de Madrid in Plaza de España.

Much of the cheapest accommodation in Madrid is to be

found in the wedge-shaped zone between **c/de Atocha** and **Paseo del Prado** and in the *barrios* of **Chueca** and **Malasaña**. Similarly, the huge old buildings along **Gran Vía** hide a vast array of hotels and *hostales* at every price, often with a delightfully decayed elegance. After dark, however, the area can feel somewhat seedy.

In the very heart of the city – **Sol, Opera and Plaza Mayor** – there are a surprising number of reasonably priced options, and if you want to be right in the thick of Madrid's nightlife, you'll find plenty of good choices around **Plaza de Santa Ana**.

North of Gran Vía, there are further clusters of *hostales* on and around **c/de Fuencarral** and **c/de Hortaleza**, although the streets around the southern end of Fuencarral form a red-light district, so take care after dark. Further north towards Bilbao is another nightlife centre; the most pleasant options here are around Plaza Santa Bárbara.

The city's most expensive hotels are grouped around **Paseo del Prado**, **Recoletos** and in **Salamanca**, although even in these upmarket districts you'll find several more modest options.

....

The telephone code for Madrid is ☎91. Calling Madrid from abroad dial your international access code then 34-1, followed by the subscriber's number.

....

HOTELS

Noise from the street can be a problem in the city centre, so it's a good idea to ask for a room on one of the higher floors or facing away from the street. In high summer **air conditioning** is advisable – all hotels in the ⑤ category and above will have it, while the hotel reviews will say if it

Accommodation prices

Throughout this guide, accommodation is graded on a scale from ① to ⑧. These categories show the cost per night of the cheapest double room in each establishment. In Madrid there is no high or low season, however, many upper-range hotels offer good deals at weekends and during July and August. It's also worth enquiring about the *bonos* (hotel vouchers) on sale in all travel agents which often give substantial reductions on the more upmarket options.

① Under 3000ptas	⑤ 8000–12,000ptas
② 3000–4500ptas	⑥ 12,000–18,000ptas
③ 4500–6000ptas	⑦ 18,000–25,000ptas
④ 6000–8000ptas	⑧ Over 25,000ptas

is available in any of the cheaper options. **Swimming pools** are a rarity, but you'll always be within striking distance of one of the public pools scattered around the city (see p.210). If you're arriving by car, a hotel with a **garage** is a must given the city's parking and security problems. **Breakfast** is often not included in the price of a room and it's usually much better value and more fun to go to a local café or bar.

ATOCHA AND PASEO DEL PRADO

Hotel Mediodía

Map 5, I5. Plaza del Emperador Carlos V 8 ℭ527 30 60; fax 530 70 08. Metro Atocha.

Huge 165-roomed hotel right by the Reina Sofía and Estación de Atocha. Simple, but comfortable rooms, with bathroom and TV in all – a good bargain. Directly below, the *El Brillante* café does a good cup of coffee and some basic tapas. ④.

HOTELS

Hotel Mercator

Map 5, I4. C/de Atocha 123 ℗429 05 00; fax 369 12 52. Metro Atocha.

Smart hotel well geared up for tourists, with information leaflets, money-changing facilities and café-bar. A good option if you're coming by car as it has its own car park and is easy to reach. Chintzy rooms have TVs and most have air conditioning. ⑤.

Hotel Mora

Map 5, I2. Paseo del Prado 32 ℗420 15 69; fax 420 05 64. Metro Atocha.

Friendly, recently refurbished, 62-room hotel. All rooms have air conditioning and some have pleasant views along the Paseo del Prado. The noise of the traffic isn't too bad due to double glazing. Rooms are quite small, but the hotel is perfectly positioned for all the galleries on the Paseo del Arte. ④.

Hotel Nacional

Map 5, I3. Paseo del Prado 48 ℗429 66 29; fax 369 15 64. Metro Atocha.

Large, very plush hotel, part of the NH chain, attractively situated just opposite the Jardines Botánicos. Not that pricey, given the excellent facilities and luxurious surroundings. Special offers can reduce the price substantially. ⑥.

Hotel Palace

Map 5, F4. Plaza de las Cortes 7 ℗360 80 00; fax 360 81 00. Metro Banco de España.

Colossal 440-room sumptuous hotel that has recently undergone a no-expense-spared refurbishment. Every facility including a hairdresser, beauty salon, conference rooms and

HOTELS

business services – but none of the snootiness of the *Ritz* across the road. Doubles start at 46,000ptas. **⑧**.

Hotel Asturias

Map 6, C4. C/Sevilla 2 ✆429 58 26; fax 429 40 36. Metro Sevilla.
Comfortable well-appointed hotel housed in a beautiful building only a stone's throw from Puerta del Sol. Rooms are quite large, all have air conditioning and service is courteous. **⑤**.

Hotel Carlos V

Map 3, H3. C/Maestro Vitoria 5 ✆531 41 00; fax 531 37 61.
Metro Sol.
Large, recently refurbished turn-of-the-century hotel, belonging to the Best Western chain in a pedestrianized part of town, just off c/Preciados behind the Descalzas Reales monastery. Some of the plush air-conditioned rooms on the fifth floor have quite large balconies with tables and chairs (for which you pay extra), although there isn't much of a view. There's an elegant lounge and café and the hotel has a deal with a nearby car park which guests can use at reduced rates. **⑤–⑥**.

Hotel Paris

Map 6, B3. C/de Alcalá 2 ✆521 64 96 fax 531 01 88. Metro Sol.
Smart, old-fashioned hotel right on the Puerta del Sol with spacious, pleasantly decorated rooms, half of which have air conditioning. There's a nice interior patio and a laundry on the premises. Very good value for its central position. **⑤**.

Hotel Persal

Map 6, B5. Plaza del Angel 12 ✆ 369 46 43 or 368 37 26; fax 369 19 52. Metro Sol.

HOTELS

Friendly 100-room hotel superbly located between Sol, Santa Ana and Plaza Mayor. All rooms have air conditioning, bathroom and TV. Firm mattresses and surprisingly quiet rooms should make for a good night's sleep in this excellent-value hotel. ③.

Hotel Regina

Map 6, D2. C/de Alcalá 19 521 47 25; fax 521 47 25. Metro Sol. Plush, highly practical and well-located hotel between Sol and Cibeles with very spacious rooms. Well set up for tourists with plenty of sightseeing information; popular with organized tour groups. ⑤.

Gran Hotel Reina Victoria

Map 6, C5. Plaza de Santa Ana 14 ℗531 45 00; fax 522 03 07. Metro Sol.
A giant cream cake of a hotel, perfectly placed at the top of Plaza Santa Ana, although it has lost a little of its character since it became part of the Tryp hotel chain. A favourite of bullfighters past and present, it has a taurine bar where bullfighting *tertulias* are still held during the San Isidro Festival in May and a very impressive foyer area. It comes complete with all the services you expect in this price range, including business services, currency exchange and a car park. ⑧.

Hotel Santander

Map 6, D4. C/Echegaray 1 ℗429 95 51; fax 369 1078. Metro Sevilla.
Spacious, well-decorated and spotless rooms with large bathrooms and many with a small seating area. Classy old-fashioned decor and very friendly staff. Perfectly located to sample the bars and restaurants in the Santa Ana/Huertas area. ④.

GRAN VÍA, CHUECA AND SANTA BÁRBARA

Hotel Mónaco

Map 7, I6. C/Barbieri 5 ⓒ522 46 30; fax 521 16 01. **Metro Chueca/Gran Vía.**

In a city full of many rather bland hotels this one stands out head and shoulders above the rest in terms of character. It was formally a *casa de citas* where lovers, in rather less liberal years, could arrange to meet. Since becoming a hotel in 1959 it has retained much of its original decor. Each of the wonderful Art Deco rooms is completely different, embellished with a variety of mirrors, canopies, oil paintings, and stuccoed ceilings. Room 20 with its raised bath tub was used by Alfonso XIII for his "appointments", but each room has its own particular attractions and many have been used as sets for films or video shoots. Highly recommended. ⑤.

Hotel Emperador

Map 7, D6. Gran Vía 53, ⓒ547 28 00; fax 547 2817. **Metro Callao/Plaza de España.**

The main reason to come to this hotel is the superb rooftop swimming pool with magnificent views of the Palacio Real, Casa de Campo and the packed streets of Madrid. The hotel is geared up for the organized tour market and the atmosphere is rather impersonal, but the rooms are large and nicely decorated, many with recently refurbished bathrooms. ⑦.

RECOLETOS, SALAMANCA AND CHAMBERÍ

Hotel Alcalá

Map 8, G1. C/de Alcalá 66 ⓒ435 10 60; fax 435 11 05. **Metro Príncipe de Vergara/Retiro.**

Large classy hotel just to the north of the Retiro with smart

HOTELS

well-appointed rooms, laundry facilities and a car park. Very friendly staff and an attractive location right next to the park. The wider streets and avenues in this area give it a spacious and airy feel. Excellent deals during the summer and at weekends. ⑤–⑥.

Residencia Don Diego

Map 9, F8. C/de Velázquez 45, 5Ÿ Ⓒ435 07 60; fax 431 42 63. Metro Velázquez.
This is a comfortable, friendly, medium-sized hotel in an upmarket area of town. The rooms have full facilities, including air conditioning and satellite TV. ⑤.

Galiano Residencia

Map 9, B8, C/de Alcalá Galiano 6 Ⓒ319 20 00; fax 319 99 14. Metro Colón.
Hidden away in a quiet street behind the Heron building on the Castellana, this small hotel has a sophisticated feel. There's a pleasant well-furnished salon in the entrance, staff are polite and the excellent rooms are air-conditioned. Car parking facilities. ⑤.

Hotel Santo Mauro

Map 7, K1. C/de Zurbano 36 Ⓒ 319 6900; fax 308 5477. Metro Rubén Dario.
A palace in the nineteenth century, later an embassy and now a small luxurious hotel situated in the quiet area of Chamberí, just to the west of the Castellana. The rooms have tasteful modern decor while the communal areas are more traditional, but very stylish. The excellent facilities include an indoor swimming pool, gym, sauna, beauty salon, car park and a babysitting service. ⑧.

PENSIONES AND HOSTALES

Pensiones and **hostales** are small, no-nonsense, frequently family-run establishments, sometimes with shared bathrooms and less facilities than a hotel. They are housed in large centrally located apartment blocks and in the more popular areas, you'll find two or three separate establishments, each on separate floors, in the same building. **Floors** (*pisos*) are written as 1° (first floor), 2°, etc. and often specify *izquierda* (*izqda*) or *derecha* (*dcha*), meaning to the left or right of the staircase. Some of the *hostales* in larger buildings – on Gran Vía, for example – don't always have an entryphone or doorbell at street level, making them inaccessible at night, unless you've been given a front-door key. If you book a room and intend to arrive after, say, 9pm, check that you will be able to get in.

ATOCHA AND PASEO DEL PRADO

Hostal Cervantes

Map 6, E5. C/Cervantes 34, 2° ©429 83 65 or 429 2745; fax 429 83 65. Metro Antón Martín.
If you can't get in to the *Gonzalo* on the floor above, this is an equally friendly *hostal*, although slightly more expensive. All rooms have their own bathroom, TV and ventilator and are pleasantly furnished. ③.

Hostal Gonzalo

Map 6, E5. C/de Cervantes 34, 3° ©429 27 14. Metro Antón Martín.
Very clean, recently renovated fifteen-room *hostal*; all rooms have bathroom, TV and ventilator. The charming owner, Antonio, runs a very smart place at an excellent price. Highly recommended. ③.

Pensión Mollo

Map 5, H3. C/de Atocha 104, 4° ℂ528 71 76. Metro Atocha.
The closest reasonable *hostal* to the station, although it's up a
steep hill and has no lift – not a good bet if you're heavily
laden. There are seven clean rooms; all of the doubles have en-
suite showers. ②.

Hostal Aguilar

Map 6, D4. C/de San Jerónimo 32, 2° ℂ429 59 26; fax 429 26 61.
Metro Sevilla.
Large *hostal*, with airy rooms all with bath, TV and air
conditioning. Specializes in multi-bed rooms offering very
good prices for quadruples (8500ptas), making it an ideal
budget place for families. ③.

Hostal Americano

Map 6, B3. Puerta del Sol 11, 2° ℂ522 28 22; fax 522 111 92.
Metro Sol.
Right beside the statue of Madrid's emblem, *El Oso y
Madroño*, in Puerta del Sol – you couldn't get nearer to the
city centre. This nicely furnished *hostal* has rooms with TV,
bathroom and telephone, and there's a pleasant communal
living room. ③.

Hostal Armesto

Map 6, E5. C/San Agustín 6, 1° dcha ℂ429 09 40 or 429 90 31.
Metro Antón Martín.
A small six-room *hostal*. All rooms have bathrooms and TV and
the best ones overlook the pleasant little garden in the Casa de
Lope de Vega next door. Very well positioned for the
Huertas/Santa Ana area. ③.

Hostal La Macarena

Map 4, F2. C/Cava de San Miguel 8, 2° ©365 92 21; fax 364 27 57. Metro Sol.

Fine, family-run *hostal* in a recently pedestrianized characterful alley just off the Plaza Mayor. Rooms are quite small, but all have bathrooms, TV and ventilators. The friendly owner plans to install air conditioning. ③.

Hostal Plaza D'Ort

Map 6, B5. Plaza del Angel 13 ©429 90 41; fax 420 12 97. Metro Sol.

Next door to the *Hotel Persal;* all rooms in this very clean *hostal* have a shower or bath, TV and telephone. There are also several self-catering apartments, sleeping five or six people for 10,000ptas a night, making it a good family or group option. ③.

Hostal Rifer

Map 3, H5. C/Mayor 5, 4° ©532 31 97. Metro Sol.

Clean, bright rooms, all with en-suite facilities, in the highest – and therefore quietest – of three options in this block. The friendly owner is anxious to please. ②.

Hostal Villar

Map 6, C5. C/del Príncipe 18, 1° ©531 66 00 or 531 66 09; fax 521 50 73. Metro Sevilla.

Large *hostal* on four floors of a centrally situated building. Most of the standard rooms have small bathrooms, and all have TV and telephone. There are plans to install air conditioning in the near future. ②.

PENSIONES AND HOSTALES

GRAN VÍA, CHUECA AND SANTA BÁRBARA

Hostal Asunción

Map 7, J3. Plaza Santa Bárbara 8 ©308 23 48; fax 310 04 78.
Metro Alonso Martínez.

In a pretty position overlooking the square, this *hostal* offers
small but well-furnished rooms with bath, TV and mini-bar;
two have air conditioning. ③.

Hostal Buenos Aires

Map 7, C6. Gran Vía 61, 2° ©542 22 50; fax 542 28 69. Metro
Plaza de España.

Plenty of facilities in this well-appointed *hostal* at the Plaza de
España end of Gran Vía. Air conditioning, satellite TV, en-suite
bathrooms and a bar, but the rooms are rather plain. ④.

Hostal California

Map 7, F7. Gran Vía 38 &522 47 03; fax 531 61 01. Metro Callao.

Well-placed, friendly but somewhat pricey *hostal*. Rooms are
bright, new and relatively quiet, and all doubles have full
bathroom, TV, telephone and air conditioning. It also has its
own bar and café. ⑤.

Hostal Kryse

Map 7, G7. C/de Fuencarral 25, 1° izqda ©531 15 12; fax 522 81
53. Metro Gran Vía.

Compact ten-room *hostal*; all rooms have verandas and those
above the street have double glazing. Small bathroom, TV,
telephone and ceiling fans in all rooms. ③.

Hostal Medieval

Map 7, G5. C/de Fuencarral 46, 2° Izqda ©522 25 49. Metro Chueca.
Small well-run and friendly family *hostal*. All of the airy rooms have showers, but toilets are shared. Well-maintained building with attractive plants trailing from the verandas. ②.

Hostal El Pinar

Map 7, H7. C/San Bartolomé 2, 4° ©531 01 34. Metro Chueca.
Decent *hostal* charging some of the lowest rates in the city – perhaps because the building looks as though it's about to collapse. If you're on a tight budget and want to be right in the centre of town, this can't be beaten. Rooms have their own bathroom. Popular with students on long-term rates. ①.

Hostal Santa Bárbara

Map 7, I3. Plaza Santa Bárbara 4 ©445 73 34; fax 446 23 45. Metro Alonso Martínez.
Recently redecorated and refurbished, this is a rather upmarket *hostal* in a good location. The nice rooms all have bathrooms and there's a great Art Deco TV salon. English-speaking Italian owner. ⑤.

EATING

E ating out in Madrid is one of the highlights of any visit to the city. There's plenty to suit every pocket from budget backstreet bars to high-class designer restaurants, and a bewildering range of cuisines encompassing tapas, traditional *Madrileño* and Spanish regional dishes as well as international cooking.

Breakfast is a pretty light affair, usually a cup of coffee and a *tostada* (toast and marmalade), but the traditional *Madrileño* breakfast of *chocolate con churros* – a glutinous dark chocolate with deep-fried hoops of batter – is sometimes taken, especially after a night out on the tiles (see p.175). A mid-morning snack of a *bocadillo* (a French bread sandwich) or a *sandwich mixto* (a toasted ham and cheese sandwich) should keep hunger at bay until *aperitivos* and a few tapas at any time from 1pm onwards. **Lunch** (*la comida*) is taken very late with few *Madrileños* starting before 2pm, and is often a long drawn-out affair. **Dinner** (*la cena*), which again may be preceded by some tapas, will usually begin around 10pm, although, most people tend to arrive for dinner by 10.30pm and you may not be admitted much later. There are quite a number of **late-night options**, however, and the listings magazines all have sections for restaurants open past midnight (*después de medianoche/de madrugada* – see box p.144).

> Opening hours have been given for all establishments, but be warned that bars often open and close according to how busy they are or the mood of the staff working that night. Many restaurants close on Sunday and/or Monday and for all or part of August.

The streets around **Puerta del Sol** are packed with places to eat and drink. You should spend at least one evening sampling the historic, tiled bars **of Santa Ana/Huertas**, while to the south, in the tiny streets of **La Latina** and **Lavapiés** there's an appealing neighbourhood feel to the bars and restaurants. On **Gran Vía**, burger bars fill most of the gaps between shops and cinemas but, head a few blocks north, and there's plenty on offer, including a good cluster of ethnic restaurants on c/San Bernardino (north of the Plaza de España). **Chueca**, **Santa Bárbara** and **Malasaña** further north, have some superb traditional old bars and bright new restaurants serving some of the most creative food in the city, while the smarter districts of **Recoletos and Salamanca** contain few bars of note, but some extremely good restaurants.

The recommendations given here include *bares*, *cafés*, *cervecerías* (beer halls), *marisquerías* (seafood bars) and *restaurantes*, but have been divided simply into "Tapas bars" and "Restaurants", depending on whether they concentrate more on bar food or sit-down meals; many will actually have a bar area where you can get tapas, together with a more formal *comedor* (canteen) or *restaurante* out the back or upstairs.

Children are nearly always welcome and most restaurants will make special arrangements for them. Restaurants are full to the brim at weekends so it is vital to **book** at least a day ahead and even during the week it's advisable to reserve a table to avoid having to wait.

Tapas Glossary

Pincho	Mouthful
Tapa	Saucerful
Ración	Small plateful

Standard tapas and *raciones* might include :

Aceitunas	Olives
Ahumados	Smoked fish
Albóndigas	Meatballs
Almejas	Clams
Anchoas	Anchovies
Bacalao	Cod (often salted)
Berberechos	Cockles
Boquerones	Small, sardine-like fish usually served in vinegar
Calamares	Squid
Callos	Tripe, often served in a spicy tomato sauce
Cangrejos de río	Freshwater crayfish
Caracoles	Snails
Champiñones	Mushrooms, usually fried in garlic
Chistorra	Sausage with paprika
Chorizo	Spicy sausage
Cocido	Stew
Empanadilla	Fish / Meat pasty
Ensaladilla	Russian salad (diced vegetables in mayonnaise)
Escalibada	Aubergine (eggplant) and pepper salad
Gambas	Prawns
Hígado	Liver
Jamón serrano	Cured ham

Jamón de York	Regular ham
Mejillones	Mussels
Mollejas	Sweetbreads
Morcilla	Black pudding
Navajas	Razor clams
Patatas alioli	Potatoes in garlic mayonnaise
Patatas bravas	Spicy fried potatoes
Pimientos	Peppers
Pincho moruno	Kebab
Pulpo	Octopus
Riñones al Jerez	Kidneys in sherry
Salchicha	Sausage
Sepia	Cuttlefish
Sesos	Brains
Tortilla española	Potato omelette
Tortilla francesa	Plain omelette
Zarajo	Grilled sheep's intestine wound around a stick, poached in brandy and wine and fried in olive oil.

TAPAS

Madrid is renowned for its **tapas** (usually three or four chunks of fish or meat, or a dollop of salad), which traditionally were served up free with a drink. These days you have to pay for anything more than a few olives (where you do get free food now, it will often be called a *pincho*), but a single helping rarely costs more than 200–400ptas unless you're somewhere very flashy. The procession from one bar to the next sampling its speciality has evolved into a culinary ritual in the city. Fortunately the best tapas bars are clustered together, particularly in the streets between **Puerta del Sol** and **Plaza de Santa Ana**, **La Latina** and **Lavapiés**. One of the main advantages of tapas is that you can experiment, and in many places food is laid out in glass display cases so you can eat whatever takes your fancy even if you don't know what it's called.

....

**Madrid's own speciality tapas include *patatas bravas*
(chunks of deep fried potato coated in a bright
orange spicy sauce), *orejas* (pigs' ears), and *callos*
(tripe in a hot tomato sauce).**

....

Raciones are simply bigger plates of the same, and can be enough in themselves for a light meal; *pinchos morunos* (small kebabs) are often also available. When ordering, make sure you make it clear whether you want a *ración* or just a *tapa*. The more people you're with the better; half a dozen *tapas* or *pinchos* and three *raciones* can make a varied and quite filling meal for three or four people.

SOL, PLAZA MAYOR AND OPERA

El Anciano Rey de Los Vinos

Map 6, A4. C/de la Paz 4. Metro Sol.
Mon–Thurs & Sun 9.30am–4pm & 6.30pm–11.30pm, Fri & Sat
9.30am–4pm & 6pm–midnight. Closed Aug.
The "Old Man King of Wines" is a great old bar near to the Puerta del Sol. The wines are excellent, and for the sweet-toothed, the *torrijas* (deep-fried bread doused in wine and sprinkled with sugar and spices) is a must. A host of other tapas is available, including fine *callos* and *albóndigas*.

Las Bravas

Map 6, C5 & B5. C/Alvarez Gato 3 & c/Espoz y Mina 13. Both
Metro Sol.
Daily noon–4pm & 7pm–midnight.
As the name suggests, *patatas bravas* is the thing to try at this

bar, just south of Puerta del Sol. The *tortilla and pulpo* are tasty, too. The outside of the bar is covered with novelty mirrors, which are said to have inspired a story by Valle Inclán and are a hangover from when this was a barber shop. There's another branch just around the corner.

Casa del Abuelo

Map 6, C4. C/de la Victoria 12. Metro Sol.
Daily 11.30am–3.30pm & 6.30–11.30pm.
Tiny, highly atmospheric bar serving sweet, rich red house wine and cooked prawns – try them *al ajillo* (in garlic) or *a la plancha* (grilled). Use your free wine voucher to get a drink at the nearby El Abuelo.

Casa del Labra

Map 6, A3. C/de Tetuán 12 ✆531 00 81. Metro Sol.
Mon–Sat 11am–3.30pm & 5.30–11pm, Sun 1–4pm & 8.15–11.15pm.
A great, traditional place dating from 1869 and retaining much of its original interior. This is where the Spanish Socialist Party was founded in 1879. Order a drink at the bar and a *ración* of cod fried in batter (*bacalao*) at the counter to the right of the door. There's also a restaurant through the bar on the right – an old panelled room, serving classic *Madrileño* food.

Lhardy

Map 6, C3. Carrera de San Jerónimo 8 ✆521 33 85. Metro Sol.
Shop: Mon–Sat 9.30am–3pm & 5–9.30pm, Sun 9am–2.30pm.
Restaurant: Mon–Sat 1–3.30pm & 9–11.30pm, Sun 1–3.30pm.
Lhardy is one of Madrid's most famous and expensive restaurants. Once the haunt of royalty, it's a beautiful place but greatly overpriced – expect to pay upwards of 7000ptas per head for a three-course meal. Downstairs, however, there's a wonderful

bar/shop, seemingly preserved in aspic, where you can snack on canapés, *fino* and *consomé* – without breaking the bank – serving yourself from the glass cabinets and gleaming silver urn.

Mejillonera El Pasaje

Map 6, B4. Pasaje Matheu. Metro Sol.
Daily except Tues noon–midnight.
Mussels (*mejillones*) served in every way imaginable in a bar-packed pedestrian-only alleyway between c/Espoz y Mina and c/de la Victoria, south of Puerta del Sol.

Museo del Jamón

Map 6, B3. Carrera de San Jerónimo 6. Metro Sol.
Mon–Sat 9am–midnight, Sun 10am–midnight.
The largest branch of this Madrid chain, from whose ceilings are suspended hundreds of *jamones* (hams). The best (and they're not cheap) are the *jabugos* from the Sierra Morena, though a ham croissant will set you back under 200ptas.

La Oreja de Oro

Map 6, C4. C/de la Victoria. Metro Sol.
May–July & Sept Mon–Sat 1–4pm & 8pm–1am; Oct–April Tues–Sun 1–4pm & 8pm–1am. Closed Aug.
Standing room only in this bar just opposite *La Casa del Abuelo*. Go for the excellent *pulpo a la Gallega* (sliced octopus served on a bed of potatoes fried in olive oil and seasoned with cayenne pepper) washed down with Ribeiro wine served in terracotta bowls. Plenty of other sea food tapas on offer too.

El Oso y El Madroño

Map 6, A5. C/de la Bolsa 4. Metro Sol.
Mon–Sat 10am–midnight.

A tiny *castizo* bar where you can have a drink to the accompaniment of the *Madrileño chotis* and chat to the traditionally attired barmen who appear to have been here forever. Speciality *cocido*, snails, sangría and Jerez.

Casa Alberto

Map 6, C6. C/de las Huertas 18 ©**429 93 56. Metro Antón Martín.** Tues–Thurs noon–1am, Fri & Sat noon–2am, Sun noon–4pm.
Traditional *tasca* with a zinc and marble bar which has resisted the passage of time since it was founded back in 1827. Good *caracoles*, *gambas* and a great anchovy canapé, ideally accompanied by a glass of house vermouth. There's a small dining room at the back.

La Costa de Vejer

Map 6, C5. Corner of c/Núñez de Arce & c/Alvarez del Gato. Metro Sol.
Tues–Sun noon–midnight.
The speciality here is prawns (*gambas*), grilled with garlic – an absolute must. Service is friendly and there's plenty of room to sit down at the back if you want to linger a little longer and try out some of the other tapas.

El Lacón

Map 6, D5. C/Manuel Fernández y González 8 ©**429 3698. Metro Sol.**
Daily noon–4pm & 8pm–midnight, Fri–Sun till 1.30am. Closed Aug.
Large Galician bar-restaurant with plenty of seats upstairs. Great *pulpo*, *caldo gallego* (meat and vegetable broth) and *empanadas* (pastry slices filled with tuna and vegetables).

La Taberna de Dolores

Map 6, F6. Plaza de Jesús 4. Metro Antón Martín.
Daily 11am–midnight.

Splendid canapés at this popular and friendly tiled bar at the bottom of Huertas. Decorated with beer bottles from around the world, the beer is really good, and the food specialities include roquefort and anchovy, and smoked-salmon canapés. Get here early if you want a space at the bar.

Viña P

Map 6, C5. Plaza de Santa Ana 3. Metro Sol.
Daily 1–4pm & 8pm–12.30am.

Very friendly staff serving a great range of tapas in a bar decked out with bullfighting mementos and posters. Try the asparagus, stuffed mussels and the mouthwatering *almejas a la marinera* (clams in a garlic and white wine sauce).

LA LATINA AND LAVAPIÉS

Almendro 13

Map 4, E5. C/del Almendro 13. Metro La Latina.
Tues 1–5pm, Weds–Sun 1–5pm & 8pm–midnight.

Fashionable wooden panelled bar that serves great *fino* from chilled black bottles. Help yourself to the glasses from the racks on the wall and tuck into original tapas of *huevos rotos* (fried eggs on a bed of crisps) and *roscas rellenas* (rings of bread stuffed with various meats).

El Almendro

Map 4, E5. C/del Almendro 27. Metro La Latina.
Daily except Tues 1–4.30pm & 8.30pm–midnight.

On the corner of the Plaza de San Andrés, this is just the place for highly original seated tapas. Fill in a card ticking your orders and choose from, among other dishes, an excellent asparagus in avocado sauce, wafer-thin chips and *chorizo*, three cheese salad and *tortilla de bacalao*. Imaginatively presented and very tasty.

El Bonanno

Map 4, E5. Plaza del Humilladero 4. Metro La Latina.
Mon–Sat 1–4pm & 8pm–1.30am.

Street and bar blend into one in this tiny place as people spill out through the door and window to form a spontaneous *terraza*. The ideal place for a slice of *pastel de merluza* (a delicious fish pie) and some homemade vermouth. Give the goat's cheese in olive oil a try too.

Los Caracoles

Map 5, A5. C/de Toledo 106. Metro Puerta de Toledo.
Tues–Sat 9am–10.30pm, Sun 9am–4pm. Closed July.

A continual supply of snails in spicy sauce is issued from the sizzling pan in this rough and ready local bar, all washed down with the local *vermút del grifo*.

La Taberna Angosta

Map 4, C5. C/de Mancebos 6. Metro La Latina.
Mon–Thurs 6pm–2.30am, Fri–Sun noon–3.30am.

Fantastic homemade patés – the *paté de ave al vino blanco* is especially good – accompanied by great wines in this friendly bar in the heart of the old Moorish quarter of Madrid. There's a small *terraza* on the pavement opposite in the summer.

Taberna de Antonio Sánchez

Map 4, H6. C/Mesón de Paredes 13. Metro Tirso de Molina.
Mon–Sat noon–4pm & 8pm–midnight.

Said to be the oldest *taberna* in Madrid, this seventeenth-century bar has a stuffed bull's head (to commemorate Antonio Sánchez, the son of the founder, who was killed by a bull) and a wooden interior. Lots of *finos* on offer, plus *jamón* and *queso* tapas or *tortilla de San Isidro* (with salted cod) and *callos*.

La Taberna de los Cien Vinos

Map 4, E4. C/del Nuncio 16. Metro La Latina.
Tues–Sun 1–3.45pm & 8–11.45pm.

A vast selection of Spanish wines plus plenty to choose from on the constantly changing tapas menu, including excellent leek pie, smoked salmon and *pinchos* of roast beef. Every month they sell a different selection of whites and reds. The owner also goes on regular journeys around Spain to discover new wines. Not suitable for the indecisive.

La Taberna de Zapatero

Map 4, E5. C/del Almendro 22. Metro La Latina.
Tues–Sat 1–4pm & 8pm–midnight, Sun 1–4pm.

Excellent Ribera del Duero and original tapas in this friendly local haunt. Try the tooth-tingling *cazuelita de cabrales* (strong blue cheese mixed with cider) and the mild curry-flavoured chicken *pollo zapateado*.

GRAN VÍA, CHUECA AND SANTA BÁRBARA

Santander

Map 7, H6. C/de Augusto Figueroa 25. Metro Chueca.
Mon–Sat 10.45am–4pm & 7.30–11pm. Closed Aug.

It's worth a visit to this bar in the heart of Chueca for the range of tapas, including *empanadas*, *tortillas* and quiche lorraine, as well as a huge variety of fresh homemade canapés at reasonable prices.

Stop Madrid

Map 7, G7. C/de Hortaleza 11. Metro Gran Vía.
Mon–Sat noon–4pm & 7pm–midnight.
An old-time spit-and-sawdust bar, revitalized with Belgian, Mexican and German beers as well as *vermut* on tap. Tapas are largely *jamón* and *chorizo*, with the Canapé Stop of ham and tomato doused in olive oil well worth a try.

Taberna Angel Sierra

Map 7, I6. C/de Gravina 11, on Plaza Chueca. Metro Chueca.
Daily except Wed 10.30am–4pm & 7–11pm.
One of the great bars of Madrid, with a traditional zinc counter which is constantly washed down. Everyone drinks *vermut*, which is on tap and delicious, and free tapas of the most exquisite *boquerones en vinagre* are despatched. *Raciones* are also available, though they're expensive.

MALASAÑA AND BILBAO

Chipén

Map 7, G1. C/del Cardenal Cisneros 39. Metro Bilbao.
Daily noon–4pm & 7.30pm–midnight/1am.
A totally *castizo* bar, decorated with tiles portraying famous city sights and serving a range of tapas from a menu written in *Madrileño* slang. Specialities include *chipén* (smoked-salmon canapé) and *fetén* (blue cheese canapé). Also serves frog's legs and draught vermouth.

La Camocha

Map 7, G1. C/de Fuencarral 15 (Metro Bilbao) & c/de Fuencarral 95 (Metro Tribunal).
Daily 7am–2am.

TAPAS: MALASAÑA AND BILBAO

Asturian cider bar serving splendid *pulpo* and *almejas a la sidra*. You can use the special cider-pouring instruments stuck to the wall to make sure it is properly aerated.

Taberna del Foro

Map 7, F2. C/de San Andrés 38. Metro Bilbao.
Daily 7am–2/3am.

An annex to the *Café del Foro* serving splendid hot *bocaditos* (little sandwiches) with typical *Madrileño* name tags such as the *pasodoble* (bacon and cheese), *chotis* (tuna and peppers) and *cibeles* (sardines and tomato).

RECOLETOS AND SALAMANCA

Alkalde

Map 2, K3. C/de Jorge Juan 10. Metro Serrano.
Mon–Fri 1–4pm & 8.30pm–midnight, Sat 1–4pm.

This pricey, but very popular bar serves up Basque tapas, a real treat which you could turn into a tasty meal. Look out for the *empanadas* and the *tortillas* filled with peppers.

Hevia

Map 9, E2. C/de Serrano 118. Metro Núñez de Balboa.
Mon–Sat 9am–1.30am.

Plush venue and clientele for pricey, but excellent tapas and canapés – the hot Camembert is a must.

José Luis

Map 9, E1. C/de Serrano 89. Metro Núñez de Balboa.
Mon–Sat 9am–1am, Sun noon–11am.

The best of this chain of smart bar-restaurants originally established by a Basque who came to the city in the late 1950s.

An unstoppable success with branches now in Seville, Valencia, Barcelona and Montreal. Dainty and delicious sandwiches are laid out along the bar, together with canapés of *cangrejo* (crab), *morcilla* (black pudding) and steak.

RESTAURANTS

Madrid's restaurants offer every regional style of **Spanish cooking**: Castilian for roasts (*horno de asar* is a wood-burning oven) and stews, *Gallego* for seafood, *Andaluz* for fried fish, Levantine (Valencia/Alicante) for paella and other rice-based (*arroz*) dishes, Asturian for winter stews such as *fabada* and Basque for the ultimate gastronomy (and high prices).

Over the last few years, dozens of **foreign cuisines** have also appeared. There are some good Peruvian, Argentinian and Italian places and a scattering of enjoyable Indonesian

Restaurant prices

Restaurants have been graded as inexpensive (under 2000ptas a head for a three-course meal and wine), moderate (2000–3500ptas), expensive (3500–6000ptas) and very expensive (over 6000ptas). You can of course pay very different amounts at any restaurant depending on what you order and when. Fish and seafood generally boost the bill, while a set lunchtime **menú del día** is often amazingly cheap (from as little as 900ptas for three courses and house wine). If service is not included, a **tip** of somewhere between five and ten percent is sufficient, but never more than 500ptas in total.

Most – but by no means all – of the restaurants listed as "moderate" or above will accept **credit/charge cards** (*tarjetas*). If in doubt, phone ahead to check.

and Japanese restaurants. With few exceptions, though, Indian and Chinese restaurants are fairly dire, as, too, are most of the Mexican and Brazilian ones.

Traditional **Madrileño food** consists of robust mixed stews (such as the meat and chickpea *cocido*) and offal dishes, but the capital is also renowned for its quality seafood despite its distance from the sea – the best produce from Galicia is packed straight onto the train for Madrid each day.

SOL, PLAZA MAYOR AND OPERA

El Botín

Map 4, G2. C/Cuchilleros 17 ©366 42 17. Metro Sol/Tirso de Molina.

Daily 1–4pm & 8pm–midnight. Expensive.

Established in 1725, and highly picturesque with its tiled and wooden panels, this place features in the *Guinness Book of Records* as Europe's oldest restaurant. Favoured by Hemingway among others, it's inevitably a tourist haunt, but not such a bad one. Highlights are the traditional Castilian roasts – especially suckling pigs (*cochinillo*) and lamb (*cordero lechal*). Good house wine. The *menú del día* is around 4000ptas, but you could eat for less.

Casa Ciriaco

Map 4, C2. C/Mayor 84 ©548 50 66. Metro Opera.

Daily except Wed 1.30–4pm & 8.30–1.30pm. Closed Aug. Moderate.

Attractive, old-style *taberna*, long reputed for traditional Castilian dishes – trout *en escabeche* (marinated in vinegar and garlic) chicken *en pepitoria* (in almond sauce) and *cocido*, served up in old-style portions. The *menú* is 2100ptas; main *carta* dishes are a bit less. If you're not planning on a sit-down meal, you can still sample some of the excellent wine in the front bar.

Casa Gallega

Map 3, G2. C/Bordadores 11 ⓒ541 90 55 & Plaza San Miguel 8 ⓒ547 30 55. Both Metro Opera/Sol.
Daily 1–4pm & 8pm–midnight. Expensive.

An airy and welcoming *marisquería* that has been importing seafood on overnight trains from Galicia since it opened in 1915. Costs vary greatly according to the rarity of the fish or shellfish that you order. Gallego staples such as *pulpo* (octopus) and *pimientos de Padrón* (tiny, randomly piquant peppers) are brilliantly done and inexpensive, but the more exotic seasonal delights will raise a bill for two well into five figures.

Taberna del Alabardero

Map 3, E2. C/de Felipe V 6 ⓒ547 25 77. Metro Opera.
Daily 1–4pm & 9pm–midnight. Moderate–expensive.

A fine *taberna* in one of the nicest streets in this area, just behind the Plaza de Oriente. The cooking is Basque and, considering this, prices are relatively low, with a *menú del día* at 1100ptas. The *pimientos del piquillo rellenos de bacalao* (spicy peppers stuffed with cod) and the *merluza con almejas* (hake with clams) are recommended.

SANTA ANA AND HUERTAS

El Cenador del Prado

Map 6, D5. C/ del Prado 4 ⓒ429 15 61. Metro Antón Martín.
Mon–Fri 1.30–4pm & 9pm–midnight, Sat 9pm–midnight. Closed Aug. Expensive.

Set in a sort of relaxing greenhouse room with imaginative cuisine

RESTAURANTS: SANTA ANA AND HUERTAS

combining Spanish, Mediterranean and Oriental influences. There's a *menú de degustación* at 3500ptas and some spectacular desserts.

Champagnería Gala

Map 6, E7. C/de Moratín 22 ©429 25 62. Metro Antón Martín.
Daily 1.30–4.30pm & 9pm–1.30am, Fri & Sat eve bar only.
Inexpensive–moderate.

Fantastic-value restaurant run by a group of women, specializing in paellas and *fideuás* (like paella, only made with noodles instead of rice) and with excellent *pan tumaca* (toasted bread with tomato and garlic). Book ahead and try to get a table in the verdant indoor patio at the back. In the evenings, champagne accompanied by chocolate is served – a sophisticated oasis of calm if you want to relax after a taxing bar crawl.

Domine Cabra

Map 6, E6. C/de las Huertas 54 ©429 43 65. Metro Antón Martín.
Mon–Sat 2–4pm & 9–11.30pm, Sun 2–4pm. Closed second half of
Aug. Moderate.

Interesting mix of traditional and modern, with *Madrileño* standards given the *nueva cocina* treatment. Good sauces – a rarity in Spain – and look out for the steak with blue cheese sauce (*entrecot con crema de cabrales*) and the roasted scallops in white wine (*vieiras gratinadas al vino Albariño*).

Donzoko

Map 6, D4. C/de Echegaray 3 ©429 57 20. Metro Sevilla.
Mon–Sat 1.30–3.30pm & 8.30–11.30pm. Moderate.

Very reasonable-value Japanese restaurant with helpful service, decent *sushi* and delicious *tempura*. If you're in a group the *sukiyaki* (strips of meat and vegetables fried in a wok on the table) is a good bet.

La Sanabresa

Map 5, G2. C/Amor de Dios 12 ©429 03 38. Metro Antón Martín.
Mon–Sat 1–4pm & 8–11.30pm, Fri & Sat till midnight. Inexpensive.
A real local with a TV in one corner and an endless supply of
customers who come for its excellent and reasonably priced
dishes. Don't miss the grilled aubergines (*berenjenas a la plancha*).

LA LATINA AND LAVAPIÉS

La Burbuja que Ríe

Map 4, C7. C/del Angel 16 ©366 51 67. Metro Puerta de Toledo.
Tues 1–5pm, Wed–Sun 1–5pm & 8pm–midnight. Moderate.
Very popular noisy Asturian restaurant with a young clientele.
Huge servings of mussels, excellent selection of Asturian
cheeses and a very tasty *mero a la crema de anchoas* (grouper in
anchovy sauce). Get here early for a table.

Casa Lastra Sidrería

Map 5, E2. C/del Olivar 3 ©369 08 37. Metro Antón Martín/Tirso de
Molina.
Mon, Tues & Thurs–Sat 1–5pm & 8pm–midnight, Sun 1–5pm.
Closed July. Moderate.
Very popular restaurant serving classic Asturian fare: *chorizo a la
sidra* (chorizo in cider), *entrecot al cabrales* (steak in a strong blue
cheese sauce), *fabada* (a warming winter stew of beans, *chorizo*
and *morcilla*) and, of course, *sidra natural* (cider).

Casa Lucio

Map 4, F4. Cava Baja 35 ©365 32 52. Metro La Latina.
Mon–Fri & Sun 1–4pm & 9–11.30pm, Sat 9–11.30pm. Closed Aug.
Expensive.
Madrileños come here for Castilian dishes such as *cocido*, *callos*

(tripe) and roasts, cooked to perfection. Prices have gone up a bit since the king visited but you can still eat well for under 4000ptas if you're careful. Booking is essential.

El Económico/Soldermersol

Map 5, F5. C/de Argumosa 9 ©539 41 65. Metro Lavapiés. Daily except Sat 1–5pm & 9pm–midnight. Closed mid-Aug to mid-Sept. Inexpensive.

Traditional family-run workmen's *comedor* set in what looks like the front room of a house, in a pleasant tree-lined street near the Reina Sofía. An unbeatable 800ptas lunchtime *menú*

After Midnight

If you're desperate for that late-night stomach filler to keep you going into the early hours, the following places are strategically situated in the key night-time areas of the city.

La Carreta, Map 7, I7. C/Barbieri 10 (Metro Chueca; ©532 70 42). The latest opening of all – you can order up till 4.30am – and you get a show thrown in too. Tango dancing and grilled meats South American style should satisfy even the most serious insomniac reveller. Daily 1–5pm & 9pm–5am. Moderate.

La Farfalla, Map 6, E7. C/Santa María 17 (Metro Antón Martín; ©369 46 91). The place to go for late-night food and a lively party atmosphere in the Huertas area. Good range of tasty pizzas and Argentinian-style meat. Daily 9pm–3am; Fri & Sat till 4am. Inexpensive.

Palacio de Anglona, Map 4, D4. C/Segovia 13 (Metro La Latina; ©366 37 53). Italian-style dishes served up in this trendy joint situated in the cellars of an old palace. Daily 8.30pm–3am. Moderate.

offering a surpringly large choice, friendly service and very tasty food.

Posada de la Villa

Map 4, F4. Cava Baja 9 ©366 18 60. Metro La Latina.
Mon–Sat 1–4pm & 8pm–midnight, Sun 1–4pm. Closed Aug.
Expensive.

The most attractive-looking restaurant in Latina, spread over three floors of a seventeenth-century mansion. Cooking is typically *Madrileño*, including superb wood-roast lamb and suckling pig. Reckon on a good 6000ptas per person for the works – though you could get away with less.

Viuda de Vacas

Map 4, F5. Cava Alta 23 ©366 58 47. Metro La Latina.
Daily except Thurs 1.30–4.30pm & 9pm–midnight. Closed early Aug.
Inexpensive–moderate.

Highly traditional cosy restaurant with quality Castilian fare. Better value than the more celebrated *tabernas* in Cava Baja. Try the *merluza al horno* (baked hake).

GRAN VÍA, CHUECA AND SANTA BÁRBARA

El 26 de Libertad

Map 7, I6. C/de la Libertad 26 ©522 25 22. Metro Chueca.
Daily 1–4pm & 9pm–midnight. Closed Sun eve in July & Aug.
Moderate.

Imaginative cuisine served up in an attentive, but unfussy manner in this brightly decorated restaurant popular with the Chueca locals. Peppers stuffed with seafood, mushrooms in blue cheese and ostrich steaks in raspberry are some of the highlights.

El Buey

Map 7, B7. Plaza de la Marina Española 1 ©541 30 41 (Metro Santo Domingo) & c/General Pardiñas 10 ©431 44 92 (Metro Príncipe de Vergara).

Mon–Sat 1–4pm & 9pm–midnight. Moderate.

A meat eaters' paradise specializing in steak which you fry up yourself on a hotplate. Very good side dishes, including a great leek and seafood pie and excellent homemade desserts. Help yourself to wine and cheese in the tiny bar while you wait to be seated.

Carmencita

Map 7, I7. C/de la Libertad 16 ©531 66 12. Metro Chueca.

Mon–Fri 1–4pm & 9pm–midnight, Sat 1–4pm. Inexpensive to moderate.

Beautiful old restaurant, dating back to 1830, with panelling, brass, marble tables – and a new Basque-influenced chef. Popular with politicians and the literary crowd. The lunch *menú* is a bargain at 1200ptas.

La Chocolatería

Map 7, I6. C/Barbieri 15 ©521 00 23. Metro Chueca.

Daily 1.45–3.45pm & 9pm–1.30am. Closed Aug. Moderate.

Not just chocolate here in this romantic old-world setting; in fact a very imaginative menu with specials including *codillo en salsa de ciruela* (pork knuckle in plum sauce), well-cooked vegetables, interesting salads and a range of homemade desserts.

El Comunista (Tienda de Vinos)

Map 7, I6. C/Augusto Figueroa 35 ©521 70 12. Metro Chueca.

Mon–Sat 1–4.30pm & 9.30–11.45pm, Sun 9.30–11.45pm. Closed mid-Aug to mid-Sept. Inexpensive.

Long-established, popular *comedor* that has changed little since it was given its unofficial (but always used) name as a student haunt under Franco. The garlic soup (*sopa de ajo*) is recommended.

Nova Galicia

Map 7, C4. C/de Conde Duque 3 ©559 42 60. Metro Plaza de España.
Mon–Sat 7am–midnight, Sun 7am–4pm. Closed second half of Aug. Moderate.
Excellent-value Galician restaurant specializing in seafood tapas and *arroz con bogavante* (rice with lobster). Pass through the ordinary-looking front bar and into the dining room hidden behind. Very good for large parties when they will do a special *queimada* (flaming Galician liquor served in small terracotta bowls).

Salvador

Map 7, I7. C/Barbieri 12 ©521 45 24. Metro Chueca.
Mon–Sat 1.30–5pm & 9pm–midnight. Closed Aug. Expensive.
Bullfighting decor and traditional specialities such as *rabo de toro* (bull's tail), *gallina en pepitoria (chicken fricassee)*, fried *merluza (hake)* and *arroz con leche* (rice pudding) which are all excellent.

La Tasca Suprema

Map 7, J4. C/de Argensola 7 ©308 03 47. Metro Alonso Martínez.
Mon–Sat 1.30–4pm. Closed Aug. Inexpensive.
Very popular family-run local only open at lunchtimes and worth booking ahead for. Perfect Castilian home cooking, including *callos*, and on Monday and Thursday, *cocido*.

MALASAÑA AND BILBAO

Balear

C/Sagunto 18 ©447 91 15. Metro Iglesia.
Mon 1.30–4pm, Tues–Sat 1.30–4pm & 8.30pm–midnight, Sun 1.30–4pm. Moderate.

RESTAURANTS: MALASAÑA AND BILBAO

Madrid's Vegetarian Restaurants

Madrid can be an intimidating city for veggies, given the mass of pigs, fish and seafood on display in bar and restaurant windows and on counters. However, you can order vegetables separately at just about any restaurant in the city – although make sure you specify that you do not want stray pieces of ham included – and there is good pizza and pasta to be had at a number of Italian places. You can even find the odd vegetarian paella. As for **tapas**, *champiñones*, *patatas bravas*, *patatas ali oli*, *pimientos de padrón* and *tortilla* are probably the best bets.

More crucially, the capital now has half a dozen decent and inexpensive **vegetarian restaurants**, scattered around the centre. These include:

Artemisa, Map 6, D4. C/Ventura de la Vega 4 (Metro Sevilla; ©429 50 92). A popular place (you may have to wait for a table), best for its veggie pizzas, stuffed aubergines and an imaginative range of salads. No smoking – even more of a novelty than vegetarian food in Madrid. Mon–Sat 1.30–4pm & 9pm–midnight, Sun 1.30–4pm. Moderate.

El Estragón, Map 4, D4. Plaza de La Paja 10 (Metro La Latina; ©365 89 82). Good vegetarian tapas, leek pie and chocolate cake. Economical *menú del día* at 1000ptas and a fine setting on the edge of this ancient plaza. Daily 12.30–4.30pm & 8.30–midnight. Inexpensive–moderate.

El Granero de Lavapiés, Map 5, G5. C/de Argumosa 10 (Metro Lavapiés; ©467 76 11). Excellent macrobiotic and vegetarian food, including spinach soup and veggie burgers. Situated in a pleasant tree-lined Lavapiés street. Mon–Fri 1–4pm. Closed Aug. Inexpensive.

La Granja, Map 7, F3. C/de San Andrés 11 (Metro Bilbao/ Tribunal; ©532 87 93). Good-value set menu that changes

every day offering a choice of soup, salad, a main dish of vegetables, rice and fruits topped with sauce, dessert and drinks).
Mon-Wed 1.30–4.30pm & 9pm–midnight, Thurs–Sun
1.30–4.30pm. Inexpensive.

Vegetariano, **Map 7, F4**. C/de Marqués de Santa Ana 34
(Metro Tribunal; ℗532 09 27). Excellent salads and
Mediterranean vegetables. No smoking. Tues–Sat 1.30–4pm &
9–11.30pm, Sun 1.30–4pm. Inexpensive.

This relaxed Levantine restaurant serves only rice-based dishes
– fifteen different types of paella – but they're superb. There's
an inexpensive *cava* and you can turn up any time before
midnight.

La Giralda

Map 7, G1. C/Hartzenbush 12 ℗445 77 79. Metro Bilbao.
Mon–Sat 1–4.30pm & 8pm–midnight. Moderate to expensive.
A little slice of Andalucía serving *Andaluz* fish and seafood
of very high quality. Perfectly cooked *chipirones* (small squid
fried in batter), *calamares* and all the standards, plus
wonderful *mero* (grouper). A second branch, across the road
at no. 15, does a similarly accomplished job on *pescados
fritos*.

La Glorieta

Map 7, E2. C/Manuela Malasaña 37 ℗448 40 16. Metro Bilbao.
Mon–Sat 1.30–5pm & 9pm–midnight. Closed Aug 10–25. Moderate.
Modern Spanish cooking with Basque and French influences –
imaginative and tasty. Very good-value *menú del día* at 1000ptas,
which includes a better than average bottle of wine, tasty
lemon cheesecake, coffee and a *copita* of high powered Galician
orujo.

MADRID'S VEGETARIAN RESTAURANTS

Ribeira Do Miño

Map 7, H5. C/de Santa Brígida 1 ©521 98 54. Metro Tribunal.
Daily 1–5pm & 8pm–1am. Moderate.
Great-value *marisquería* near the Museo Municipal, serving a
mariscada (shellfish platter) for two at only 3500ptas; go for the
slightly more expensive Galician white wine, *Albariño*, to
accompany it.

Taberna Griega

Map 7, E4. C/del Tesoro 6 ©532 18 92. Metro Tribunal.
Tues–Sun 8.30pm–midnight and beyond. Closed Aug. Inexpensive.
Enjoyable Greek restaurant, with live *bouzouki* music most
nights. A tasty *moussaka* and plentiful *metzes* are stalwarts of the
menu. At weekends there's Greek dancing accompanied by
obligatory plate smashing.

RECOLETOS AND SALAMANCA

Al Mounia

Map 7, K7. Paseo de Recoletos 5 ©435 08 28. Metro Banco de
España.
Tues–Sat 1.30–3.30pm & 9pm–midnight. Closed Aug. Expensive.
Moroccan cooking at its very best at the most established
Arabic restaurant in town, offering an atmospheric and
romantic setting with impeccable service. The *bastilla* (pigeon
pie) and desserts are a must.

El Amparo

Map 2, K3. Callejón Puigcerdá 8 ©431 64 56. Metro Serrano.
Mon–Fri 1.30–3.30pm & 9–11.30pm, Sat 9–11.30pm. Expensive.
Most critics rate this designer restaurant among the top five in

Madrid and you'll need to book a couple of weeks ahead to get a
table. Faultless Basque cooking by Carmen Guasp, with main
dishes around the 3000ptas mark. Expect a bill of at least 6000ptas a
head.

Casa Portal

C/Dr Castelo 26 ℘574 20 26. Metro Retiro.
Mon–Sat 1.30–4pm & 8.30–11.30pm. Closed Aug. Moderate.
Superlative Asturian cooking – go for the *fabada* (beans,
chorizo and morcilla stew) or *besugo* (bream) washed down
with some natural cider. The shellfish is excellent too.

Paradis Madrid

Map 6, F3. C/Marqués de Cubas 14 ℘429 73 03. Metro Banco
de España.
Mon–Fri 1.30–4pm & 9pm–midnight, Sat 9pm–midnight. Closed
Easter & Aug. Expensive.
Part of a chain of restaurants run by a Catalan duo with branches
in Barcelona and New York. Designerish details include a menu
for olive oils. The cooking is light, Mediterranean and tasty; try
the wonderful *arroz negro* with seafood.

Viridiana

Map 6, H3. C/Juan de Mena 14 ℘523 44 78. Metro Retiro.
Mon–Sat 1.30–4pm & 9pm–midnight. Closed Easter & Aug. Very
expensive.
Bizarre temple of Madrid *nueva cocina*, offering mouthwatering
creations like *solomillo* (sirloin) with black truffles and *mero* with
crèpes, while also conducting pyrotechnic experiments – dishes
often arrive decorated with small incendiary devices. Superb
selection of wine. Main courses are around 2500ptas and no
cards are accepted.

RESTAURANTS: RECOLETOS AND SALAMANCA

Zalacaín

C/Alvarez de Baena 4 ©561 59 35. Metro Rubén Darío.
Mon–Fri 1.15–4pm & 9pm–midnight, Sat 9pm–midnight. Closed Aug. Very expensive.

Luxurious setting for the best restaurant in town and the only one with three Michelin stars. As you'd expect, the Basque-style cooking of master chef Benjamín Urdaín is topnotch and wines are superb. You pay for the pleasure, but the set menu at 6950ptas is still good value.

ARGÜELLES

Casa Mingo

Paseo de la Florida 2 ©547 79 18. Metro Príncipe Pío.
Daily 11am–midnight. Closed Aug. Inexpensive.

Next to the Ermita de Antonio de la Florida, this is a great-value, noisy and crowded Asturian chicken and cider house. Tables on the pavement or in the barn-like interior are like gold dust so loiter close by with your bottle of *sidra natural* in hand ready to jump in when someone finishes. The spit-roast chicken is the practically compulsory main course, while the *chorizo* cooked in cider and *cabrales* (blue cheese) are also very good. You can also buy a takeaway for a picnic in the Casa de Campo, if you prefer.

La Vaca Argentina

Map 2, A1. Paseo del Pintor Rosales 52 ©559 66 05. Metro Argüelles.
Daily 1–5pm & 9pm–midnight. Moderate.

Good views and great grilled steaks (*churrasco*) at this Argentinian restaurant overlooking the Parque del Oeste. Its terrace is a very pleasant place to eat in summer.

DRINKING

W ith over 12,000 **bars** in the city, it's clear that the bar – and its close cousins, the café and *terraza* – is a central feature of *Madrileño* life. There's a bewildering variety to choose from: *cervecerías* (beer special-ists), *coctelerías* (cocktail bars), *champagnerías* (champagne bars), *tabernas* (old-style taverns), *bares de copas* (bars mainly serving spirits) and a new wave of Irish bars. You'll also find *discobares* and *pubs* where music is the primary attraction; these are covered in a separate chapter (see *Nightlife*).

"Bar hanging" is one of the best, and most pleasant, ways to get the feel of the city and its people, although you'll need to adopt *Madrileño* bar **customs** as quickly as possible. Don't get put off or feel uncomfortable if the barman or waiter appears to ignore you; just give a firm shout of "*oiga*" which, although it sounds rude to English-speaking ears, is in fact the polite way of calling the bar-man's attention. Once you have ordered don't be in a hurry to thrust your pesetas into the barman's hand; instead wait until you are ready to go and then ask for "*la cuenta*". Leave a few small coins as a tip if you wish and remember that you normally pay a little more for sitting at a table with waiter service than for standing at the bar. You won't often find bins for your bar detritus of olive

Drinking – The Essentials

Drinking out needn't be expensive, especially if you stick to the more down-to-earth local bars and, even better, get to know the barman. If you venture into cocktail bars and *bares de copas* you will pay a lot more for both beers and spirits, although measures are very generous indeed and it's usually up to you to tell the barman to stop pouring. It's worth remembering that imported beers and spirits (*importación*) are always a good deal more expensive than the Spanish equivalents (*nacional*).

Beer

Cerveza, lager-type beer, is generally of very good quality. It comes bottled in *tercios* (a third of a litre) or smaller *botellines*, and on draught (*de barril*), in *cañas* (small glasses), *dobles* (larger glasses), *jarras* (jugs) or even *pintas* (pints). Non-alcoholic beers (*cerveza sin alcohol*) are available by the bottle in all bars.

Wine and liqueurs

Wines (*tinto* – red, *blanco* – white and *rosado* – rosé) are a very cheap option and many bars have a fine selection, so ask for it by name as you will tend to get the cheapest if you don't specify. **Sherries** are also worth trying, especially the chilled dry *fino* or fuller bodied *palo cortado* served in many Andaluz bars, as is *vermút de barril* (draught vermouth), all of which make an ideal aperitif. Catalan champagne-like sparkling wine (**cava**) is good value and can be ordered at specialist wine bars and *champagnerías*. **Sangría**, a deceptively strong, but refreshing punch-like mixture of red wine, fruit and lemonade is common in summer. A variety of after-dinner drinks and **liqueurs** are available including locally produced *anís* (aniseed), *pacharán* (another more fruity aniseed drink from Navarra) and *orujo* (a powerful schnapps-type drink).

Soft drinks

As you'd expect, all the major brand-name soft drinks are available, but also worth trying are the specifically Spanish soft drinks such as **horchata** (a milky drink made from crushed nuts) and **granizado** (crushed ice with lemon, orange or coffee). When ordering **water** specify if you want it still (*sin gas*) or sparkling (*con gas*).

Coffee and tea

Coffee is usually of excellent quality and generally served black in a small cup (*café solo*). If you want a larger, more dilute black coffee ask for an *americano*; with a drop of milk it's *café cortado*, and white with lots of hot milk it's *café con leche*. For decaffinated ask for *descafeinado*. **Tea** (*té*) is usually poor and ordering it with milk will often get you a glass of milk with a tea bag floating on top, so it's best to order the two separately.

stones, paper napkins, toothpicks, etc. so it is usual to throw them on the floor.

Most cafés and bars serve some sort of food, but if this is their primary attraction we have listed them under 'Tapas bars' in the *Eating* chapter. There is, however, no absolute dividing line and you will often find excellent snacks in the places listed in this chapter. Many bars, and especially nightclubs, set up outdoor *terrazas* in summer. For details of these see p.178.

SOL AND SANTA ANA

Aloque

Map 5, F3. C/Torrecilla del Real 20. Metro Antón Martín.
Daily 7.30pm–1am.
Relaxed wine bar where you can try top-quality wines by the

glass. Its owner, Paco Parejo, is a science professor and expert on viticulture. Regular wine-tasting sessions and a wine connoisseurs' *tertulia* (Tues) are held here.

El Anciano

Map 3, C6. C/de Bailén 19. Metro Opera.
Daily except Wed 10am–3pm & 5.30–11pm; Fri & Sat till 12.30am. Closed Aug.
Pleasant bar across the road from the Palacio Real, and just the place to refresh yourself after some hard work on the tourist trail. Tasty beer and a good range of wines in an old-fashioned environment dating back to 1907.

Café de Oriente

Map 3, D4. Plaza de Oriente 2. Metro Opera.
Daily 8.30am–1.30am; Fri & Sat till 2.30am.
Elegant, traditional-style café founded a decade or so ago by priest, Luis Lezama, to finance a charity rehab programme for ex-convicts. Plenty of mirrors, marble tabletops and candlesticks with occasional accompaniment from the pianist. A popular *terraza* in summer looks out on the newly renovated Plaza de Oriente.

Cervecería Alemana

Map 6, C5. Plaza de Santa Ana 6. Metro Sol.
Daily except Tues 10am–12.30am; Fri & Sat till 2am.
Stylish old beer house founded in 1904 with dark wooden panels, white marble tables and a packed bar. Frequented in times past by Hemingway and, these days, seemingly every other American tourist. Order a *caña* and go easy on the tapas, as the bill can mount up fast.

Cervecería Santa Ana

Map 6, C5. Plaza de Santa Ana 10. Metro Sol.
Daily 11am–1.30am; Fri & Sat till 2.30am.
Cheaper than the *Alemana*, with tables outside but few inside.
Good beer, friendly service and a fine selection of tapas.
Always packed at night.

Cuevas del Sésamo

Map 6, C4. C/del Príncipe 7. Metro Sevilla.
Daily 6.30pm–2am.
Originally opened in 1950, the caves below were discovered
the following year, and today the walls are replete with poetry
and literary phrases. Great acoustics for the resident pianist and
impromptu poetry readings. The Japanese have built an exact
replica in Kyoto.

Los Gabrieles

Map 6, D5. C/de Echegaray 17. Metro Sol.
Daily 2.30pm–2.30am.
This impressively tiled bar, which includes scenes from *Don
Quixote* and a version of Velázquez's *Los Borrachos*, is a Madrid
monument and it's worth going earlier than is cool to
appreciate the fabulous tableaux, created by sherry companies
in the 1880s. Drinks are reasonable, considering the venue.
Very crowded after 10pm, especially at weekends.

Naturbier

Map 6, C5. Plaza de Santa Ana 9. Metro Sol.
Daily 8pm–3am.
Next door to the *cervecerías Alemana* and *Santa Ana*, the
Naturbier Bar brews its own tasty, cloudy beer and serves a
variety of German sausages to accompany it. There's usually

room to sit in the cellar down below if the top bar is too crowded.

Salón del Prado

Map 6, D5. C/del Prado 4. Metro Sol.
Daily 2pm–2am; Fri & Sat till 2.30am; Sun till 1am.
Elegant Parisian-style café-bar serving great coffee and hosting classical concerts on Thursday night at 11pm. Turn up early if you want a table.

La Venencia

Map 6, D4. C/de Echegaray 7. Metro Sol/Sevilla.
Daily 7pm–1.30am. Closed Aug.
This rather delapidated, narrow, wooden-panelled bar covered in yellowing advertising posters is great for sherry sampling. The whole range is here, served from wooden barrels, and accompanied by delicious olives and *mojama* (dry, salted tuna). Atmospheric and authentic.

Viva Madrid

Map 6, D5. C/Manuel Fernández y González 7. Metro Antón Martín.
Daily noon–2am; Fri & Sat till 3am.
Another fabulous tiled bar – both outside and in – offering wines and sherry, plus basic tapas. Get here early if you want to see the tiles in their full glory, as it gets very crowded. Quite pricey, but certainly worth a stop.

LA LATINA AND LAVAPIÉS

Alquezar

Map REF C/Lavapiés 53. Metro Lavapiés.
Daily 1pm–1am; Fri & Sat till 3am.

Las Tertulias

Everywhere people meet to chat and argue, but only in Spain – a country where conversation is considered to be one of the fine arts – has this simple custom been converted into an established ritual with rules and regulations. To earn the name **tertulia**, a regular time and place must be fixed – usually in a café or bar – and participants must come prepared to speak, interrupt, contradict and generally intensify the discussion. Subject matter can range from politics, philosophy and literature through to bullfighting and flamenco.

The first *tertulias* began with the eighteenth-century Enlightenment and were largely political with liberals and absolutists – supporters and opponents – of the French Revolution, arguing out their differences. In the late nineteenth and early twentieth centuries, with the rise of the literary groups, the "Generation of '98" and subsequent "Generation of '27", they became a forum for intellectual and artistic ideas, with participants including the poet Federico García Lorca and painter José Gutiérrez de Solana (whose famous painting of the *tertulia* at the **Café del Pombo** hangs in the Reina Sofía art gallery). Hemingway, however, refused to go to the **Café Gijón** because he hated all literary *tertulias* and regarded the people who attended them as "a load of show-offs".

Cafés such as *Gijón*, *El Lion* and *El Parnasillo* built their reputations on the standard of their *tertulias*, and as one old *contertulio* said, "In life there are only three fundamental choices: marital state, profession and café." However, many were silenced during the Civil War and afterwards under Franco, when meetings of more than five people were seen as suspect. They reappeared in the late 1940s with the emergence of *Juventud Creadora* (Creative Youth) in *Café Gijón* headed by Nobel Prize Winner, Camilo José Cela, and to this day, although they have declined in importance and may not reach the intellectual heights of the past, they are still alive and well in a number of the city's old cafés and bars.

An Arabian atmosphere is created with walls adorned with camels and mosques, background music and sweet-smelling tea served from silver-plated teapots. If you get peckish try the Arab pastries.

Café del Nuncio

Map 4, E4. C/de Segovia 9. Metro La Latina.
Daily 12.30pm–2.30am; Fri & Sat till 3am.

A great place for cocktails, alcoholic coffees and the house speciality, *Agua de Valencia* (a sort of bucks fizz). Good cakes and biscuits too and a very pleasant *terraza* in summer.

El 21

Map 4, G3. C/de Toledo 21. Metro La Latina.
Daily 11am–3.30pm & 7–11pm. Closed Aug.

Excellent *chupito* (a thimbleful of spirits) bar, serving a vast range of mini cocktails (including non-alcoholic) with evocative names such as *Erótico*, *Medias de seda* (Silk stockings), *Terremoto* (Earthquake) and *Volcán* (Volcano). The cheap and cheerful alternative to a full-scale cocktail bar; all drinks are 150–200ptas.

María Panadora

Map 4, B4. Plaza Gabriel Miró 1. Metro La Latina.
Tues–Sun 4pm–1.30am; Fri & Sat till 4.30am. Closed second half of Aug.

An incongruous mixture of *champagnería* and bookshop, where quality *cava* can be enjoyed with the perfect accompaniment of chocolate-covered tapas and strawberries – a decadent and highly enjoyable little outing.

Nuevo Café Barbieri

Map 4, F4. C/de Ave María 45. Metro Lavapiés.
Daily 3pm–2am; Fri & Sat till 3am.

Ever so slightly seedy, well-known café with a vaguely intellectual reputation, situated just off the Plaza de Lavapiés. It's a relaxed place with unobtrusive music, lots of wooden tables, old-style decor, newspapers and a wide selection of coffees.

Pastelería-Licorería El Madroño

Map 4, E4. C/de Caravaca 10. Metro Lavapiés.
Tues–Sun 10am–2pm & 6pm–midnight; Fri & Sat till 2am. Closed Aug.

The place to go for Madrid's own liqueur made from the berries of the *madroño* tree; you can pick up a slice of seaweed cake, too, while you're here.

El Tempranillo

Map 4, E5. C/Cava Baja 38. Metro La Latina.
Daily noon–4pm & 9pm–2am.

Excellent little wine bar serving a vast range of Spanish wines by the glass. Although only recently established, it has the air of having been here for years and has already established a faithful clientele. A great place to discover your favourite Spanish wine.

GRAN VÍA, CHUECA AND SANTA BÁRBARA

Café Moderno

Map 7, D3. Plaza de las Comendadoras 1. Metro Noviciado.
Daily 3pm–2am; Fri & Sat till 3am; June–Sept from noon.

Hidden away in a quiet, hippyish square alongside the Convento de las Comendadoras is this mock Art Deco café. Activities include musical recitals, tarot card reading, theatrical performances and Arabian dancing. Plenty of different coffees and herbal teas.

Carpe Diem

Map 7, D5. Plaza Conde de Toreno 2. Metro Plaza de España/ Noviciado.
Tues–Sat 9pm–3am.

A part of the takings of this bar goes towards overseas projects and it often stages markets in aid of developing countries. The single-roomed bar is decorated with Pop Art and cartoons, while noticeboards keep the clientele informed of upcoming events. Happy hour goes on until midnight, with a variety of Spanish pop and salsa played.

La Cervecería Internacional

Map 7, I5. C/Regueros 8. Metro Alonso Martínez.
Daily 1–5pm & 8pm–1am; Fri & Sat till 2.30am.

Large beer hall masquerading as a beer festival, situated in the heart of the teenage disco belt around Plaza Santa Bárbara. Plenty of different draught beers, music videos and good tapas.

Círculo de Bellas Artes

Map 7, I8. C/de Alcalá 42. Metro Banco de España.
Daily 8am–2am; Fri & Sat till 3am.

You pay 100ptas for day membership to the Círculo, which gives access to the exhibitions (see p.49) and to a luxurious bar complete with reclining nude sculpture and sofas. Outside is a year-round *terraza*.

El Cock

Map 7, H7. C/de la Reina 16, just behind Museo Chicote. Metro Gran Vía.
Daily 7pm–3am.

Formerly connected to the Museo Chicote (see below) by a

secret corridor, this is now a smart and very *moda* bar, styled like a gentlemen's club, and you have to knock to get in. Attracting an arty crowd late at night, the music is good, but there's no dancing. *Cañas* or wine cost around 600ptas, cocktails 900ptas.

Del Diego

Map 7, H7. C/de la Reina 12. Metro Gran Vía.
Mon–Sat 9pm–3am. Closed Aug.

Another Art Deco cocktail bar set up by a former Chicote waiter who personally mixes all the cocktails. Friendly, unhurried atmosphere and open until the early hours. The house special, vodka-based *Del Diego,* is the one to go for.

Museo Chicote

Map 7, H7. Gran Vía 12. Metro Gran Vía.
June–Sept 5pm–3am (Fri & Sat till 4am); Oct–May noon–3am (Fri & Sat till 4am).

The place to go if you've got a bit of imagination and want to wallow in nostalgia. Opened in 1931 and still full of Art Deco lines and pistacho-coloured booths, this bar was opened by Perico Chicote, ex-barman at the *Ritz*. At the back he set up a museum to house his collection of over ten thousand special bottles, including original Napoleon brandy, Chinese chrysanthemum liquor and vodka from the Tsar. Sophia Loren, Frank Sinatra, Ava Gardner, Luis Buñuel, Orson Wells and the ubiquitous Hemingway have all passed through its doors. The collection has, alas, long gone, sold by Perico's descendants and then auctioned off bottle by bottle in 1984. Nowadays they will mix you any (expensive) cocktail while you savour the memories. Busiest after midnight.

Irish Pubs

One recent phenomena on the Madrid bar scene has been the emergence of the **Irish Pub**. Although a pint of the "black stuff" has long been available in the capital, specialist Irish pubs have sprung up all over the city in the last few years. Having bought up the Spanish brewery, *Cruzcampo*, in 1991 *Guinness* has been more heavily involved in establishing its presence across the city, setting up and supplying pubs, whilst other individual ventures have followed in their wake. Theme pubs based on village shops, Dublin streets, country cottages and breweries have all appeared, while the Celtic music scene has taken off in a big way with a number of bands now firmly established on the pub circuit. Popular with the city's large British community, young *Madrileños* also form a substantial section of their clientele. If you want to be assured of a great St Patrick's night or just feel a little homesick you could try some of the following:

Finbars, **Map 2, B1.** C/ Marqués de Urquijo 10 (Metro Argüelles). Good range of live music on most nights in this self-styled pub/music shop. Drop by on Thursday night if you want a game of rugby for the local ex-pats team, the Madrid Lions. Sky TV sports. Mon–Sat 11am–3am, Sun noon–3am.

Finnegans, **Map 7, J5.** Plaza de las Salesas 9 (Metro Colón). Large bar with several rooms complete with bar fittings and wooden floors brought over from Ireland. English-speaking staff and TV sports. Mon–Thurs & Sun 12.30pm–2am, Fri & Sat 1pm–3am.

La Fontana de Oro, **Map 6, C4.** C/de la Victoria 1 (Metro Sol). Although it's a heresy to have turned this ancient bar (dating back over 200 years and which featured in Benito Pérez

Galdós's book of the same name) into an Irish pub, it's an attractive and lively venue with some swinging Celtic sounds. Daily 9am–5am.

The Irish Rover, Avda. Brasil 7 (Metro Lima). On an Irish street behind the concrete jungle of the Azca centre, off the Castellana. Popular with young *Madrileños* and packed at weekends. Daily noon–4am.

The Quiet Man, Map 7, G5. C/Valverde 44 (Metro Tribunal). One of the first on the scene, designed in the style of a turn of the century Dublin pub and full of authentic fittings. Mon–Thurs 5.30pm–2am, Fri–Sun 1pm–3.30am.

Net Café

Map 7, E2. C/de San Bernardo 81. Metro San Bernardo.
Mon–Thurs 8pm–2am, Fri & Sat 4pm–3.30am, Sun 4pm–1am.

If you really can't bear to be away from the computer screen while you're on holiday, this is the place for you. Surf the Net, play the latest games and chat to other nerds.

MALASAÑA AND BILBAO

Café Comercial

Map 7, G2. Glorieta de Bilbao 7. Metro Bilbao.
Daily 8am–1am; Fri & Sat till 2am.

A *Madrileño* institution and one of the city's most popular meeting points. This is a lovely traditional café full of mirrors, substantial tables and the whole cross section of Madrid society. Settle in, relax and listen to the piano player on Friday and Saturday nights. Regular *tertulias* on Monday at 6pm and bi-monthly meetings for English writers on Saturday evening. Well placed for the Chueca/Santa Bárbara area.

Café del Foro

Map 7, F3. C/de San Andrés 38. Metro Tribunal.
Daily 7pm–3am; Fri & Sat till 4am.
Expensive but enjoyable bar with live music or some form of entertainment most nights. Attracts a slightly older, fairly smart crowd. The decor is designed by Costus, Almodóvar's sidekick.

Café de Ruiz

Map 7, F2. C/de Ruiz 11. Metro Bilbao.
Daily 3pm–3am.
Classic old-fashioned café in the midst of Malasaña – a great place to while away an afternoon reading the paper. Discreet background music and good cakes and biscuits.

Casa Quemada

C/de Cardenal Cisneros 56. Metro Quevedo.
Daily 8pm–late.
Unusual for this bar-packed area in that it's old (all-wood decor) and very peaceful. You can't miss it as there's a car stuck in the window – one of the first assembly-line models produced in the country. *Sangría* at a modest 900ptas a jug.

Medina Magerit

Map 7, F3. C/Divino Pastor 21. Metro Bilbao.
Daily 7pm–2am.
Original bar with a friendly and enthusiastic owner serving an interesting and creative selection of drinks, including *Tisana India con zumos* (fruit juices with herbs and seeds), *Agua de Cebada* (a crushed ice and barley concoction) and delicious *mojito cubanos* (rum cocktails). A selection of board games is available to pass the time and downstairs there's a very small, but atmospheric cellar where traditional flamenco is sometimes performed.

DRINKING: MALASAÑA AND BILBAO

RECOLETOS AND SALAMANCA

Café el Espejo

Map 7, L6. Paseo de Recoletos 31. Metro Colón.
Daily 10am–2am; Fri & Sat till 3am.

Opened in 1978, but you wouldn't guess it given its antiquated decor. Mirrors, gilt and a wonderful extravagant glass pavilion, plus a leafy outside *terraza*. Just the place to buy a coffee and watch the world go by.

Café Gijón

Map 7, K6. Paseo de Recoletos 21. Metro Banco de España.
Daily 8am–1.30am; Sat till 2am.

Famous literary café dating from 1888, decked out in Cuban mahogany and mirrors. A centre of the intellectual/arty *movida* in the 1980s. Best for morning or late afternoon coffee as tables are turned over for the set menu at lunchtime. There's also a cellar restaurant and a very pleasant summer *terraza*. Regular artistic *tertulias* are still held here (see box, p.159).

El Gato Persa

Map 7, K5. C/de Bárbara de Braganza 10. Metro Colón.
Daily 10am–1am. Closed second half of Aug.

This tearoom, set in a small library with comfortable seats, soft lighting and Baroque music (jazz at night), makes a very relaxing escape from the bustle of the city. A wide range of fruit and floral teas is on offer, including *mil y una noches*, a combination of black tea and wild flowers.

NIGHTLIFE

Madrid's renowned **late-night scene** really took off with **la movida madrileña** in the late 1970s, when the end of the Franco era produced an explosion of artistic creativity combined with a long-suppressed desire to indulge in pure hedonistic enjoyment. Although the true *movida* has passed, nightlife still remains a pretty serious phenomenon – this is the only city in Europe where you can get caught in traffic jams at 4am, when clubbers are either going home or moving on to the dance-past-dawn discos. Madrid's bar and club scene has, if anything, got more frenetic over the past few years, largely due to the appearance of **bakalao**, a Spanish (originally Ibizan) version of house music which is especially prominent in the zone around Bilbao.

As with everything *Madrileño*, there is a bewildering variety of types of nightlife. The mainstays of the Madrid scene are the **discobares** – bars of all musical and sexual persuasion, whose unifying feature is background (occasionally live) rock, dance or salsa music and usually a small dance floor. These don't generally make an admission charge, but drinks are more expensive than in other bars; they get going around 11pm and stay open till 2am or 3am. **Discotecas** are rarely worth investigating until around 1 or 2am. They aren't always that different from *discobares*, though they tend to be bigger and flashier, with a lot of attention to lights, sound system and decor, and they stay open very late – most until 4am, some till 6am. If you're up for it **"After Hours" venues** open at between 5 and 6am and keep going until late morning when you can grab some *chocolate con churros* before finally heading home to bed (see p.175).

Venues with regular live music – rock, jazz, flamenco, salsa and classical – are covered in the *Live Music* chapter, see p.187.

In summer, many of the trendier clubs suspend operations and set up all-night outdoor **terrazas**, which are effectively open-air discos. They change location from year to year as they are pursued by the local authorities for breaches of local bye-laws on noise, traffic and obstruction, but they still pop up every summer in and around the Castellana.

DISCOBARES

Discobares are scattered all over the city, but each area has its own very particular identity. The magnet for the teenage crowd is **Alonso Martínez**, while **Argüelles** and **Moncloa** are student hangouts, and **Salamanca** is the place for chic bars and high prices. If you want to be at the cutting edge of trendiness, head for **Malasaña** and **Chueca**, while you'll find a more eclectic mix in the streets around **Sol** and **Santa Ana**.

SOL, OPERA AND SANTA ANA

La Comedia

Map 6, C4. C/del Príncipe 16. Metro Sol.
Daily 9pm–4am; Fri & Sat till 9am.
Modern, relaxing bar for a quiet drink by day, which gets

livelier as the night progresses. Good selection of varied and danceable music, and it's a favourite haunt for staff from earlier-closing bars as its open until 9am at the weekends. Entry charge of 1000ptas at night.

No se lo digas a nadie

Map 6, D4. C/Ventura de la Vega 7. Metro Sol.
Mon–Sat 8pm–2am; Fri & Sat till 5am.

Founded (and still run) by a women's co-op, though this bar has mellowed a bit in recent years (the toilets no longer proclaim *nosotras* and *ellos* – "us" and "them"). Nonetheless, it retains a political edge, hosting benefit events from time to time. There's no door policy or dress code and drinks are reasonably priced. Upstairs you'll find six pool tables and plenty of places to sit; downstairs there's a disco playing mainly dance music.

Villa Rosa

Map 6, C5. Plaza de Santa Ana 5. Metro Sol.
Mon–Sat 11pm–5am.

Formerly a famous flamenco club which later featured in Pedro Almodóvar's *High Heels*, the exterior of this dance bar is adorned with beautiful *azulejos* of famous Spanish cities and the interior is straight out of the Alhambra, with its *Mudéjar* arches and ceilings. Monday and Tuesday are salsa nights, Wednesday flamenco and the rest of the week is mainstream disco.

GRAN VÍA, CHUECA AND SANTA BÁRBARA

Big Bamboo

Map 7, J7. C/del Barquillo 42. Metro Alonso Martínez.
Daily 10.30pm–5am; Fri & Sat till 6am.

Reggae music and great cocktails, including an upside-down margarita poured directly down the throat – mixing takes place by vigorous shaking of the head before you swallow. Plenty of room for dancing.

Cliché

Map 7, J6. C/del Barquillo. Metro Chueca.
Daily 11pm–3am.

The best of many bars along this street – a relaxed yet funky place, with clientele as eclectic as the decor and aged 15 to 50.

Impacto

Map 7, J3. C/Campoamor 3. Metro Alonso Martínez.
Daily 11pm–3am.

Inside, this place is a mini-labyrinth with little rooms and bars around every corner. A fairly trendy, slightly older crowd, reasonably priced drinks and a good variety of music, despite the lack of a dance floor. Door policy of sorts.

Kingston's

Map 7, J5. C/del Barquillo 29. Metro Chueca/Alonso Martínez.
Daily 10pm–5am.

Relaxed multicultural *discobar* with colourful ethnic designs portraying plants and exotic animals. Music ranges from soul and funk to reggae and rap. At the weekend professional dancers get things going.

El Morocco

Map 7, D6. C/Marqués de Leganés 7. Metro Santo Domingo.
Daily 11pm–5am.

Latest venture by rock singer Alaska, long-time mover of the *movida* and mate of Pedro Almodóvar. The crowds here could well be from an Almodóvar movie and it's likely that some, at least, have acted in one. Cabaret show at 2am, the odd (and

DISCOBARES: GRAN VÍA, CHUECA AND SANTA BÁRBARA

171

odd is the word) band, and a pulsing dance floor. There's an occasional entrance charge and you'll need to look the part to get past the doorman.

MALASAÑA AND BILBAO

Al Lab'Oratorio

Map 7, G5. C/de Colón 14. Metro Tribunal.
Tues–Sat 9pm–3am; Fri & Sat till 6am.
Famous 1980s bar with very loud rock music on the sound system. Often stages live gigs for up and coming groups on a little stage downstairs. Young studenty clientele.

Tupperware

Map 7, F6. C/Corredera Alta de San Pablo 26. Metro Tribunal.
Fri & Sat 8pm–5am.
The place to go for the latest on the indie scene, with a mixture of grunge, Brit pop and old classics from the punk era.

La Vaca Austera

Map 7, F3. C/de la Palma 20. Metro Tribunal.
Daily 10pm–3.30am; Fri & Sat till 4.30am.
American style rock bar playing punk/indie classics, with pool tables, mixed clientele and friendly atmosphere.

Vía Lactea

Map 7, F3. C/de Velarde 18. Metro Tribunal.
Daily 8pm–3am.
Call in here to see where the *movida* began. A Malasaña classic, *Vía Lactea* was a key meeting place for Spain's designers, directors, pop stars and painters in the 1980s, and it retains its original decor from the time, billiard tables included.

Warhol's Club

Map 7, H1. C/de Luchana 20. Metro Bilbao.
Wed & Thurs 7pm–1am, Fri & Sat 7pm–10am.

Very popular *discobar* spread over two floors, with lots of chrome, glass, video screens and ultra-violet lighting. Attracts an early-20s crowd. No door policy.

SALAMANCA

Teatriz

Map 9, E9. C/de Hermosilla 15. Metro Serrano.
Mon–Sat café noon–3pm, bars 9pm–3am. Closed Sat lunch & Aug.

This former theatre, redesigned by the Catalan, Mariscal, together with Philippe Starck, is as elegant a venue as any in Europe. There are bars on the main theatre levels, watched over by a restaurant in the circle. Down in the basement there's a library-like area and small disco; look out too for the futuristic toilets. Drinks are fairly pricey (1500ptas for spirits), but there's no entrance charge.

Vanitas Vanitatis

C/de Velázquez 128. Metro Avenida América.
Daily 8.30pm–2am; Fri & Sat till 5am.

Upmarket hangout with a pretty strict door policy. Loud British and US dance music, but with a pleasant interior terrace if it all gets too much for you.

DISCOTECAS

Discotecas are usually the last stop on a *Madrileño* night out, visited long after the metro has closed, hence public transport can be a problem. Fortunately most are situated in the central areas, so the best bet is to hop into a taxi or go on foot. Although **dress codes** are not, in general, particularly strict, some of the more upmarket joints are fairly selective about who they let in and you may at times need to ingratiate yourself with the doorman. Being foreign, oddly enough, seems to make it easier to get in. Long queues are also frequent, so it may be worth arriving slightly earlier than is cool. **Entry charges** are quite common and quite hefty (600–3000ptas), but tend to cover you for a first drink. Be aware that many *discotecas* in Spain are fairly ephemeral institutions and frequently only last a season before opening up somewhere else under a different name, so it's a good idea to consult *La Guía del Ocio* or *Metropóli* (see p.7) for the very latest information.

SOL, OPERA AND SANTA ANA

Joy Eslava

Map 3, G4. C/de Arenal 11. Metro Sol.
Daily 11.30pm–5.30am, Fri–Sun till 6am; 1500–2000ptas.
This big-name disco is frequented by musicians, models, media folk and footballers. Home to the thirty- something yuppie crowd. If you can't get in (3–5am is the hippest time to come), console yourself at the *Chocolatería San Ginés* (see box opposite), on the street behind.

Kapital

Map 5, I4. C/de Atocha 125. Metro Atocha.
Thurs–Sat midnight–5.30am.
Seven floors catering for most tastes, with two dance floors, a cinema and a top-floor terrace. Varied musical menu of disco, merengue, salsa, *sevillanas* and even some karaoke.

Palacio de Gaviria

Map 3, H5. C/de Arenal 9. Metro Opera/Sol.
Daily 11pm–late; Mon–Thurs 1500ptas, Fri–Sun 1800ptas including your first drink.

Aristocratic, nineteenth-century palace where you can wander through a sequence of extravagant Baroque salons, listen to a chamber concert in the ballroom, watch a live show or simply dance the night away. It hosts regular "International Parties", has dance classes and is a fantastic setting in which to have a late drink. A frequent stopping-off point before going into *Joy Eslava*, just down the road. Expect to pay 1500ptas a drink.

GRAN VÍA, CHUECA, MALASAÑA AND SANTA BÁRBARA

Arena

Map 7, B5. C/de la Princesa 1. Metro Plaza de España.
Wed–Sun midnight–6am; 1500–2000ptas including first drink.

Chocolate Before Bed

If you stay up through a Madrid night, then you must try one of the city's great institutions, the **Chocolatería San Ginés** on Pasadizo de San Ginés, off c/de Arenal between the Puerta del Sol and Teatro Real. Established in 1894, this serves *chocolate con churros* (dark chocolate with deep-fried batter) to perfection – just the thing after a night's excess. There's an almost mythical *Madrileño* custom of winding up at San Ginés after the clubs close (not that they all do any longer), before heading home for a shower and then off to work.

San Ginés is open Tues–Sun 1am–7.30am, also Fri–Sun 7–10pm for weekend shoppers when the *chocolate* is half-price.

CHOCOLATE BEFORE BED

Big, modern and very popular former cinema, hosted at weekends by the minor Italian royal, Conde Lecquio, a man famous for being famous. Reggae and funk progresses to house music during the night. The current "in" place.

El Calentito

Map 7, D7. C/Jacometrezo 15. Metro Callao.

Daily 11pm–5am.

A fine place to experience wild, abandoned Madrid. It's tiny and cramped with strictly South American sounds: be prepared to dance with anyone! The entrance is easily missed, however – look out for the painted window. Drinks are modestly priced.

Davai

Map 7, C6. C/Flor Baja 1, cnr Gran Vía 59. Metro Santo Domingo/Plaza de España.

Wed–Sat 10pm–5am, Sun 9am–2pm & midnight–6am; 800–1000ptas including first drink.

A multi-club operating under several different names during the week. The undoubted highlight is Thursday night when the Seventies are revived under the name Starsky and Hutch. The perfect opportunity to dust off your flares and platforms and wallow in great disco and funk classics.

Pachá

Map 7, H3. C/de Barceló 11. Metro Tribunal.

Wed–Sat 11.30pm–5am; 1500–2000ptas including first drink.

An eternal survivor on the Madrid disco scene. Once a theatre and still very theatrical, it is exceptionally cool during the week, less so at the weekend when the out-of-towners take over. Good if you like techno.

El Sol

Map 7, G8. C/Jardines 3. Metro Gran Vía.
Daily 11.30pm–5am, Fri & Sat till 5.30am; 1000–2000ptas.
Hosts around twenty live concerts a month, but continues
afterwards (usually about 1.30am) as a disco with danceable
house, soul and acid jazz. Very good acoustics and well
ventilated.

Speakeasy

Map 7, I4. C/de Fernando VI 6. Metro Alonso Martínez.
Mon–Wed 8pm–1am, Thurs–Sat 8pm--5am;
free or 100ptas including first drink.
Good-value, friendly disco that holds "International Parties"
for foreigners new to the city. Good resident DJ.

OUT OF THE CENTRE

Aqualung Universal

**Paseo de la Ermita del Santo 40–48. Metro Puerta de
Toledo/Marqués de Vadillo.**
Mon–Sat midnight–3am, Fri & Sat till 5am; 1000–3000ptas.
Disco and aquapark for all-night raving. You can cool off in the
swimming pool when the dance floor gets too hot, and there
are rooms set aside for go-go girls, magicians and karaoke.
Located across the river, over the Puente de Segovia, it's a ten-
minute drive from the centre and about fifteen minutes' walk
from the Puerta de Toledo metro.

Cats

C/de Julián Romea 4. Metro Guzmán El Bueno.
Daily 10pm–5.30am.
Situated in Moncloa, a popular student area, towards the end of
c/de la Princesa, with a good range of bars and discos, *Cats* is a

DISCOTECAS: OUT OF THE CENTRE

Terrazas and Chiringuitos

Madrid is a different city during summer: temperatures soar, and life moves outside and becomes even more late night. In July and August, those *Madrileños* who haven't headed for the coast meet up with each other from 10pm onwards, at one or other of the city's immensely popular **terrazas**. These can range from a few tables set up outside a café, or alongside a **chiringuito** (a makeshift bar) in one of the squares, to extremely trendy, and very expensive, designer bars, which form the summer annexe of a club or *discoteca*.

Paseo de Recoletos and Paseo la Castellana

The biggest concentration of *terrazas* is to be found up and down the grass strip in the middle of the Paseo de Recoletos and its continuation, Paseo de la Castellana. On the nearer reaches of Paseo de Recoletos are *terrazas* of the old-style cafés *Gran* (no. 8), *Gijón* (no. 21) and *Espejo* (no. 31), which are popular meeting points for *Madrileños* of all kinds.

Past Plaza de Colón, the trendier terrazas begin, most pumping out music, and some offering entertainment, especially midweek, when they need to attract custom. They are extremely posey places, with clubbers dressing up for a night's cruise along the length – an expensive operation, with cocktails at 1000ptas a shot, and even a *caña* costing 600ptas.

Elsewhere in Madrid

Antiguo Cuartel del Conde Duque, **Map 7, C3.** Metro Ventura Rodríguez. This is a beautiful patio, inside an old military barracks. The council puts on weekly flamenco recitals and concerts in July and August, with a small admission charge, but most nights entry is free.

Jardines de Conde Duque, **Map 7, C3.** Corner of c/de Conde Duque 11 and c/Santa Cruz del Marcenado. Metro Ventura Rodríguez. Close to the Centro Cultural where the *Veranos de Villa* concerts are based in the summer months.

Jardines de las Vistillas, **Map 4, B4.** C/de Bailén, on the south side of the viaduct. Metro La Latina. This area, due south of the Palacio Real, has a number of *terrazas* and *chiringuitos*. It's named for the "little vistas" to be enjoyed in the direction of the Guadarrama mountains to the northwest.

Paseo del Pintor Rosales, **Map 2, A2.** Metro Argüelles. There's a clutch of late-night *terrazas* at the base of the Teleférico, with views over the river to the Casa de Campo.

Plaza de las Comendadoras, **Map 7, B3.** Metro Ventura Rodríguez. One of the city's nicest squares, this has a couple of *terrazas* attached to the *Café Moderno* and a Mexican restaurant.

Plaza Dos de Mayo, **Map 7, F3.** Metro Tribunal. The *chiringuito* on Malasaña's main square is always diverting, though the square is known as a hangout for drug addicts.

Plaza de Olavide, Metro Quevedo. An attractive neighbourhood square, with more or less year-round *terrazas* attached to four or five cafés and tapas bars.

Plaza de Oriente, **Map 3, D4.** Metro Opera. The *Café de Oriente terraza* is a station of Madrid nightlife.

Plaza de Santa Ana, **Map 6, C5.** Metro Sol. Several of the *cervecerías* here have seats outside and there's a *chiringuito* in the middle of the square from June to September.

La Vieja Estación, **Map 2, J9.** Avda. Ciudad de Barcelona. Metro Atocha. A massive multi-*terraza* just behind Estación de Atocha, this attracts a glamorous clientele ranging from football stars to TV personalities. If you don't fancy people-watching, there are concerts, talent contests and exhibitions.

TERRAZAS AND CHIRINGUITOS

large bar surrounded by various dance floors, podiums and chill-out areas. Attracts a young crowd and the emphasis is firmly on dancing to a varied selection of music.

Galileo Galilei

C/Galileo 100. Metro Rios Rosas.

Mon–Sat 3.30pm–3am; Sat till 4am.

Bar, concert venue and disco all rolled into one. Check the *Guía del Ocio* to find out whether it's the night for cabaret, salsa or a singer-songwriter.

Space of Sound

Estación de Chamartín. Metro Chamartín.

Sat, Sun & public holidays 6.30am–noon.

If you've still got energy left, this After Hours club on top of the Chamartín train station will allow you to strut your stuff all morning; if you can take the constant bombardment of *bakalao*, that is.

DISCOTECAS: OUT OF THE CENTRE

GAY MADRID

Recent years have witnessed a significant expansion in the **gay scene** in the capital. The area around Plaza Chueca remains at the heart of the action, but gay clubs are beginning to open up in other areas too. The **lesbian scene** has experienced a similar expansion and shares many of the places listed with gay men. There are, however, a few exclusively lesbian clubs listed separately below. Madrid nightlife in general, though, has a strong gay presence and most of the clubs and bars listed in the *Nightlife* chapter have a very mixed clientele.

Around **Plaza Chueca**, graffiti-plastered walls proclaim the existence of a *zona gay*, and the surrounding streets, especially **c/de Pelayo**, harbour at least a dozen exclusively gay bars and clubs, as well as a well-known gay café, the **Café Figueroa**. During **Carnaval** (the week before Lent), Chueca is especially lively with the gay community joining in the fancy dress parades and general over-indulgence.

Despite the high level of integration in Madrid's nightlife and social scene, there is a remarkably reactionary attitude from many quarters of Spanish society towards homosexuality in general. As a result, the gay community is becoming more organized and groups such as **Coordinadora**

Information Services

Coordinadora Gay de Madrid, Map 7, E4. C/Espíritu Santo 37 (Metro Noviciado; ℡523 00 70). The main gay organization in Madrid giving information on health, leisure and gay rights. Mon–Fri 5–9pm; Aug from 7pm.

Berkana, Map 7, I6. C/Gravina 11 (Metro Chueca). Gay and lesbian bookshop that's one of the best places to find out what's happening on the gay scene. Mon–Sat 10.30am–2pm & 5–8.30pm.

Centro de La Mujer, Map 7, J5. C/del Barquillo 44, 1° izq (Metro Alonso Martínez; ℡319 36 89). Feminist and lesbian groups all share this centre and it's the best stop for information on anything to do with the lesbian community.

Gay de Madrid are actively involved in pushing for gay rights. They also help organize **Gay Pride Week** held at the end of June.

Two **publications** are worth picking up while you're in the city: *Revista Mensual*, a gay listings magazine covering the whole of Spain available from most newspaper stands, and *Shangay Express*, a free newspaper avaliable in most gay clubs and bars.

CAFÉS AND RESTAURANTS

A Brasileira

Map 7, H6. C/de Pelayo 49 ℡308 36 25. Metro Chueca.
Mon–Sat 1–5pm & 9pm–2am.
Small Brazilian restaurant offering a very tasty selection of South American dishes. Expect to pay around 2000ptas per person.

Café Acuarela

Map 7, I6. C/Gravina 10. Metro Chueca.
Daily 4pm–2am; Fri & Sat till 4am.
Very comfortable café, stylish decor and the perfect place for a quiet drink.

Café Figueroa

Map 7, I6. C/Augusto Figueroa 17. Metro Chueca.
Mon–Sat noon–1am; Fri & Sat till 2.30am.
Opened sixteen years ago, this is an established institution on the *Madrileño* gay scene. Regulars of all ages. Pool table upstairs and great parties during *Carnaval*.

Gula Gula

Map 7, H8. Gran Vía 1 ☏522 87 64 (Metro Gran Vía) & c/Infante 5 ☏420 29 19 (Metro Antón Martín).
Mon–Sat 1–4.30pm & 9pm–2am; Fri & Sat till 3am.
Spacious salad bar type restaurant that does an eat-as-much-as-you-can self-service buffet for 1500ptas. Live shows featuring drag queens and dancers every night. Popular for "hen nights" as well as with the gay crowd.

GAY BARS AND DISCOTECAS

Angels of Xenon

Map 5, F2. C/de Atocha 38. Metro Antón Martín.
Fri & Sat midnight–6am; 1500ptas including first drink.
Mainly, but not exclusively, gay crowd. House music, scantily clad go-go girls and drag queens in this massive over-the-top venue with a huge dance floor, lasers and smoke machines.

GAY BARS AND DISCOTECAS

Bar LL

Map 7, H6. **C/de Pelayo 11. Metro Chueca.**
Daily 6pm–3am.
Fairly recent addition to the Chueca gay scene. Upstairs there's a bar which has live acts at the weekend (striptease and drag queens). Downstairs there's a more intimate room, where people sit around and talk or watch hard-core gay porn on the video screen. Attracts a slightly older crowd, mainly singles.

Black and White

Map 7, I6. **C/de Libertad 34. Metro Chueca.**
Daily 9pm–4am; Fri & Sat till 5am.
Very popular strip shows upstairs and a disco downstairs at this well-established nightspot.

Cruising

Map 7, H6. **C/Pérez Galdós 5. Metro Chueca.**
Daily 8pm–3.30am; Fri & Sat till 4.30am.
This *discobar* is strictly for leather boys, with a dark room showing porn films and a bar upstairs. Downstairs is a disco playing a good variety of danceable music.

Heaven

Map 3, G2. **C/Veneras 2. Metro Santo Domingo/Callao.**
Daily midnight–late; 1000ptas.
Just behind Plaza Callao, this mixed disco becomes very popular with the gay crowd as an "After Hours" venue. Good DJs playing a selection of house music. During the week it organizes parties, live acts and strip shows.

La Lupe

Map 5, F3. **C/ Torrecilla del Leal 12. Metro Antón Martín.**

Daily 9pm–2.30am.

Mixed gay and lesbian bar. Good music, cheap drinks. and occasional cabaret.

New Leather Bar

Map 7, I5. C/de Pelayo 42. Metro Chueca.
Daily 8pm–3am; Fri & Sat till 4am.

A bar on two floors with a mixed gay crowd. Dance floor, darkened rooms, erotic parties and strip shows.

Ricks

Map 7, I7. C/de las Infantas 26. Metro Banco de España.
Daily 11pm–5am.

Mixed straight/gay *discobar* which gets wild at weekends when every available space is used for dancing. Open and light, with a friendly atmosphere and fine music ranging from house classics to disco to hi-NRG – plus table football at the back. Pricey drinks.

Shangay Tea Dance

Map 3, I2. C/Mesonero Romanos 13. Metro Callao.
Sun 9pm–2am; 1000ptas including first drink.

A compulsory Sunday night stop, featuring live shows and 70s disco hits.

LESBIAN BARS AND DISCOTECAS

Ambient

Map 7, H4. C/San Mateo 21. Metro Alonso Martínez.
Tues–Thurs & Sun 8pm– 4am, Fri & Sat 9pm–5am.

Thriving lesbian bar, serving decent pizzas. Also pool, table football, exhibitions, occasional live acts and a market on Sunday.

Medea

Map 5, E2. C/de la Cabeza 33. Metro Lavapiés/Antón Martín.

Daily Tues–Sun 11pm–5am; 900ptas.

The city's premier lesbian disco – though accompanied men are admitted. Cabaret on Thursday & Sunday, smart decor, great music and a pool table.

La Rosa

Map 6, B2. C/Tetuán 27. Metro Sol.

Daily 11pm–6am; 800ptas.

Lesbian disco run by a women's collective, although men are admitted if accompanied. Good selection of music and friendly atmosphere.

LIVE MUSIC

Madrid's music scene is as varied as anything else in the city and there are opportunities to see almost every kind of music, from classical and opera to salsa and flamenco. Often, it's the smaller, off-beat clubs that are the more enjoyable, though there are plenty of large auditoria – including the sports stadiums and bullring – for big-name concerts. In summer, events are supplemented by the council's **Veranos de la Villa** cultural programme and in autumn by the Festival de Otoño.

Forthcoming events are well covered in
Madrid's listings magazines; see p.7.

For **classical music** and **opera**, the **Teatro Real**, Plaza Isabel II (Metro Opera; box office ✆516 06 06), the city's newly refurbished and reopened opera house, along with the **Auditorio Nacional de Música**, c/Príncipe de Vergara 146 (Metro Cruz del Rayo; box office ✆337 01 00), home of the Orquesta Nacional de España, are the two major venues. The **Teatro Monumental**, c/de Atocha 65 (Metro Atocha; box office ✆429 81 19) also hosts regular classical performances. Several smaller venues also present classical recitals including the **Círculo de Bellas Artes**, c/Marqués de Casa Riera 2 (Metro Banco de España; box office ℗531 77 00) and the **Fundación Juan March**, c/Castelló 99 (Metro Núñez de Balboa; box office 435 42 40). For a more relaxed ambience, there are a few **cafés and bars** where chamber music is played; try the *Salón del Prado*, c/del Prado 4 (Metro Sol) on Thursday night at 11pm and *La Fídula*, c/de las Huertas 57 (Metro Antón Martín) most nights at 11.30pm and 1am. Make sure you arrive on time as the doors are closed during performances. The city's main venue for Spanish **operetta** (*zarzuela*) is the **Teatro de la Zarzuela**, c/Jovellanos 4 (Metro Sevilla; box office ℗429 82 25).

FLAMENCO

Flamenco has undergone something of a revival in Madrid in the 1990s, in large part due to the "new flamenco" artists, like Joaquín Cortés, who are unafraid to mix it with a bit of blues, jazz, even rock. The following club and café listings span the range from purist flamenco to crossover experiments, and some host performances from the major stars. Opening hours are variable and those given below are only a rough guideline.

In addition, you can try the **Salas Rocieras**, places where the public get up and perform *sevillanas*, the complex and sensual courtship dance of southern Spain. Even if you don't want to have a go yourself, it's worth paying a visit just to watch the spectacle. Drinks and food are, however, very pricey. Good options are *Al Andalús*, c/Capitán Haya 19 (Metro Lima; Mon–Sat 11pm–6am; minimum bar/tapas charge of 2000–3000ptas) and *Almonte*, c/Juan Bravo 35 (Metro Núñez de Balboa; daily 9pm–6am).

Candela

Map 5, F3. C/del Olmo 2 ©467 33 82. Metro Antón Molina.
Daily 10.30pm–late.

A legendary bar frequented by musicians, with occasional shows too. The late, great Camarón de la Isla is reputed to have sung here until 11am on one occasion. The cellar area is only accessible by invitation.

Café de Chinitas

Map 3, E1. C/Torija 7 ©559 51 35. Metro Santo Domingo.
Mon–Sat 9pm–2am, Fri & Sat till 3am; 4200ptas.

One of the oldest flamenco clubs in Madrid, hosting a dinner-dance spectacular. It's expensive, but the music is authentic and the audience is predominantly Spanish. Reservations are essential, though you may get in late when people start to leave about an hour before closing (at this time you don't have to eat and the entrance fee includes your first drink).

Caracol

C/Bernardino Obregón 18 ©530 80 55. Metro Embajadores.
Daily 9.30pm–2am; 500–4000ptas.

The top names tend to appear here in a place popular with the young crowd, so it's worth making a reservation here as soon as possible after you arrive. Flamenco is often mixed with jazz and blues; for pure flamenco, come on Thursday night.

Casa Patas

Map 5, E2. C/Cañizares 10 ©369 04 96. Metro Antón Martín.
Daily midnight–3am; 1500–3000ptas.

Small club with bar and restaurant that gets its share of big names. The best nights are Thursday and Friday.

FLAMENCO

Corral de la Morería

Map 4, B4. C/de la Morería 17 ⓒ365 84 46. Metro La Latina.
Daily 9pm–3am; 4000ptas.

This is a good venue for some serious flamenco acts, but again expensive at about 4000ptas for the show plus a drink. Worth staying until late on in case there are any spontaneous contributions from the audience. Frank Sinatra and Ava Gardener are among the celebrities who have signed the guest book.

Peña Chaquetón

C/Canarias 39 ⓒ671 27 77. Metro Palos de la Frontera.
Fri 11.30pm only; 800–1500ptas.

The place for purists – just one show weekly, but it's a good one. Turn up early if there's a big name or you won't get in, and try and make yourself comfortable in the spartan surroundings (don't worry about the Members Only sign outside).

La Soleá

Map 4, F4. C/Cava Baja 27. Metro La Latina.
Mon–Sat 8.30pm–3am.

This brilliant, long-established flamenco bar is the genuine article. People sit around in the tiny salon, pick up a guitar or start to sing and gradually the atmosphere builds up until everyone is clapping or dancing. Has to be seen to be believed.

ROCK AND BLUES

Madrid is very much on the international rock tour circuit and you can catch big (and small) American and British acts playing to enthusiastic audiences. **Tickets** for most big rock concerts are sold by Madrid Rock, Gran Vía 25 and Fnac, c/Preciados 28 (both Metro Callao; daily 10am–10pm; all cards).

> **You'll find a thriving Celtic music scene in many of Madrid's Irish pubs; see box on p.164.**

Madrid has also long been the heart of the Spanish rock scene, and in the smaller clubs you'll see a very wide range of local bands. In most cases you can just turn up and pay on the door – keep an eye out for posters scattered around the city and check the *Guía del Ocio*.

CLUBS

La Coquette

Map 3, G4. C/de Arenal 22, entrance on c/de la Hileras. Metro Opera.
Daily 8pm–2.30am. Closed Aug.
Small, smoky blues bar, where people sit around in the near dark watching bands perform on a tiny stage. Live music most nights.

Maravillas

Map 7, F4. C/de San Vicente Ferrer 33. Metro Tribunal.
Thurs–Sat 9pm–late.
Small but usually uncrowded indie venue, a favourite with the young crowd, where bands play anything from jazz to funk to reggae, often till around 4am.

Siroco

Map 7, D3. C/San Dimas 3. Metro San Bernardo/Noviciado.
Tues–Thurs 9.30pm–3am, Fri–Sun 10pm–6am.
Live local bands most nights at this popular little club, just

ROCK AND BLUES: CLUBS

north of Gran Vía. Music ranges from soul and funk to rock and indie.

Swing

Map 7, F4. C/de San Vicente Ferrer 23. Metro Tribunal.
Daily 10pm–5am.
Large rock haunt which features live bands playing anything from rock and roll to folk. Plenty of quieter areas if you want to chat.

MAJOR CONCERT VENUES

Aqualung Universal

Paseo de la Ermita del Santo 40–48. Metro Puerta de Toledo/Marqués de Vadillo.
Rock and salsa concerts are often held at this disco and aquapark, located across the river, over the Puente de Segovia. It's a ten-minute taxi ride from the centre of town and fifteen minutes' walk from the Puerta de Toledo metro. Primal Scream, Ocean Colour Scene and Björk have played here in recent years.

Canciller 2

Pobladura del Valle 21. Metro San Blas.
Primarily a heavy rock venue, but also hosts blues and Celtic music gigs. If there isn't a concert scheduled it serves as a bar and meeting place for Madrid's headbangers.

La Katedral

C/Fundadores 7. Metro Manuel Becerra/O'Donnell.
New venue, which has taken over from the now defunct Revólver, kicking off with recent concerts by indie bands including Echobelly and Supergrass.

> The two football stadiums, Estadio Santiago Bernabéu and Estadio Vicente Calderón, are also used for gigs. See *Sport* for transport details.

Palacio de Deportes

Avda Felipe II. Metro Goya.

Large indoor sports arena usually used by Madrid's basketball teams and increasingly by the big-name artists on the Spanish leg of their European tours. Fifteen thousand capacity, but the acoustics leave a lot to be desired. Oasis and the Spice Girls have appeared here.

Plaza de Toros de las Ventas

Las Ventas. Metro Ventas.

The bullring is a pretty good concert venue, put to use during the summer festival. Tickets are usually all one price, though the best reserved seats (*asiento reservado*) often carry an extra charge.

La Riviera

Map 2, A7. Paseo Bajo Virgen del Puerto s/n, Puente de Segovia. Metro Puerta del Angel.
Fri–Sun 11pm–5am.

Fun disco and concert venue right next to the river that has hosted some of the big names in recent years, from the trendy Lenny Kravitz to the not-so-trendy Lynyrd Skynyrd.

LATIN MUSIC

Madrid attracts big-name Latin artists and if you happen to coincide with the summer festival you'll stand a good chance of catching someone of the stature of salsa legend Joe Arroyo, or – a huge star in Spain – Juan Luis Guerra from the Dominican Republic. Gigs by the likes of these tend to take place at the rock venues listed on pp.192–3. The local scene is a good deal more low-key but there's enjoyable salsa, nonetheless, in a handful of clubs.

Las Noches del Cuplé

Map 7, E3. C/Palma 51. Metro Tribunal.
Daily except Wed 9.30pm–1am; Fri & Sat till 2am.
A 6500ptas entry charge here entitles you to food and live music, while 3000ptas will get you a drink and the show. The former is good value as long as you're into traditional music-hall Spanish, French songs and tangos.

Oba-Oba

Map 3, G1. C/Jacometrezo 4. Metro Callao.
Daily 11pm–5.30am.
Live Brazilian music as you refine your samba and lambada technique with the help of lethal Brazilian *caipirinhas* from the bar.

Salsipuedes

Map 7, F6. C/Puebla 6. Metro Callao/Gran Vía.
Daily 11pm–6am; 1000ptas including first drink.
Serious salsa dancing to a live orchestra most weekdays in a "tropical" setting in this large venue. You need to be smartly dressed to get in.

JAZZ

Madrid doesn't rank with London, Paris or New York on the jazz front, but the clubs are friendly, unpretentious places. Look out for the annual jazz festival staged at a variety of venues in November.

Café Central

Map 6, B5. Plaza del Angel 10. Metro Sol.
Mon–Sat noon–1.30am, Fri & Sat till 2.30am; 800–1200ptas.
This was voted no. 6 in a recent "Best Jazz Clubs of the
World" poll in *Wire* magazine. It's certainly an attractive venue
– small, relaxed and covered in mirrors – and it gets the
occasional big name, plus strong local talent. The Art Deco
café is worth a visit in its own right.

Café Jazz Populart

Map 6, C6. C/de las Huertas 22. Metro Antón Martín.
Daily 6pm–2am; 600ptas charge on first drink.
Nightly sets from jazz and blues bands. Another friendly and
relaxed venue. Tends to start a little earlier than the *Café Central*
which is a few minutes away, so you can combine the two if
you fancy an overdose of laid-back rhythms.

Segundo Jazz

C/Comandante Zorita 8. Metro Nuevos Ministerios.
Daily 7pm–3.30am.
Jazz on most nights of the week, but also some Latin sounds
(usually Wed & Thurs). Shows normally get going at around
midnight. No entry charge, but you are obliged to buy a drink.

Triskel Tavern

Map 7, F4. C/de San Vicente Ferrer 3. Metro Tribunal.
Daily 10am–3am.
This Irish bar has a jazz night on Tuesday and it's worth
popping in to see what's on.

JAZZ

THEATRE AND CINEMA

I n a city that has been home to so many of the country's great writers and dramatists it is not surprising that Madrid's theatrical tradition is strong. In the Golden Age writers such as **Cervantes**, **Lope de Vega** and **Tirso de Molina** all lived in the streets in and around Plaza de Santa Ana, and later, the literary heritage was maintained by the convergence on the city of great poets and writers, such as **García Lorca** and **Antonio Machado**. *Madrileños* have always been enthusiastic theatregoers and today you can catch anything from the classics to contemporary experimental productions, cabaret and comedy acts.

Ticketing systems have traditionally been pretty archaic and it is only very recently that venues have started to introduce telephone and credit card bookings. It's often best to go directly to the theatre and buy the tickets on the spot. Prices range from 1000ptas to 4000ptas, but many venues operate a **día del espectador** (usually Mon or Wed) when prices are halved – demand is high so try to book as early as possible.

....
See Directory, p.237 for details of ticket agencies.
....

Details of performances, which usually begin after 9pm, are to be found in the *Guía del Ocio* and the Friday supplement of *El Mundo*. Look out also for what's on offer in the annual *Festival de Otoño* (late Sept to Nov) sponsored by the Comunidad de Madrid. This is often the time when international shows and performers visit the city.

Berlin Cabaret

Map 4, E4. Costanilla de San Pedro 11 ©366 20 34. Metro La Latina.
Mon–Sat 11pm–3am, Fri & Sat till 4am.
Varied cabaret and comedy in a traditional, slightly seedy club setting. Admission is normally free, but drinks are expensive.

Círculo de Bellas Artes

Map 6, E2. C/de Alcalá 42 ©531 77 00. Metro Banco de España.
The Círculo (see p.49) houses a beautiful old theatre which puts on adventurous productions.

Centro Cultural de la Villa

Map 2, J3. Plaza de Colón ©575 60 80. Metro Colón.
Arts centre directly under the waterfall in the plaza where you're likely to see some of the more experimental companies on tour as well as popular works and *zarzuela* performances.

Teatro Español

Map 6, D5. C/del Príncipe 25 ©429 62 97. Metro Sol/Sevilla.
Classic Spanish theatre performed in this majestic venue at one end of Plaza de Santa Ana. The theatre is built on the site of one of the original *corrales* (courtyards) where drama was first

THEATRE

performed for ordinary *Madrileños* in the Golden Age. Works by Lope de Vega, Calderón de la Barca and Tirso de Molina often feature on the programme.

Teatro María Guerrero

Map 7, K6. C/Tamayo y Baus 4 ©319 47 69. Metro Colón.
This is the headquarters of the Centro Dramático Nacional which stages high-quality Spanish and international productions in a beautiful neo-Mudéjar interior.

Teatro Nuevo Apolo

Map 5, D2. Plaza Tirso de Molina 1 ©429 52 38. Metro Tirso de Molina.
An old music hall style venue with traditional decor and a good atmosphere, if a little cramped. Madrid's principal venue for major musicals and recent host to the successful tour by the Harlem Gospel Singers.

CINEMA

Spaniards, and *Madrileños* in particular, are enthusiastic and knowledgeable movie devotees. They flock to the openings of Spanish and international films in the city, lap up the extensive press and TV coverage and seem to know all the latest gossip about the stars of the screen.

The city itself has been a star in its own right: the elegant apartment blocks on the edge of the Retiro, sleazy night-clubs and bars in the centre and the decaying slum areas on the outskirts have all featured as backdrops in the post-*movida* films of **Pedro Almodóvar**. While Almodóvar blazed the trail in the 1980s, a new generation of young directors have followed in the 1990s, including Alex de la Iglesia, whose *El día de la Bestia* was a big box office hit, and more recently the young student, Alejandro Amenábar, with his thrilling debut *Tesis*.

Cinemas (*cines*) can be found all over the central area. Major releases are dubbed into Spanish, though a number of cinemas have regular **original language** screenings, with subtitles; these are listed in a separate *versión original subtitulada* (*v.o.*) section in the newspapers and *Guía del Ocio*. **Tickets** for films cost around 700ptas, but most cinemas have a *día del espectador* (usually Mon or Wed) when admission is 400ptas. Be warned that on Sunday night half of Madrid goes to the movies and queues can be long – it's usually best to buy tickets early and then spend some time in a bar before the show starts.

Alphaville, Renoir & Lumière

Map 7, A4. C/de Martín de los Heros ⌀559 38 36/⌀559 57 60/⌀542 11 72. Metro Plaza de España.
A trio of multi-screen cinemas, within 200m of each other just beside Plaza de España. *V.O.* new releases and old classics make up the majority of films. The Lumière has early sessions for children-orientated films, The Alphaville has a good basement café and the Renoir does informative film notes, although it doesn't allow food or drink inside.

Bellas Artes

Map 6, E2. C/Marqués de Casa Riera 2 ⌀522 50 92. Metro Banco de España.
A varied diet of mainstream releases and art-house productions. Comfortable environment and pleasant café.

California

C/Andrés Mellado 53 ⌀544 00 58. Metro Moncloa.
Giant single-screen cinema in the midst of studenty Moncloa.

CINEMA

After a brief experiment showing dubbed foreign films it has reverted once again to *v.o.* only.

Cines Ideal

Map 6, B6. C/Doctor Cortezo 6 ⓒ369 25 18. Metro Sol/Tirso de Molina.

A massive nine-screen complex south of Sol with something for everyone – a mixture of mainstream, art-house, independent and Spanish films.

Filmoteca/Cine Doré

Map 5, F2. C/Santa Isabel 3 ⓒ369 11 25. Metro Antón Martín.

Beautiful old cinema, now home to an art film centre, with imaginative programmes of classic and contemporary films. In summer, there are open-air screenings on a little *terraza* – they're very popular, so buy tickets in advance. See p.41 for more on the Cine Doré.

CINEMA

FESTIVALS

I t's always worth checking out which **festivals** (*fiestas*) your visit to Madrid coincides with. There are dozens throughout the year, some involving the whole city, others just an individual *barrio*. The more important dates are listed below.

Religious dates aside, the city council organizes cultural festivals, in particular the **Veranos de la Villa** (July–Sept) and **Festival de Otoño** (Sept–Nov) concerts (classical, rock, flamenco), theatre and cinema events. Many events are free and they're often open air, taking place in the city's parks and squares. Full programmes are published in the monthly *En Madrid* tourist hand-out.

JANUARY

Cabalgata de los Reyes (Cavalcade of the Three Kings)

January 5. An evening procession through the city centre in which children are showered with sweets.

FEBRUARY

Carnaval

In the week before Lent this is an excuse for a lot of partying and fancy-dress parades. The end of *Carnaval* is marked by the bizarre and entertaining *Entierro de la Sardina* (Burial of the Sardine) on the Paseo de la Florida.

MARCH/APRIL

Semana Santa

Easter Week is celebrated with traditional processions of penitents in Madrid, although they're not as impressive as those in Toledo.

MAY

Fiesta del Dos de Mayo

May 2. In Malasaña particularly featuring bands and partying around the Plaza Dos de Mayo. It was the funkiest festival in the city during the 1980s, but has been a bit low-key in recent years.

Fiestas de San Isidro

May 15. The festival of Madrid's patron saint is spread for a week either side of May 15, and is one of the biggest festivals in Spain. There's a non-stop round of carnival: bands, parades and loads of free entertainment. Bands play every night in the Jardines de las Vistillas (south of the Palacio Real), and the evenings are full of *chotis* music and dancing (a dance typical of Madrid). The fiestas also herald the start of the bullfighting season.

La Feria del Libro

At the end of May, Madrid's great book fair takes place with hundreds of stands set up in El Retiro.

JUNE

Fiesta de la Ermita de San Antonio de la Florida

June 13. Events based around the church (see p.107).

Fiestas de San Juan

June 17–24. Bonfires and fireworks in El Retiro.

JULY

La Virgen del Carmen

July 9–16. Local fiesta in Chamberí.

AUGUST

Castizo fiestas

August 6–15. Traditional *fiestas* of *San Cayetano*, *San Lorenzo* and *La Virgen de la Paloma* in La Latina and Lavapiés *barrios*. Much of the activity takes place around the Plaza de la Paja and Las Vistillas.

DECEMBER

Nochevieja

December 31. New Year's Eve is celebrated at bars, restaurants and parties all over the city, with bands in some of the squares. Puerta del Sol is the traditional place to gather, waiting for the strokes of the clock – it is traditional to swallow a grape on each strike.

SPORT AND BULLFIGHTING

Spaniards, and *Madrileños* in particular, are **sport crazy**. Basketball, cycling, handball, tennis and motorcycling all generate plenty of interest – and Madrid itself plans a bid for the 2008 Olympics – but without doubt, the great national obsession is **fútbol** (*el deporte rey*, the king of sports). The biggest-selling daily paper in Spain is the sports tabloid *Marca*, and ninety percent of its pages are taken up with football (mainly coverage of Real Madrid). Fierce rivalry between Madrid and Barcelona dominates the two major sports of football and basketball, but there is also severe competition within the city between the main clubs, **Real Madrid** and **Atlético Madrid** (in football) and Real Madrid and Estudiantes (in basketball).

Sports facilities in Madrid are good, although very heavily used. You shouldn't have too much difficulty finding somewhere to swim (in summer), play tennis or go running – there are plenty of *polideportivos* (sports centres) run by the council and scattered across the city and its suburbs – but even the most obscure sports can be tracked down through the Consejo Superior de Deportes (©589 67 00; fax 589 66 14).

While many Spaniards regard **bullfighting** as more of a refined art form than a sport, it does have much in common with professional sport with its multi-million dollar turnover, highly paid preening stars and massive exposure on television. It's a phenomenon linked very closely to the history, culture and character of Spain.

FOOTBALL

Madrid has two football clubs in the *Primera División* (First Division), **Atlético Madrid** and **Real Madrid**. In addition, in the Second Division (*Segunda A*) it has Rayo Vallecano, recently relegated from the First Division; Leganés, local stalwarts from the tough industrial suburb whose name they bear; and Atlético Madrid B, Atlético's second team. The **season** runs from September to May and league matches are usually played on Sunday afternoon at either 5pm or 7pm depending on the time of year. Some of the bigger matches are shown live on TV and these are played on Saturday at 8.30pm. There's also a live match on Monday evening at 9.30pm.

In the post-Bosman era there has been a massive influx of expensive foreign imports, mostly from South America and Eastern Europe, including Roberto Carlos, Mijatovic, Seedorf and Suker for Real, and Juninho, Vieri and Bejbl for Atlético. However, there are also plenty of classy **Spanish players** on the scene notably Atlético's Lardin and Kiko and Real's Raul and Hierro. Entertainment on the pitch is matched by the antics off it, with larger-than-life club chairmen such as Atlético's Jesús Gil and Real's Lorenzo Sanz continually embroiled in disputes with each other or with the Spanish football federation – Gil even managed to floor Compostela's chairman with a punch in 1996.

The ticketing system is remarkably primitive with **tickets** usually only going on sale a couple of days before matches. Massive queues build up outside the stadium box offices and there are no other outlets or credit card lines. For the smaller games (those that are not Madrid derbies or don't involve Barcelona), tickets can be obtained quite easily, but for big matches you may have to resort to the touts, who can be knocked down quite substantially if you're prepared to bargain.

Fans tend to congregate in the bars that ring the stadiums well before kick-off as **alcohol** is banned inside the ground, although it's a common sight to see a *bota* (hide pouch full of cheap red wine) being passed around the crowd. At half-time there's a general rustle of tin foil as almost everyone settles down to enjoy their homemade *jamón* or *tortilla bocadillo* – the food inside the grounds is pretty poor.

Atlético Madrid

Estadio Vicente Calderón, Paseo de la Virgen del Puerto 67
Ⓒ**366 47 07. Metro Pirámides.**
Ticket office Mon–Fri 5–8pm; two days before each match also
11am–2pm. Tickets from 3000ptas.

Atlético Madrid, given the not so glamorous nickname of *Los Colchoneros* (The Mattress Makers) due to the colours of their shirts which resemble the formerly ubiquitous red and white Spanish mattresses, have always been the rather poor relations of the city. Originally set up by young Basques and *Madrileños* as a branch of Athletic de Bilbao, the club soon became independent (although its strip is still the same colour as the Basque club) and has enjoyed considerable success during its 94-year history. They have won nine league titles and nine cups as well as the Cup Winners' Cup in 1962, the high point being the *doblete* (league and cup double) in the 1995–96 season when their loyal and long-suffering fans at last had an excuse to celebrate in the Neptuno fountain just down the road from Cibeles. Although not as impressive as the Bernabéu, the **Vicente Calderón Stadium** has a not unsubstantial 60,000 capacity and usually enjoys a far better atmosphere than its more glamorous neighbour.

Real Madrid

Estadio Santiago Bernabéu, c/Concha Espina s/n ©344 00 52. Metro Lima.

Ticket office Mon–Fri 6–9pm; match days 11am–1.30pm. Tickets from 2000ptas go on sale three days before each match.

Of the three main Madrid football clubs, the one with the best record and richest heritage is **Real Madrid**, six times winners of the European Cup and 27 times winners of the Spanish League. *El Equipo Merengue* (The Meringues), after their traditional all-white strip have, in recent times, been eclipsed by the successes of their arch rivals, Barcelona, but in their heyday dominated not just Spanish, but also European and world football with players of the quality of Puskás, Di Stefano and Gento. Real also participated in arguably the greatest football match on British soil, the 7–3 humbling of Eintracht Frankfurt in the final of the European Cup at Hampden Park in 1960. Under Franco's regime they became the showpiece of Spanish sport and have always enjoyed a privileged financial position compared to their local rivals, despite recent financial crises. They have a small but repellent neo-fascist group of hooligan followers known as the *Ultra Sur*, but they are

FOOTBALL

heavily outnumbered by vast numbers of decent fans at the frequently packed ground. Their magnificent **Santiago Bernabéu Stadium**, venue of the 1982 World Cup Final, is one of the greatest grounds in the world, with its recently enlarged capacity of 105,000. Whenever they have something to celebrate, Real fans throng to the fountain of Cibeles at the top of Paseo del Prado, some 300,000 choosing to do so when they won the 1996–97 championship.

Rayo Vallecano

Nuevo Estadio de Vallecas, Avda Payaso Fofó s/n ⓒ478 22 53. Metro Portazgo.
Ticket office Mon–Sat 5.30–8.30pm & two hours before each match. Tickets from 2000ptas.

Rayo Vallecano have endured successive seasons teetering on the brink of relegation, finally to succumb to the Second Division in the 1996–97 season. Their modest stadium in the working-class suburb of Vallecas holds a mere 20,000, but there is still plenty of atmosphere. They openly admit they cannot compete financially with big brothers Real and Atlético and frequently reschedule games for Sunday mornings so as not to clash with their neighbours' fixtures. The best position they have managed in the league was tenth in 1977–78. Their eccentric presidential husband-and-wife partnership of José María Ruiz Mateos and María Teresa Rivero adds a little colour to this local club.

BASKETBALL

Basketball is the second most popular spectator sport in Spain, and Madrid has two top-class teams, **Estudiantes** and **Real Madrid** (part of the football club), who play at the Palacio de Deportes, Avda. Felipe II 19 (Metro Goya; ticket office daily 11am–2pm & 5–8pm; ©401 91 00; tickets from 1000ptas) and the Pabellón de Deportes del Real Madrid, Paseo de la Castellana 259 (Metro Begoña; ©315 00 46) respectively. The **season** runs from September to May, the high points being the playoffs from April onwards and the Torneo de Navidad in the last week in December.

**There are several polideportivos (sports centres)
catering for most sports scattered throughout the
city: Polideportivo de la Chopera, Parque del
Retiro (Metro Atocha; daily 8.30am–9.30pm; ©420
11 54); Estadio de Vallehermoso, Avda Islas
Filipinas s/n (Metro Cuatro Caminos/Ríos Rosas;
daily 8am–10pm; ©534 77 23); Parque Deportivo
La Ermita, c/Sepúlveda 3–5 (Metro Puerta del
Angel; Mon–Fri 9am–11pm, Sat 10am–8pm, Sun
10am–3pm; ©470 01 11).**

BOWLING

You'll find plenty of ten-pin **bowling alleys** in Madrid. Two of the largest are Bowling Azca, Paseo de la Castellana 77 (Metro Nuevos Ministerios; daily 11am–midnight, Fri & Sat till 2am; ©555 76 26; 300–600ptas) and AMF Bowling Centre, La Vaguada (Metro Herrera Oria/Barrio del Pilar; daily 10pm–1am, Fri & Sat till 4am; ©730 18 11; 400–650ptas).

GOLF

Golf is prohibitively expensive at the private clubs in Madrid. The main public facilities are the two courses (18

and 9 holes) at Olivar de la Hinojosa on the eastern outskirts of the city – Avda. de Dublin s/n, Campo de las
Naciones (Metro Canillejas or bus #122 from Arturo Soria
Metro; daily 8.30am–8pm; ℂ721 18 89). It costs 5800ptas
for eighteen holes.

GYMS AND FITNESS CENTRES

Some private gyms provide short-term membership; try
Club Abascal, c/José Abascal 46 (ℂ442 07 49); Palestra
c/Bravo Murillo 5 (ℂ448 98 22) or Holiday Gym, Plaza
Carlos Trías Bertrán 4, c/Serrano Jover 3 (ℂ640 11 11).

RUNNING

There are plenty of places to run in the major parks, Parque
del Oeste, Casa de Campo and the Retiro; the last two have
specially marked out routes for *footing*, the one in the Casa
de Campo is by the lake and the one in the Retiro is on the
north side of the park.

SWIMMING

Madrid is well supplied with **open-air pools** (*piscinas*),
which is just as well given that summer temperatures can
soar above 40°C. Most have shade and pleasant sun-
bathing areas, and some offer other activities such as vol-
leyball. Most open-air pools are open from mid-May to
mid-September daily 10.30am–8pm and admission is usually 500ptas. Another option is the rooftop pool at the
Hotel Emperador, Gran Vía 53 (Metro Gran Vía; ℂ547 28
00). It'll cost you 1500ptas, but you get spectacular views
of the city as you swim. In addition, there are indoor
pools at Moratalaz, c/ Valdebernardo (Metro Pavones;

closed Aug; ©772 7121). For **aquaparks**, see *Kids' Madrid*, p.231.

The most central open-air pools include: Barrio del Pilar, c/ Monforte de Lemos (Metro Barrio del Pilar/Begoña; ©314 79 43); Canal de Isabel II, Avda. de las Islas Filipinas 54 (Metro Ríos Rosas; ©533 96 42); Casa de Campo, Avda. del Angel (Metro Lago; ©463 00 50); Concepción, c/José del Hierro (Metro Concepción/Quintana; ©403 90 20); La Elipa, Parque de la Elipa, c/ O'Donnell s/n (Metro Estrella; ©430 35 11); Chamartín, Plaza del Perú (Metro Pío XII; ©350 12 23); **La Latina**, Plaza de la Cebada 1 (Metro La Latina; ©365 80 31).

TENNIS

Most of the *polideportivos* and the Casa de Campo (Metro Lago, near the lake) have a variety of courts for rent at around 500ptas an hour, but you'll need your own equipment.

BULLFIGHTING

Bullfighting (*los toros*) is a multi-billion peseta business and it is estimated that around half a million Spaniards are employed either directly or indirectly in the bullfighting world. Nevertheless there are many Spaniards who have never been to a bullfight and may only have seen one on TV; there is even some opposition to the activity from animal welfare groups, but it is not widespread. Despite claims that bullfighting was beginning to die out, the 1990s have seen it become even more fashionable – audiences include a full cross section of society from farmers and villagers to show business stars and politicians. *Los toros* is culture and ritual rolled into one, where the emphasis is on the way man and bull "perform" together – the art is at issue rather than the cruelty. *Aficionados* argue that the life of a bull destined for the ring is infinitely preferable and more honourable than that of the majority which end ignominiously in the slaughterhouse. Whatever your view and whether or not you decide to go and see a **corrida** is entirely a matter of individual feeling, but if you are in Madrid during one of the *ferias* you are more than likely to come across one on TV.

Regular *corridas* are also held in the smaller bullrings of a number of towns surrounding Madrid during their *fiestas*. Many also feature **encierros**, where young bulls pursue often rather drunken runners making a mad dash along a set route into the *plaza de toros*. The more famous of these *ferias* (all late Aug) include: **Chinchón**, a picturesque setting in the ancient plaza; **Colmenar Viejo**, a prestigious *feria* in he heart of bull-breeding country; **Manzanares el Real**; and **San Sebastián de los Reyes**, which features highly rated *encierros*. Towns to the north and west of Madrid, such as Pozuelo and Las Rozas, hold their *ferias* in September.

Alongside the established and popular **matadores** – Enrique Ponce, César Rincón, Curro Romero, Joselito, Litri, Jesulín de Ubrique, Ortega Cano, José María Manzanares and Finito de Córdoba – are two new stars, El Cordobés, a young pretender of spectacular technique, who claims to be his legendary namesake's illegitimate son, and Cristina Sánchez, the first woman to make it into the top flight for many decades.

Plaza de Toros de Las Ventas

C/de Alcalá 237 ©726 4800 or 356 2200. Metro Ventas. Box office March–Oct Thurs–Sun 10am–2pm & 5–8pm; tickets 2000–12,000ptas.

Madrid's neo-*Mudéjar* bullring, **Las Ventas**, with its 23,000 capacity, is probably the most illustrious in the world. The season lasts from March to October and *corridas* are held every Sunday at 7pm and every day during the three main ferias: *La Comunidad* (early May), *San Isidro* (mid-May to June) and *Otoño* (late Sept to Oct). **Tickets** go on sale at the ring only a couple of days in advance with many already allocated to season-ticket holders. The cheapest seats are *gradas*, the highest rows at the back, from where you can see everything that happens without too much of the detail; the front rows are known as the *barreras*. Seats are also divided into *sol* (sun), *sombra* (shade), and *sol y sombra* (shaded after a while). The *sombra* seats are more expensive, not so much for the spectators' personal comfort as the fact that most of the action takes place in the shade. On the way in, you can rent cushions – two hours sitting on concrete is not much fun. Beer and soft drinks are sold inside.

SHOPPING

S hopping districts in Madrid are pretty defined. The biggest range of shops is along Gran Vía and around Puerta del Sol, and this is where you'll find the **department stores** such as El Corte Inglés. In addition, Marks & Spencer has a branch at c/de Serrano 52 in Salamanca and C&A has one in the La Vaguada shopping centre (Metro Barrio del Pilar). Although Madrid has its fair share of stylish designer shops it has also managed to retain many of its **traditional establishments**, and it is these eccentric little shops, still serving the local community, that provide the greatest interest value for casual browsers and shopaholics alike.

For **fashion** (*moda*), the smartest addresses are c/de Serrano, c/de Goya, c/Ortega y Gasset and c/de Velázquez in Salamanca, north of the Retiro, while more alternative designers are to be found in Malasaña and Chueca (along c/Almirante, especially). For shoes the road to head for is c/de Augusto Figueroa in Chueca where there are a number of factory outlets selling a wide range at very good prices. Anything **electrical**, particularly sound systems, can be found in nearby c/del Barquillo. The **antiques** trade is centred down towards the Rastro, on and around c/Ribera de Curtidores, or in the Puerta de Toledo shopping centre,

Opening hours

Usual **opening hours** are Monday–Friday 9.30am–2pm & 5–8pm, Saturday 10am–2pm, but there are also two chains of late-night shops – Vip's and 7 Eleven – that stay open into the hours and on Sundays. Each branch sells newspapers, ciga- rettes, groceries, books, CDs – all the things you need to pop in for at 3am. Larger branches also have café-restaurants, one-hour photo developing and other services. Nearly all shops are closed on Sunday, but the larger stores do open on the first Sunday of each month (not in Aug). All the larger stores take credit cards.

while for truly idiosyncratic items, it's hard to beat the shops just off Plaza Mayor, where luminous saints rub shoulders with surgical supports and fascist memorabilia. The cheap- est, trashiest **souvenirs** can be collected at the Todo a Cien Pesetas (Everything 100ptas) shops scattered all over the city.

For more on the Rastro see box, p.38.

Most areas of the city have their own *mercados del barrio* (indoor **markets**), devoted mainly to food. Among the best are those in Plaza San Miguel (just west of Plaza Mayor); La Cebada in Plaza de la Cebada (Metro La Latina); Antón Martín in c/Santa Isabel (Metro Antón Martín), and Maravillas, c/Bravo Murillo 122 (Metro Cuatro Caminos). The city's biggest market is, of course, the **Rastro** – the flea market – which takes place on Sunday in the area south of Plaza Mayor. Other specialized markets include a second- hand **book market** on the Cuesta de Moyano, at the southwest corner of El Retiro (see p.85) and the stamp and coin market in Plaza Mayor every Sunday (Metro Sol; 9am–2pm) where collectors gather to buy, sell and inspect.

BOOKS, MAPS AND POSTERS

In addition to specialist bookstores, the museum and art gallery shops, especially in the Reina Sofía, all have a good range of posters, prints and books.

Booksellers

C/José Abascal 48. Metro Ríos Rosas.
Mon–Fri 9.30am–2pm & 5–8pm, Sat 10am–2pm.
Specializes in English-language books, also stocks videos and has a decent childrens' section.

Casa del Libro

Map 7, F7. Gran Vía 29 & Maestro Victoria 3. Both Metro Callao.
Mon–Sat 9.30am–9.30pm.
The city's biggest bookstore, with four floors covering just about everything, including a wide range of fiction in English and translations of classic Spanish works from Lope de Vega to Benito Pérez Galdós. The branch at Maestro Victoria has a good section on maps, guides and books about Madrid.

Crisol

C/Juan Bravo 38. Metro Diego de León.
Mon–Sat 10am–10pm, Sun & public holidays 11am–3pm & 5–9pm.
Good selection of English-language books. Records and foreign newspapers too.

La Librería

Map 3, D6. C/Mayor 78. Metro Sol.
Mon–Fri 10am–2pm & 4.30-7.30pm; Sat 11pm-2pm.
Tiny bookshop full of books just about Madrid. Also a good place to pick up old postcards, historic maps and photos of the city.

La Tienda Verde

C/Maudes 23 & 38. Metro Cuatro Caminos.
Mon–Sat 9.30am–2pm & 4.30–8pm.
A small shop crammed with trekking and mountain books, guides and survey (*topográfico*) maps. The helpful staff will point you in the right direction.

CLOTHES AND SHOES

Chain stores selling good-value clothes can be found all over the city; look out for Massimo Dutti, Springfield, Milano Trajes for men, and Zara and Mango for women, while Cortefiel caters for both sexes.

Adolfo Domínguez

Map 9, D6 & E3. C/José Ortega y Gasset 4 & c/de Serrano 96. **Both Metro Serrano.**
Mon–Sat 10am–2pm & 5–8.30pm. The c/Serrano branch doesn't close for lunch.
The classic modern Spanish look – sober colours, little extra decoration and free lines. Domínguez's designs are quite pricey, but he has a cheaper *Básico* range. Men's clothes only at the Ortega y Gasset branch. Expect to pay in the region of 10,000ptas for a shirt.

Ararat

Map 7, K6 & J6. C/Conde Xiquena 13 & c/Almirante 10 & 11. **Both Metro Chueca.**
Mon–Sat 11am–2pm & 5–8.30pm.
A trio of shops with clubby Spanish and foreign designs at reasonably modest prices. Men's clothes are at c/Conde

Xiquena 13, women's in c/Almirante. No. 10 specializes in more formal wear, while no. 11 goes for a younger more modern look.

Berlín

Map 7, J6. C/Almirante 10. Metro Chueca.
Mon–Sat 11am–2pm & 5–8.30pm.
Next door to *Ararat*. Women's clothes from a selection of vanguard European and American designers as well as Spaniard Roberto Torretta. Trousers start at around 15,000ptas, dresses at 35,000ptas and shoes will soon be available too.

Camper

Map 7, D6. C/Gran Vía 54. Metro Callao.
Mon–Sat 10am–2pm & 5–8.30pm.
Spain's best shoe shop chain, selling practical and comfortable designs at modest prices, with the odd quirky fabric and unusual heel thrown in. There are lots of other branches around the city. Men and women.

Ekseptión

Map 2, L3. C/de Velázquez 28. Metro Velázquez.
Mon–Sat 10.30am–2.30pm & 5–8.30pm.
A dramatic walkway bathed in spotlights gives on to some of the most *moderno* clothes in Madrid, from Sybilla and Antoni Miró, among others. Versace, Jean Paul Gaultier et al are also represented. Men and women.

Excrupulus Net

Map 7, J6. C/Almirante 7. Metro Chueca.
Mon–Sat 11am–2pm & 5–8.30pm.

Groovy shoes from Spanish designers, Muxart and Looky, starting at 15,000ptas. Also sells some original and stylish accessories. Men and women.

Glam

Map 7, G6 & H6. C/de Fuencarral 35 (Metro Gran Vía/Chueca) & c/Hortaleza 62 (Metro Chueca).
Mon–Sat 10am–2pm & 5–9pm.

Club, street-style clothes. The clientele and the clothes wouldn't look out of place in an Almodóvar film. Good value with shirts and tops around 5000ptas.

Hernanz

Map 4, G3. C/de Toledo 30. Metro Tirso de Molina.
Mon–Fri 9.30am–1.30pm & 5–8.30pm, Sat 9.30am–1.30pm; no cards.

This shoe shop stocks *alpargatas* (espadrilles) in just about every imaginable colour and style, including ones with shiny silver trimming for evening wear. The king reputedly buys his here, so they must be good. Prices range from 900 to 3000ptas.

Sybilla

Map 2, K3. C/Jorge Juan 12. Metro Retiro.
Mon–Sat 10am–2pm & 4.30–8.30pm.

Sybilla was Spain's top designer of the 1980s – a Vivienne Westwood of Madrid. She remains at the forefront of the scene, and her prices show it. The shop is a comfortable place to while away the time, with its armchairs and sofas, clashing with Sybilla's trademark vivid colours. Women's clothes only.

CHILDREN

Bazar Mila

Map 7, F7. Gran Vía 33. Metro Gran Vía/Callao.
Mon–Sat 9.30am–8.30pm.
Standard toy shop that is just the place to get your Spanish set of *Monopoly* or your plastic models of Real or Atlético players.

Caramelos Paco

Map 4, F5. C/de Toledo 55. Metro La Latina.
Mon–Sat 9.30am–2pm & 5–8pm, Sun 11am–3pm.
A child's dream and a dentist's nightmare with a window crammed full of every imaginable sugary sweet. Giant lollipops, sugar-coated figures and almond-flavoured sticks of rock are among the delights.

Prénatal

Map 7, G7. C/de Fuencarral 17. Metro Quevedo.
Mon–Sat 10am–1.45pm & 4.30–8pm.
Madrid isn't a particularly good place for kids' clothes, but if you need something in an emergency this is your best bet.

Puck

C/Duque de Sesto 30. Metro Goya.
Mon 4.30–8pm, Tues–Sat 10am–1.30pm & 4.30–8pm.
An old-fashioned toy shop now celebrating 25 years in business. The fabulous dolls' houses are complete down to the very smallest detail, and customers can select their own decor. A refreshing absence of Transformers and Ninja Turtles.

CRAFTS AND SOUVENIRS

El Arco de los Cuchilleros

Map 4, G2. Plaza Mayor 9. Metro Sol.
Mon–Sat 11am–8pm, Sun 11am–2.30pm.

El Arco houses thirty or so workshops and artesans, who reflect
Spanish *artesanía* at its most innovative and contemporary.
Ceramics, leather, wood, jewellery and textiles. There's a
gallery space used for five or six exhibitions each year. Prices
are very reasonable and staff very helpful.

Casa Jiménez

Map 3, G2. C/de Preciados 42. Metro Callao.
Mon–Sat 10am–1.30pm & 5–8pm. Closed Sat afternoon in July and
all day Sat in Aug.

One of the oldest established shops in Spain. Here you can buy
elaborately embroidered *mantones* (shawls) made in Seville with
prices ranging from 17,000 to 100,000 ptas, as well as gorgeous
fans from around 6000ptas.

Casa Yustas

Map 4, G1. Plaza Mayor 30. Metro Sol.
Mon–Fri 9.45am–1.30pm & 4.30–8pm, Sat 9.45am–1.30pm; no cards.

Madrid's oldest hat shop, established in 1894. Every
conceivable model and price from pith helmets and commando
berets to panamas and bowlers.

Fútbol Total

C/de Cardenal Cisneros 80. Metro Quevedo.
Mon–Sat: July–Sept 10.30am–2pm & 5.30–8.30pm; Oct–June
10.30am–2pm & 5–9pm.

Just the place to get your Real, Atlético or even Rayo shirt. In fact the strip of practically every Spanish team is available, for around 7000ptas.

Alvarez Gómez

Map 2, J4. C/de Serrano 14. Metro Serrano.
Mon–Sat 9.30am–2pm & 4.45–8.15pm.
Gómez has been making the same perfumes in the same bottles for the last century. The fragrances – carnation, rose and violet – are as simple and straight as they come. The elegant shop complete with its chandeliers also sells stylish toilet bags, hats and umbrellas.

Palomeque

Map 3, G4. C/Hileras 12. Metro Opera.
Mon–Fri 10–2pm & 5–8pm, Sat 10–2pm.
A religious department store stocking rosary beads and habits to your very own plastic baby Jesus. If you want to complete your postcard collection of Spanish saints and virgins, this is for you.

José Ramírez

Map 4, H3. C/Concepción Jerónima. Metro Sol/Tirso de Molina.
Mon–Fri 9.30am–2pm & 5–8pm, Sat 10am–2pm.
One of the most renowned guitar workshops in Spain; it even has a museum of antique instruments. Prices start at around 15,000ptas and head skywards for the quality models and fancy woods. Famous clients include Segovia.

Seseña

Map 6, B4. C/de la Cruz 23. Metro Sol.
Mon–Sat 10am–1.30pm & 4.30–8pm.
Tailor specializing in traditional *Madrileño* capes for royalty and celebrities. Clients have included Luis Buñuel and Gary Cooper.

DEPARTMENT STORES

El Corte Inglés

Map 3, I4. C/de Preciados 1–4. Metro Sol. Branches at c/de la Princesa 42 (Metro Argüelles); c/de Goya 76 & 87 (Metro Goya); Paseo de la Castellana 71 & 85 (Metro Nuevos Ministerios). Mon–Sat 10am–9.30pm.

The Spanish department store *par excellence*. It's not cheap, but the quality is very good and the advantage is that you can get practically anything you want under one roof. Highly professional staff (the majority of whom speak English) and a classy food department. Good for sports equipment and not bad for CDs.

Fnac

Map 3, H2. C/de Preciados 28. Metro Callao. Mon–Sat 10am–9.30pm, Sun noon–9.30pm.

Not really a true department store, but it does have excellent sections for books, videos, CDs and electrical equipment. Also sells concert tickets. The book department is good for English-language fiction and has a decent section for English-language teachers/learners. The store has a price promise that it will return your money if you find any article cheaper anywhere else.

FOOD AND DRINK

Baco – La Boutique del Vino

C/de San Bernardo 117. Metro Quevedo. Mon–Fri 11am–2pm & 5–8pm, Sat 10am–2pm; no cards.

Supermarket-type wine store with a good-value range of quality Spanish wines, *cavas*, brandies and also Asturian cider (*sidra*). It's certainly worth splashing out on one of the *reservas* from Ribera del Duero or Rioja. Look out too for good reds from Navarra and Valdepeñas and whites from Rueda and Galicia.

Bruin

Map 2, A1. Paseo del Pintor Rosales 48. Metro Argüelles.
Daily 10am–midnight.
Great ice-cream parlour with a nice *terraza* next to Parque del Oeste. Over twenty different different flavours, plus the full range of chilled drinks.

Casa Mira

Map 6, D4. Carrera de San Jerónimo 30. Metro Sevilla.
Mon–Sat 10am–2pm & 5pm–9pm.
The place to go for *turrón* (flavoured nougat) – eaten by nearly all Spaniards at Christmas – and marzipan. The family business has been open for nearly 150 years since the founder, Luis Mira, arrived from Asturias and set up a stall in Puerta del Sol.

Mallorca

Map 2, J4. C/de Serrano 6. Metro Serrano.
Daily 9.30am–9pm.
The main branch of Madrid's best deli chain – a pricey but fabulous treasure trove for picnics, cakes and chocolates for presents. All branches have small bars serving drinks and canapés.

La Mallorquina

Map 3, I5. Puerta del Sol 2. Metro Sol.
Mon–Sat 9am–9.45pm.
Wonderful-smelling pastry shop and café selling everything

you've always been told not to eat. Try the small ball-shaped *buñuelos* filled with cream or the tray of assorted *pasteles*. Upstairs there's a salon which overlooks Puerta del Sol – a great place for people watching while sampling a milky coffee and a slice of truffle cake.

Mariano Aguado

Map 6, D5. C/de Echegaray 19. Metro Sevilla.
Mon–Fri 9.30am–2pm & 5.30–8.30pm, Sat 9.30am–2pm.
Atmospheric wine sellers with an assuringly musty atmosphere. Fine selection of Spanish wines and, especially, sherries (*vinos de Jerez*) at prices to suit any pocket.

Mariano Madrueño

Map 3, H3. C/Postigo San Martín 3. Metro Callao.
Mon–Fri 9.30am–2pm & 5–8pm, Sat 9.30am–2pm.
Great traditional wine sellers established back in 1895. There's an overpowering smell of grapes as you peruse its vintage-crammed shelves. Intriguing tipples include powerful *Licor de Hierbas* from Galicia and homemade *Pacharán* sloe gin.

Museo del Jamón

Map 6, B3. Carrera de San Jerónimo 6. Metro Sol.
Mon–Sat 9am–midnight, Sun & public holidays 10am–midnight.
A fantastic range of hams hanging from the ceiling, but it'll set you back a bit – a quality *Jamón de Jabugo* from pigs fed exclusively on acorns weighs in at 8000ptas a kilo while the more industrially manufactured *Jamón de Serrano* is a mere 2500ptas. At the very least stay for a glass of red wine and sample one of the selection plates available. Staff are always willing to provide advice. Branches all over town.

SHOPPING: FOOD AND DRINK

Tienda Olivarero

Map 7, I4. C/Mejía Lequerica 1. Metro Alonso Martinez.
Mon–Sat 9.30am–2.30pm & 5.30–7.30pm.

Outlet for an olive growers' co-operative, with information sheets to guide you towards purchasing the best olive oils. A vast range of grades and quantities are available from all over the peninsula.

RECORDS AND CDs

Madrid Rock

Map 7, G3. Gran Vía 25. Metro Callao.
Daily 10am–10pm.

By Spanish standards this is a huge record store, selling a good range of rock, jazz, Pop Español and flamenco CDs. Tickets for most concerts are available here.

La Metralleta

Map 3, G3. Plaza de San Martín. Metro Opera.
Mon–Sat 10am–2.30pm & 4.30–8.30pm.

Down the steps on the edge of the plaza, La Metralleta buys and sells CDs, records, film posters, calendars and anything connected with the entertainment industry. Lots of bargains, with CDs at around 900ptas – a good place to find more obscure stuff.

KIDS' MADRID

Although many of the main sights and museums in Madrid lack child-specific services or activities, there is plenty in the city to keep children occupied and interested for a short stay. Most of the **parks** have playgrounds, and, in addition to the city's swimming pools (see p.210), there are a couple of **aquaparks** situated out of town. The colourful parades and events during **fiestas** are also worth investigating, particularly during *Carnaval* (Feb) and at Christmas.

Children are, in general, doted on in Spain and are welcome in nearly all cafés and restaurants. Most are more than willing to provide special child portions, while the *VIPs* chain of café/restaurants and all the burger bars provide children's menus. Spanish children stay up later than in many other countries and frequently accompany parents for a late evening stroll or drinks at a *terraza*.

Acuarium de Madrid

Map 3, H4. C/Maestro Vitoria 8 ℗531 81 72. Metro Callao/Sol.
Daily 11am–2pm & 5–9pm; 375ptas.
A small-scale, but quite intriguing exhibition of fish, reptiles and spiders located in the heart of the shopping zone of Madrid. Instant distraction for bored children.

Imax Madrid

Parque Tierno Galván, Meneses ☏467 48 00. Metro Méndez Alvaro.
Continuous shows: Mon–Fri 11.20am–1pm & 3.45pm–1am, Sat & Sun 11.20am–2.15pm & 3.45pm–1am; 850–1000ptas.

Three different types of screen at this futuristic cinema – a giant flat one, a dome-shaped one for all-round viewing and one for 3D projections.

Laser City

Map 7, B5. C/de la Princesa. Metro Plaza de España.
Mon–Thurs 6pm–1am, Fri & Sat noon–3pm & 6pm–4am, Sun noon–3pm & 6pm–1am; 700ptas for 15min, 1000ptas for 30min.

Kids will be familiar with this – it involves running around a sort of intergalactic maze trying to target everyone else with your laser gun. You get a read-out detailing your sharp-shooting exploits afterwards. Pricey, but popular.

Mirador del Faro

Avda. del Arco de la Victoria. Metro Moncloa.
Tues–Sun: Sept–May 10.30am–2pm & 5.30–8pm; June–Aug 11am–1.45pm & 5.30–8.45pm; 200ptas.

The futuristic *mirador* (viewing gallery) provides fantastic views over the city and is very popular with children.

Museo de Cera (Wax Museum)

Map 7, L4. Paseo de Recoletos 41 ☏308 08 25. Metro Colón.
Daily 10.30am–2pm & 4–8.30pm; 900ptas, under-12s & over-65s 600ptas, under-4s free.

Over 450 different personalities and a chamber of horrors feature in this expensive and tacky museum, which is nevertheless popular with children.

Museo de Ciencias Naturales

C/José Gutiérrez Abascal 2 ©411 13 28. Metro Nuevos
Ministerios.
Tues–Fri 10am–6pm, Sat 10am–8pm, Sun 10am–2.30pm; 400ptas,
under-14s 300ptas.

The Natural History Museum is the most interactive of the
traditional musems in the city centre, with audio-visual displays
on the evolution of life on earth and plenty of dinosaur
exhibits.

Parque de Atracciones

Casa de Campo ©526 80 30 or ©463 29 00. Metro Batán/bus #33
& #65.
July & Aug daily noon–1am, Fri & Sat till 2am; Sept–June daily
noon–11pm, Sat till 1am. Entry without rides 475ptas; entry with
unlimited access to rides (*Calco Supernapy*) 1800ptas; under-7s
(*Calco Infantil*) 1000ptas.

A theme park full of rides and attractions. The latest
additions include the vertical drop (*la lanzadera*), the
stomach-churning *la máquina*, and the white-water raft ride,
los rápidos. Spanish singers and groups perform in the open-
air auditorium during the summer months and there are
frequent parades. Plenty of places to eat and drink of the
burger/pizza variety.

Planetario

Avda. del Planetario 16, Parque Tierno Galván ©467 38 98.
Metro Méndez Alvaro.
Tues–Fri shows at 5.30pm & 6.45pm, Sat & Sun 11.30am, 12.45pm,
5.30pm & 6.45pm; 450ptas. under-14s 200ptas.

Exhibition halls, audio-visual displays and projections on a
variety of astronomical themes (all in Spanish).

Teleférico

Map 2, A2. Paseo Pintor Rosales ©541 74 50. **Metro Argüelles.**
April–Sept daily 11am–2.30 & 4.30pm–dusk; Oct–March Sat, Sun &
public holidays only; 355ptas single, 505ptas return.

A popular cable car ride over to the restaurant-bar on the far
side of Casa de Campo, with great views of the city. You can't
use it to get to the zoo or Parque de Atracciones, however, as
they're on the other side of the park.

Zoo-Aquarium

Casa de Campo ©711 99 50. **Metro Batán/bus #33.**
Daily 10am–9.30pm; 1560ptas, under-7s 1255ptas, under-3s free.

The zoo, situated on the southwestern edge of Casa de Campo,
is laid out in sections corresponding to the five continents.
Most animals are kept in by moats and they have plenty of
space to move around. There are over 2,000 different species, a
dolphinarium with regular shows, an aquarium which includes
sharks, pavilions dedicated to venomous snakes and the
"mysteries of nature", as well as a children's zoo and parrot
show. Boats are available for rent and there are train tours of the
site, as well as self-service restaurants and hamburger stalls.

PARKS AND GARDENS

Casa de Campo

Metro Lago/Batán.
The Zoo, Parque de Atracciones and boating lake are all here.
However, be aware that the park has become increasingly
populated by prostitutes and their clients (see p.108).

Parque del Oeste

Map 2, A2. Metro Moncloa/Príncipe Pío.
Very pleasant shady parkland with a small river, the Egyptian
Templo de Debod and the starting point of the Teleférico cable
car (see p.106).

Parque del Retiro

Map 8. Metro Retiro/Ibiza/Atocha.
Plenty of activities for children, including a boating lake,
puppet shows and playgrounds. Room for rollerskating and
cycling, too (see p.80).

AQUAPARKS

Aquamadrid

Carretera de Barcelona (N-II) km 15.5 ℗673 10 13. Bus
Continental Auto #281, #282, #284, or #385 from Avda. de
América. Train *Cercanías* C-2 or C-7 to San Fernando.
June–Sept Mon–Fri noon–8pm; Sat & Sun 11am–8pm; Mon–Fri
1200ptas, under-12s 900ptas; Sat & Sun 1500ptas; under-12s 1100ptas;
half-day entry (after 4pm) Mon–Fri 950ptas, Sat & Sun 1250ptas.
Busy waterpark with the usual monster slides and large lake,
plus toddlers' pool and night-time disco.

Aquópolis

Villanueva de la Cañada, Carretera de la Coruña (N-VI) km 25
℗815 69 11. Bus Autoperiferia 581 from Estación Sur.
June–Sept daily noon–8pm; Mon–Fri 1600ptas, under-10s
1000ptas; Sat & Sun 1800ptas, under-10s 1200ptas.
The largest of the waterparks with a variety of giant slides, a
wave machine, a water-based assault course and plenty of grass
for a picnic. Smaller rides for younger kids too.

DIRECTORY

AIRLINES Most airlines have their offices along the Gran Vía or on c/de la Princesa, its continuation beyond the Plaza de España. American Airlines, c/Pedro Teixeira 8, 5° (Metro Lima; ✆597 20 68 or ✆900 10 05 56); Avianca, Gran Vía 88 (Metro Plaza de España; ✆205 43 20); British Airways, c/Serrano 60 5° (Metro Serrano; ✆305 42 12 or 205 43 17); Iberia, c/Goya 29 (Metro Serrano; ✆587 81 56); KLM, Gran Vía 59 (Metro Santo Domingo; ✆247 81 00); TWA, Plaza de Colón 2 (Metro Colón; ✆310 3094) The Iberojet counter at the airport sells discounted standby seats on scheduled flights.

AIRPORT INFORMATION ✆393 60 00. See p.4 for details of airport transport.

AMERICAN EXPRESS Plaza de las Cortes 2, entrance on Marqués de Cubas (Metro Sevilla; ✆572 03 20). Open Monday–Friday 9am–5.30pm, Saturday 9am–noon for mail and transactions.

BANKS AND EXCHANGE The main Spanish banks are concentrated on c/de Alcalá and Gran Vía. Opening hours are normally Monday–Friday 9am–2pm, but they're also often open on Saturday 9am–1pm from October to May. International banks include: Bank of America, c/Capitán Haya

1 (Metro Lima); Barclays, Plaza de Colón 1 (Metro Colón); Citibank, c/José Ortega y Gasset 29 (Metro Núñez de Balboa); Lloyds, c/de Serrano 90 (Metro Núñez de Balboa). In addition to the banks, branches of El Corte Inglés department store all have exchange offices with long hours and highly competitive rates; the most central is on Puerta del Sol. Barajas airport has a 24-hour currency exchange office.

BICYCLES For rental and repairs try Bicicletas Chapinal, c/de Alcalá 242 (Metro El Carmen; Mon–Fri 10am–1.30pm & 4.30–8pm, Sat 10am–2pm; ✆404 18 53); Calmera, c/de Atocha 98 (Metro Antón Martín; Mon–Sat 9.30am–1.30pm & 4.30–8pm; ✆527 75 74); Karacol, c/Montera 32 (Metro Gran Vía/Sol; Mon–Fri 10am–2pm & 5.30–8.30pm; Sat 10.30am–2pm; ✆532 90 73).

BUSES Long-distance buses terminate at the Estación Sur de Autobuses on c/Méndez Alvaro (Metro Méndez Alvaro; ✆468 42 00). Companies and services change with great frequency and it's always worth checking schedules with the Turismo or the information line (✆435 22 66). Two of the largest companies are Auto Res (✆551 66 44) and La Sepulvedana (✆530 48 00).

CAR RENTAL Major operators have branches at Barajas airport and around the city centre: Atesa, c/Infanta Mercedes 90 (Metro Estrecho; ✆571 19 31); Avis, Gran Vía 60 (Metro Plaza de España; ✆547 20 48); Europcar, c/San Leonardo 8 (Metro Plaza de España; ✆541 88 92); Hertz, Estación de Atocha (Metro Atocha; ✆468 13 18); Rent Me, Plaza de Herradores 6, just off Plaza Mayor (Metro Sol; ✆559 08 22).

DISABILITY Madrid is not particularly well geared up for the disabled (*minusválidos*), although the situation is gradually improving. The Organizacíon Nacional de Ciegos de España (ONCE) at c/de Prado 24 (✆589 46 00 or ✆577 37 56) provides the best specialist advice. Major museums and some of the larger, more expensive hotels have adapted facilities, some buses have been altered for wheelchairs and all metro trains and buses have designated seats. However, there are no lifts in the metro and train stations. Wheelchair-adapted taxis can be ordered from Radio Taxi (©547 82 00).

DOCTORS English-speaking doctors are available at the Anglo-American Medical Unit, c/Conde de Aranda 1 (Metro Retiro; Mon–Fri 9am–8pm, Sat 10am–3pm; ©435 18 23).

ELECTRICITY 220 volts AC. Most European appliances should work as long as you have an adaptor for European-style two-pin plugs. North Americans will need this plus a transformer.

EMBASSIES Australia, Paseo de la Castellana 143 (Metro Cuzco; ©579 04 28); Britain, c/Fernando el Santo 16 (Metro Alonso Martínez; ©319 02 00); Canada, c/Núñez de Balboa 35 (Metro Núñez de Balboa; ©431 43 00); France, c/Salustiano Olozaga 9 (Metro Banco de España; ©435 55 60); Germany c/Fortuny 8 (Metro Rubén Darío; 319 91 00); Ireland, Paseo de la Castellana 46 (Metro Rubén Darío; ©577 89 31); Italy, C/Lagasca, 98 (Metro Núñez de Balboa ©577 67 69); Netherlands, Paseo de la Castellana 178 (Metro Cuzco; ©359 09 14); New Zealand, Plaza Lealtad 2 (Metro Sevilla; ©523 02 26); Norway, Paseo de la Castellana 31 (Metro Rubén Darío; ©310 31 16); South Africa, c/Claudio Coello 91 (Metro Núñez Balboa; ©435 66 88); Sweden, c/Caracas 25 (Metro Sevilla; ©308 15 35); USA, c/de Serrano 51 (Metro Serrano; ©577 40 00).

EMERGENCIES For an ambulance dial ©061, ©588 45 00 or © 522 22 22 – or get a taxi, which will be quicker, if no paramedics are necessary. For the police dial ©091 or ©092.

HEALTH Residents of European Union countries are entitled to free medical treatment and prescribed medicines under the EU Reciprocal Medical Treatment arrangement provided you have a completed E111 form (available from post offices in Britain and Social Security offices elsewhere). Citizens of non-EU countries will be charged at private hospital rates, so it is essential to take out medical insurance before travelling.

HOSPITALS The most central are: El Clínico, Plaza de Cristo Rey (Metro Moncloa; ✆330 37 47); Hospital Gregorio Marañón, c/Dr Esquerdo 46 (Metro O'Donnell; ✆586 80 00); and Ciudad Sanitaria La Paz, Paseo de la Castellana 261 (Metro Begoña; ✆358 28 31).

LANGUAGE COURSES Madrid has numerous language schools, offering intensive courses in Spanish language and culture. One of the most established is International House, c/Zurbano 8 (Metro Alonso Martínez; ✆310 13 14).

LAUNDRY Central *lavanderías* include: c/Barco 26 (Metro Gran Vía); c/de Cervantes 1–3 (Metro Sol); c/Donoso Cortés 17 (Metro Quevedo); c/de Hermosilla 121 (Metro Goya); c/de la Palma 2 (Metro Tribunal).

LEFT LUGGAGE There are *consignas* at the Estación Sur (daily 6.35am–11.45pm), Auto–Res and Continental Auto bus stations; at the airport bus terminal beneath Plaza de Colón; as well as lockers at Atocha and Chamartín train stations.

PARKING Parking is difficult in the city centre and, although the law appears to be flouted all the time, parking is banned on the main streets. If you have a car, the best bet is to leave it at your hotel or in one of the many underground car parks, especially if it has foreign plates as these are often targeted by car thieves. Illegally parked cars are towed away by the *grúa* (tow truck) and you have to ring ✆345 00 50 quoting your number plate and pay in the region of 20,000ptas to recover your vehicle.

PHARMACIES *Farmacias* are distinguished by a green cross; each district has a rota with one staying open through the night. For details call ℗098 (Spanish only) or check the notice on the door of your nearest pharmacy or the listings magazines. Madrid also has quite a number of traditional herbalists, best known of which is Maurice Mességue, c/Goya 64 (Metro Goya; Mon–Fri 10am–2pm & 5–8pm, Sat 10am–2pm).

POLICE The headquarters of the Policía Nacional are near to Plaza de España at c/Fomento 24 (℗541 71 60). If you report a crime you will have to make an official statement or *denuncia* – often a time-consuming and laborious business, especially as few policemen speak English – which you will require for any insurance claim. Other centrally located police stations [*comisarías*] are to be found at c/de la Luna 29 (Metro Callao; ℗521 12 36); c/de las Huertas 76 (Metro Antón Martín; ℗429 22 26). In an emergency call ℗091.

POST OFFICE The main one is the Palacio de Comunicaciones in the Plaza de las Cibeles (Metro Banco de España; Mon–Sat 8am–midnight, Sun 8am–10pm for stamps and telegrams; Mon–Fri 9am–8pm, Sat 9am–2pm for poste restante [*lista de correos*]). Branch offices throughout the city are open Monday–Saturday 9am–2pm, but the easiest places to buy stamps are the *estancos*, recognizable by their brown and yellow signs bearing the word *Tabacos*.

PUBLIC HOLIDAYS The main national holidays when shops and banks will be closed are: Jan 1 (*Año Nuevo*); Jan 6 (*Reyes*); Easter Thursday (*Jueves Santo*); Good Friday (*Viernes Santo*); May 1 (*Fiesta del Trabajo*); May 2 (*Día de la Comunidad*); May 15 (*San Isidro*); Aug 15 (*Virgen de la Paloma*); Oct 12 (*Día de la Hispanidad*); Nov 1 (*Todos los Santos*); Nov 9 (*Virgen de la Almudena*); Dec 6 (*Día de la Constitución*); Dec 8 (*La Inmaculada*); Dec 25 (*Navidad*).

PUBLIC TOILETS There are very few public toilets in Madrid, so your best bet is to pop into a local bar, café or department store.

TELEPHONES International calls can be made from any phone box or from any *telefónica*. The main *telefónica* at Gran Vía 30 (Metro Gran Vía) is open until midnight. To make a local call the minimum charge is 15ptas, but you won't usually get any change from a 25ptas coin. Phones that will accept coins, phonecards and credit cards are increasingly common and many have instructions in English as well as other languages. Phone cards cost 1000ptas or 2000ptas and can be bought at post offices or *estancos*. To make an international call, dial ℃07, wait for the continuous tone and then dial the country code followed by the area code – omitting initial zero – and then the number. To make a reverse charge call ask the operator for *cobro revertido*.

TICKET AGENCIES For theatre and concert tickets try Tele–Entradas (℃538 33 33) which charges no commission, or Localidades Galicia, Plaza del Carmen 1 (Metro Sol; ℃531 27 32 or 531 91 31), which sells tickets for football games, bullfights, theatres and concerts.

TRAINS ℃563 02 02 or 328 90 20; reservations ℃562 33 33. Tickets can be bought at the individual stations, or at Barajas airport arrivals and at the city-centre RENFE office, c/de Alcalá 44 (Metro Banco de España; Mon–Fri 9am–7pm, Sat 9am–1.30pm; ℃562 33 33).

TRAVEL AGENCIES Viajes Zeppelin, Plaza Santo Domingo 2 (Metro Santo Domingo; ℃542 51 54), is an English-speaking and very efficient company, offering excellent deals on flights and holidays. Nuevas Fronteras, c/Luisa Fernanda 2 (Metro Ventura Rodríguez; ℃542 39 90) and in the Torre de Madrid, Plaza de España (Metro Plaza de España; ℃247 42 00) can be good for flights, or try Top Tours, c/Capitán Haya 20 (Metro Cuzco; ℃555 06 04). Many other travel agents are concentrated on and around the Gran Vía. For student travel go to TIVE, c/Fernando el Católico 88 (Metro Moncloa; ℃543 02 08).

DAY-TRIPS FROM MADRID

EL ESCORIAL AND EL VALLE DE LOS CAÍDOS

F ifty kilometres northwest of Madrid, in the foothills of the Sierra de Guadarrama, is one of Spain's best known and most visited sights - Felipe II's vast monastery-palace complex of **El Escorial**. An exceptional building in itself, it also provides an unprecedented insight into the mindset of Spain's greatest king. The town around the monastery, **San Lorenzo del Escorial**, is an easy day-trip from Madrid and you can also take in **El Valle de los Caídos** (The Valley of the Fallen), 9km further north. This is an equally megalomaniac yet far more chilling monument: an underground basilica hewn under Franco's orders, allegedly as a monument to the Civil War dead of both sides, though in reality as a memorial to the Generalísimo and his regime.

Regular **trains** run from Estación de Atocha on the *Cercanías* line C-8a (daily 5.45am-11.30pm; 50min; 740ptas return) calling at Charmartín on the way out of the city. From the station at El Escorial take the local bus up the hill to the monastery. **Buses** (run by Autocares Herranz) leave every thirty minutes on weekdays and hourly at weekends (Mon–Fri 7.15am–10pm, Sat 9am–9.30pm, Sun & public holidays 9am–11pm) from Moncloa bus station (55min; 740ptas). The **Turismo** in San Lorenzo is at c/Floridablanca 10 (Mon–Fri 10am–2pm & 3–5pm, Sat 10am–2pm; ☎091/890 15 54).

From El Escorial to El Valle de los Caídos there's a direct local bus departing at 3.15pm and returning at 5.30pm (Tues–Sun). Tickets are sold at the *Bar Bolero*, opposite the post office just up from the monastery.

EL ESCORIAL

Tues–Sun: April–Sept 10am–6pm; Oct–March 10am–5pm; 850ptas, free Wed for EU citizens. Separate admission charge of 325ptas for the outlying lodges and formal gardens.

El Escorial was the largest Spanish building of the Renaissance. Rectangular, overbearing and severe, from the outside it resembles more a prison than a palace. Built between 1563 and 1584 by Juan Bautista de Toledo and Juan de Herrera, **Felipe II** planned the enormous complex as part monastery, part mausoleum and part palace, where he would live the life of a monk and "rule the world with two inches of paper". Seven kilometres out of town there are great views of the monastery from the Silla de Felipe (Philip's Seat), a chair carved into a rocky outcrop from where Felipe II is supposed to have watched the construction of the complex.

The monastery itself commemorates the victory over the French at St Quentin on San Lorenzo's feast day (August 10, 1557) and above the **west gateway** is a gargantuan statue of the patron saint holding the gridiron on which he was burned to death. The gridiron emblem is also present on the builders' trowels displayed in the basement exhibition in the basement, and the whole complex is said to have been designed around this pattern. Within is the **Patio de los Reyes**, named after the six statues of the kings of Israel on the facade of the basilica straight ahead. Linking the secular and religious zones of the monastery complex is the **Biblioteca**, a splendid hall with multicoloured vivid frescoes by Tibaldi showing the seven Liberal Arts. Its collections include Santa Teresa's personal diary, some gorgeously executed Arabic manuscripts, and a Florentine planetarium of 1572 demonstrating the movement of the planets according to the Ptolemaic and Copernican systems.

The enormous, cold, dark interior of the **Basílica** contains over forty altars, designed to allow simultaneous masses to be held. Behind the main altar lie some of Felipe's mammoth collection of saintly relics, including six whole bodies, over sixty heads and hundreds of bone fragments set in fabulously expensive caskets. The two bronze sculptural groups at the east end depicting Carlos V with his family and Felipe II with three of his wives were carved by the father-and-son team of Leone and Pompeo Leoni.

Many of the monastery's religious treasures are contained in the **Sacristía** and **Salas Capitulares** (Chapter Houses) and include paintings by Titian, Velázquez and José Ribera. Below these rooms is the **Panteón Real**, where deceased Spanish monarchs lie in their gilded marble tombs, while just above the entrance you pass the doorway to the **Pudrería**, a separate room in which the bodies rot for twenty years or so before the cleaned-up skeletons are moved downstairs. The royal children are laid in the **Panteón de los Infantes** and there is also a wedding-cake babies' tomb with room for sixty infants.

What remains of the Escorial's **art collection** – works by Bosch, Gerard David, Dürer, Titian, Zurbarán and many others, which escaped transfer to the Prado – is kept in the elegant suite of rooms known as the **Museos Nuevos**. Finally, there are the treasure-crammed **Salones Reales** (Royal Apartments) containing the austere quarters of Felipe II, with the chair that supported his gouty leg and the deathbed from which he was able to contemplate the high altar of the basilica.

Eating and drinking

For **refreshments** you'll need to head away from the monastery, up c/Reina Victoria into town. *La Genara*, at Plaza San Lorenzo 2, is a good-value restaurant filled with theatrical mementos, while the more expensive *Charolés*, c/Floridablanca 24, is renowned for its fish and stews. The best bar is the friendly *Cervecería Los Pescaítos*, c/Joaquín Costa 8, which also serves fish dishes.

EL VALLE DE LOS CAÍDOS

Tues–Sun: April–Sept 9.30am–7pm; Oct–March 10am–6pm; 650ptas; free Wed for EU citizens.

The **basilica complex** denies its claims of memorial "to the Civil War dead of both sides" almost at a glance. The dour, grandiose architectural forms employed, the constant inscriptions "Fallen for God and for Spain", and the proximity to El Escorial clue you in to its true function – the glorification of **General Franco** and his regime. The dictator himself lies buried behind the high altar, while the only other named tomb is that of his guru, the Falangist leader José Antonio Primo de Rivera, who was shot dead by Republicans at the beginning of the war. The "other side" is present only in the fact that the complex was built by the Republican army's survivors – political prisoners on quarrying duty.

Above the complex is a vast **cross**, reputedly the largest in the world, and visible for miles around. From the entrance to the basilica a shaky **funicular** (Tues–Sun April–Sept 11am–1.30pm & 4–6.30pm; Oct–March 11am–1.30pm & 3–5.30pm; 350ptas) ascends to its base, offering superlative views over the Sierra de Guadarrama and of the giant, grotesque figures propping up the cross.

EL VALLE DE LOS CAÍDOS

ARANJUEZ AND CHINCHÓN

A little oasis on the way to Toledo, the town of **Aranjuez** was used by the eighteenth-century Bourbon rulers as a spring and autumn retreat. Their palaces and luxuriant gardens, and the summer strawberries (served with cream - *fresas con nata* - at roadside stalls) make it an enjoyable stop. If you're travelling by train you can break your journey here and then continue on to Toledo. The nearby picturesque town of **Chinchón** is also worth a visit, home to Spain's best-known *anís* – a mainstay of breakfast drinkers across Spain.

Aranjuez is served by **trains** from Estación de Atocha (*Cercanías* line C-3 daily every 15–30min, 5am–11.55pm; 45min, 1100ptas return) and by hourly **buses** from Estación Sur (40min; 780ptas return). An old wooden **steam train**, *El Tren de la Fresa*, also makes weekend runs between Madrid and Aranjuez (mid-April to July & mid-Sept to Oct; 1hr). It leaves Atocha at 10am and returns from Aranjuez at 6.30pm (Sat & Sun). The 2900ptas fare includes a guided bus tour in Aranjuez, entry to the monuments plus strawberries on the train. The **Turismo** in Aranjuez is on Plaza del Puente (Mon–Fri 10am–2pm & 3–5pm, Sat 10am–2pm; ☎91/891 04 27).

Chinchón is connected to Aranjuez by sporadic buses (Mon–Sat) and to Madrid by hourly services on the La Veloz bus from Avda. del Mediterraneo 49 (Metro Conde de Casal; 1hr; 800ptas return).

ARANJUEZ

The beauty of **Aranjuez**, 50km from the capital, is its greenery, studded with opulent palaces and luxuriant gardens. In summer, Aranjuez functions principally as a weekend escape from Madrid and most people come out for the day as there's no accommodation.

The eighteenth-century **Palacio Real** (Tues–Sun: April–Sept 10am–6.15pm; Oct–March 10am–5.15pm; joint ticket with gardens 500ptas) and its **gardens** (daily 8am–8.30pm) were an attempt by the Spanish Bourbon monarchs to create a Versailles in Spain. Aranjuez clearly isn't in the same league but it's a pleasant place to while away a few hours. The palace is more remarkable for its interior ornamental fantasies than for any architectural virtues. The **Porcelain Room** for example is entirely covered in decorative ware from the factory which used to stand in Madrid's Retiro park, while the **Smoking Room** is a copy of one of the finest halls of the Alhambra in Granada, though executed with less subtlety. Most of the palace dates from the reign of the "nymphomaniac" Queen Isabel II, and many of the scandals and intrigues which led to her eventual abdication were played out here.

Outside, on a small island, are the fountains of the **Jardín de la Isla**. The **Jardín del Príncipe**, on the other side of the main road, is more attractive, however, with shaded

ARANJUEZ

walks along the river and plenty of spots for a siesta. At its far end stands the **Casa del Labrador** (Peasant's House; same hours as Palacio Real; 425ptas), which is anything but what the name implies, for the house is crammed with silk, marble, crystal and gold, as well as a huge collection of fancy clocks. The guided tour goes into great detail about the weight and value of every item. Also in the gardens, by the river, is the small **Casa de los Marinos** (Sailors' House; same hours as Palacio Real; 325ptas), a museum displaying the brightly coloured launches in which royalty would take to the river. You can buy a joint ticket for these two buildings for 600ptas. A bus service occasionally connects the various sites, but all are within easy walking distance of each other, and it's a lovely place to stroll around.

Eating and drinking

Casa José, c/Asbastos 32.
Tasty and expensive nouvelle cuisine.

Casa Pablete, c/Stuart.
An offshoot of *Casa Pablo* and one of the best places in town for tapas.

Casa Pablo, c/Almíbar 42.
A traditional place with walls covered with pictures of local dignitaries and bullfighters.

Mercado de San Antonio, near the Jardines Isabel II.
Just the place to buy your own food for a picnic

CHINCHÓN

Chinchón, 45km southeast of Madrid, is a highly picturesque little town with a fifteenth-century castle and a medieval Plaza Mayor encircled by wooden balconied houses, next to which stands the **Iglesia de la Asunción**, with a panel by Goya of *The Assumption of the Virgin*. Most visitors, however, come to visit the three **anis distilleries**, a couple of which are housed in the castle. After a few tastings the modestly priced *Mesón del Duende* and *Mesón del Comendador* are both good places for a **meal**, or there's the more expensive *Mesón Cuevas del Vino*, once an olive oil mill and today with its own *bodega*.

The best bet for **accommodation**, though it's not cheap, is the *parador* at c/Generalísimo 1 (©91/894 08 36; ⑦–⑧) housed in a sixteenth-century convent with wonderful Moorish-style gardens and a magnificent seventeenth-century dining room.

If you're visiting over **Easter**, you'll be treated to the townsfolk's own enactment of the *Passion of Christ*, when participants and audience process through the town. In April 1995, Chinchón launched its **Fiesta del Anís y del Vino**, an orgy of anis- and wine-tasting; understandably it was an immediate success and is now held every year in mid-April. An older annual tradition takes place on July 25, when the feast of St James (Santiago) is celebrated with a bullfight in the Plaza Mayor.

CHINCHÓN

TOLEDO

Toledo epitomizes the soul of Spain and shares many of its contradictions. From imperial greatness it declined into isolation, and from religious toleration it came to be dominated by a stark vision of Catholicism. Home to many artists including **El Greco**, and a setting for Cervantes' writing, the city is also famous for its majestic **cathedral**, its Toledan swords and the towering **Alcázar**.

Surrounded on three sides by the Río Tajo slowly meandering its way towards Lisbon, every available inch of this rugged outcrop has been built on. Churches, synagogues, mosques and houses are heaped upon one another in a haphazard spiral which the cobbled lanes infiltrate as best they can. Certainly, it's a city redolent of past glories, and is packed with sights, although the extraordinary number of day-trippers has taken the edge off what was once the most extravagant of Spanish experiences. Still, the setting is breathtaking, and if you're an El Greco fan, you'd be mad to miss this city. Toledo also hosts one of the best celebrations of **Corpus Christi** (late May/early June) in the country, with street processions and all the works. Other local festivals take place on May 25 and August 15 and 20, and the **Easter processions** here are much more impressive than those of Madrid.

To see Toledo at its best, you'll need to stay at least a night. A day-trip will leave you hard pressed to see everything and, more importantly, in the evening with the crowds gone and lit up by floodlights, resembling one of El Greco's moonlit paintings, Toledo is a completely different city. However, being such a tourist honeypot, booking a **room** in advance is important, especially at weekends and during the summer.

Getting to the city, some 70km south of Madrid, is straightforward with nine **trains** a day (fewer on Sat & Sun) from Estación de Atocha (7am–8.30pm; 1hr 15min; 1230ptas return). Toledo's train station is some way out, so either make the beautiful twenty-minute walk into town or take bus #5 or #6. **Buses** from Madrid operate every thirty minutes from Estación del Sur (6.30am–10pm; 1hr; 1140ptas return) dropping you just outside the old city, with regular buses into the heart of town. If you're driving, you'll need to park outside the old city as the streets are far too narrow inside and there are no public places to park. Toledo's main **Turismo** is also outside the city walls at Puerta de Bisagra s/n (Mon–Fri 9am–2pm & 4–6pm, Sat 9am–3pm & 4–7pm, Sun 9am–3pm; ©925/220843).

ALCÁZAR & HOSPITAL Y MUSEO DE SANTA CRUZ

Dominating the **Plaza de Zocodover**, indeed all of Toledo, is the bluff, imposing **Alcázar (**Tues–Sun 10am–1.30pm & 4–6.30pm; Oct–Apr till 5.30pm; 125ptas), entered off Cuesta del Alcázar. The present building was originated by Carlos V, though it has been burned and bombarded so often that almost nothing is original. The most recent destruction occurred in 1936 during one of the most symbolic and extraordinary episodes of the Civil War, involving a two-month siege of the Nationalist-occupied

Alcázar by the Republican town. After the war, Franco's regime completely rebuilt the fortress as a monument to the glorification of its defenders and their propaganda models and photos are still displayed.

Just north of Plaza is the **Hospital y Museo de Santa Cruz** (Mon 10am–2pm & 4–6.30pm, Tues–Sat 10am–6.30pm, Sun 10am–2pm; 200ptas), a superlative Renaissance building in itself, housing some of the greatest El Grecos in Toledo including *The Coronation of the Virgin* and *The Assumption of the Virgin*. As well as outstanding works by Goya and Ribera, the museum also contains a huge collection of ancient carpets and faded tapestries, a military display, sculpture and a small archeological collection.

THE CATHEDRAL

Mon–Sat 10.30am–1pm & 3.30–6pm, Sun 10.30am–1.30pm & 4–6pm; tickets for the Treasury, Sacristy, Chapter House and the New Museums 500ptas.

Toledo's **Catedral**, situated to the south of Plaza de Zocodover down the Calle de Comercio, really is something special, reflecting the importance of the city that for so long outshone its near neighbour, Madrid. A robust Gothic construction which took over 250 years (1227–1493) to complete, it has a richness of internal decoration in almost every conceivable style, with masterpieces of the Gothic, Renaissance and Baroque periods. The exterior is best appreciated from outside the city, where the 100-metre spire and the weighty buttressing can be seen to advantage. The cavernous interior is home to some magnificent stained glass, an outstanding **Coro** (Choir) and a wonderfully Gothic **Capilla Mayor** depicting a synopsis of the entire New Testament. Directly behind the main altar is an extraordinary piece of fantasy – the **Transparente**, a Baroque chapel, wonderfully and wildly extravagant, with its marble cherubs sitting on fluffy marble clouds. It's especially magnificent when the sun reaches through the hole punched in the roof for that purpose.

There are well over twenty **chapels** embedded in the walls, all of which are of some interest, many housing fine tombs. The **Tesoro** (Treasury), the **Sacristía** (Sacristy), the **Sala Capitular** (Chapter House) and the **Nuevos Museos** (New Museums) house hugely impressive accumulations of wealth and artistic riches including paintings by El Greco, Goya and Velázquez as well as one of El Greco's few surviving pieces of sculpture.

SANTO TOMÉ AND THE CASA DEL GRECO

Domenico Theotocopoulos, or **El Greco** (the Greek), settled in Toledo in about 1577 and it is mainly through the portrayal of the city in his extraordinary mystical paintings that the skyline of Toledo has become so famous. A tour of Toledo's El Grecos is a must and an ideal complement to viewing his other work in the Prado. El Greco's masterpiece, *The Burial of the Count of Orgaz* is housed, alone, in a small annexe to the church of **Santo Tomé** (daily: May–Sept 10am–1.45pm & 3.30–6.45pm; Oct–April till 5.45pm; 150ptas) to the west of the cathedral, and depicts the count's funeral, at which Saint Stephen and Saint Augustine appeared to lower him into the tomb. It combines El Greco's genius for the mystic, exemplified in the upper half of the picture where the count's soul is being received into heaven, with his great powers as a portrait painter and master of colour. El Greco himself, his son and Felipe II are said to be amongst the onlookers portrayed in the lower half.

The misleadingly named **Casa del Greco** just to the south of Santo Tomé in Plaza del Conde (Tues–Sat 10am–2pm & 4–6pm, Sun 10am–2pm; 400ptas) was never actually the artist's home, but is a reconstruction of a typical Toledan home of the period. It does, however, display a number of El Greco's classic works, including his famous *View and Map of Toledo*.

For thrilling, uncluttered **views** of Toledo – the skyline so familiar from various El Greco paintings – head for the Carretera de Circunvalación which runs along the south bank of the Tajo, the opposite bank from the city. It takes about an hour to walk from one of the medieval fortified bridges to the other.

THE JEWISH QUARTER

The area to the west of the Casa del Greco was once the *Judería*, the Jewish quarter of medieval Toledo. The synagogues, **El Tránsito** and **Santa María de la Blanco**, both built by *Mudéjar* craftsmen, are stunning reminders of Toledo's cosmopolitan past, while the superb church of **San Juan de los Reyes** (daily: May–Sept 10am–1.45pm & 3.30–6.45pm; Oct–April daily 10am–1.30pm & 3.30–5.45pm; 150ptas), whose exterior is bizarrely festooned with the chains worn by Christian prisoners from Granada released on the reconquest of their city, is a legacy of more intolerant times under the *Reyes Católicos*.

As you wind your way back towards Plaza de Zocodover, the **Museo de Arte Visigodo** (Tues–Sat 10am–2pm & 4–6.30pm, Sun 10am–2pm; 100ptas) stands on Calle de San Clemente in a very different, though equally impressive building – the church of San Román. Moorish and Christian elements (horseshoe arches, early murals and a splendid Renaissance dome) combine to make this the most interesting church in Toledo. Visigothic jewellery, documents and archeological fragments make up the bulk of the collection.

Northwest of Plaza de Zocodover, a short distance from Calle de la Sillería up Cuesta del Cristo de la Luz, is the tiny mosque of **Mezquita del Cristo de la Luz**. Although this is one of the oldest Moorish monuments in Spain (it was built in the tenth century on the foundations of a Visigothic church), only the nave, with its nine different cupolas, is the original Arab construction. The apse was added when the building was converted into a church, and is claimed to be the first product of the *Mudéjar* style.

HOSPITAL DE TAVERA

Situated outside the city walls to the north of the Puerta de Bisagra the private collection of the Duchess of Lerma is housed in the **Hospital de Tavera** (daily 10.30am–1.30pm & 3.30–6pm; 500ptas), a Renaissance palace with beautiful twin patios. The gloomy interior is a reconstruction of a sixteenth-century mansion and is scattered with fine paintings by Bassano, El Greco and Ribera, while the church contains the ornate marble tomb of Cardinal Tavera, the hospital's founder.

ACCOMMODATION

Fonda La Belviseña, Cuesta del Can 7 ©925/220067.
South of the Alcázar, a cheap, good-value *hostal* and hence very popular. ①.

Parador Conde de Orgaz, Cerro del Emperador ©925/221850; fax 225166.
This is Toledo's top hotel offering superb views of the city from its terrace. ⑥.

Hotel Santa Isabel, c/Santa Isabel 24 ©925/253136; fax
253136.
  The best of the mid-range hotels, right in the centre and with
  safe parking. ③.

Hotel Sol, c/Azacanes 15 ©925/213650.
  A good-value place on a quiet side street just off the main
  road up to the Plaza de Zocodover, before the Puerta del Sol.
  The owners also run the cheaper *hostal* across the street –
  ask at reception. ③.

EATING AND DRINKING

Restaurante Adolfo, c/Granada 6.
  One of the best restaurants in town, tucked behind a marzipan
  café, in an old Jewish town house (ask to see the painted
  ceiling downstairs). Expect to pay 5000ptas a head. Closed
  Sun eve.

Alex, Plaza de Amador de los Ríos, at the top end of c/Nuncio Viejo.
  Reasonable-value restaurant in a lovely location, with a much
  cheaper café at the side.

Restaurante Los Cuatro Tiempos, c/Puerta Llana, at the southeast
corner of the cathedral.
  Excellent mid-price restaurant with local specialities and good
  tapas.

Restaurante Palacios, c/Alfonso X El Sabio 3.
  Friendly and popular local restaurant, with two *menús* – the
  cheaper one costs just 900ptas.

Bar El Tropezón, Travesía de Santa Isabel 2.
  A stone's throw from the cathedral, this outdoor bar offers
  generous meals for under 1000ptas. The fish is particularly
  good.

SEGOVIA

fter Toledo, **Segovia** is the outstanding trip from Madrid. A relatively small city, strategically sited on a rocky ridge, it is deeply and haughtily Castilian, with a panoply of squares and mansions from its days of Golden Age grandeur. For a city of its size, there is an amazing number of outstanding architectural monuments. Most celebrated are the **Roman aqueduct**, the **cathedral** and the fairy-tale **Alcázar**, but the less obvious attractions – the cluster of ancient churches and the many mansions in the lanes of the old town, all in a warm, honey-coloured stone – are what really make it worth visiting. Just a few kilometres outside the city, is the Bourbon palace of **La Granja**.

Well connected by road and rail, Segovia is an easy trip from Madrid with eight **trains** daily from Atocha (6am–8pm; 2hr; 1500ptas return), as well as up to fifteen **buses** operated by Larrea from their terminal at Paseo de la Florida 11 (Metro Príncipe Pío; Mon–Sat 6.30am–10.15pm, Sun 8am–10.15; 1hr 45min; 1230ptas return). Segovia's own **train station** is some distance out of town and you'll need to take bus #3 to the Plaza Mayor. If you are driving it's best to park outside the old city below the aqueduct. The **Turismo** (May–Sept Mon–Sat

10am–2pm & 5–8pm, Sun 10am–2pm; Oct–April Mon–Fri 10am–2pm & 5–8pm, Sat 10am–2pm; ℂ921/460334), is centrally located in the Plaza Mayor.

THE CATHEDRAL AND THE ALCÁZAR

Segovia's **Catedral** (daily 9.30am–7pm; Oct–April till 6pm) was the last major Gothic building in Spain, and arguably the last in Europe. Pinnacles and flying buttresses are tacked on at every conceivable point although the interior is surprisingly bare and its space is cramped by a great green marble choir in the very centre. The treasures are almost all confined to the museum (250ptas) which opens off the cloisters.

Behind the cathedral is the **Alcázar (**daily 10am–7pm; Oct–Apr till 6pm; 375ptas), an extraordinary fantasy of a castle, with its narrow towers and flurry of turrets. It will seem eerily familiar to just about every visitor, having served as the model for the original Disneyland castle in California. Although it dates from the fourteenth and fifteenth centuries, it was almost completely destroyed by a fire in 1862 and rebuilt as a deliberately exaggerated version of the original. It's worth visiting if only for the magnificent panoramas from the tower.

THE AQUEDUCT

The most photographed site in Segovia is its stunning **Aqueduct**. Over 800m long and at its highest point towering some 30m above the Plaza de Azoguejo, it stands up without a drop of mortar or cement. No one knows exactly when it was built, but it was probably around the end of the first century AD under the Emperor Trajan. It no longer carries water from the Río Frío to the city and in recent years traffic vibration and pollution have been threatening to undermine the entire structure. Stairs beside the aqueduct lead up on to a surviving fragment of the city walls, giving an excellent view. For the best **view** of all, take the main road north for 2km or so towards Cuéllar, and a panorama of the whole city, including the aqueduct, gradually unfolds.

VERA CRUZ

The best of Segovia's ancient churches is undoubtedly **Vera Cruz** (Tues–Sun 10.30am–1.30pm & 3.30–7pm; Oct–April till 6pm; 175ptas), a remarkable twelve-sided building outside town in the valley facing the Alcázar. It was built by the Knights Templar in the early thirteenth century on the pattern of the church of the Holy Sepulchre in Jerusalem, and once housed part of the True Cross (hence its name). You can climb the tower for a highly photogenic view of the city.

Nearby is the prodigiously walled monastery of **San Juan de la Cruz** (May–Sept Tues–Sat 10am–1.30pm & 4–7pm; Oct–April Mon–Sat 4–8pm; free), where you can visit the gaudy mausoleum of its founder saint.

LA GRANJA

Just 10km southeast of Segovia on the N601 Madrid road, and connected by regular bus services, is the Bourbon summer palace of **La Granja**, built by the first Bourbon king of Spain, Felipe V, no doubt homesick for the luxuries of Versailles. Its glories are the mountain setting, and the extravagant wooded grounds and gardens, but it's worth casting a quick eye over the **palace** (June–Sept Tues–Sun 10am–6pm; Oct–May Tues–Sat 10am–1.30pm & 3–5pm,

VERA CRUZ & LA GRANJA

Sun 10am–2pm; 650ptas). The highlight of the **gardens** (daily 10am–7pm; 325ptas) is its series of fountains, which culminate in the fifteen-metre-high jet of La Fama. They're a fantastic spectacle but usually only operate at 5.30pm at weekends and on Wednesday, with special displays on May 30, July 25 and August 25 (check at the *Turismo* first).

ACCOMMODATION

Rooms can be hard to come by even out of season, so it's worth booking ahead if you're considering more than a day-trip.

Hostal Don Jaime, c/Ochoa Ondategui 8 ✆921/444787.
Excellent *hostal* near Plaza de Azoguejo. All doubles have their own bathroom. ②.

Hotel Infanta Isabel, c/Isabel la Católica 1 ✆921/443105; fax 433240.
Comfortable new hotel – and better value than the *parador* outside town – ideally positioned on Plaza Mayor. ⑤.

Hostal Juan Bravo, c/Juan Bravo 12 ✆921/435521.
Lots of big, comfortable rooms and plant-festooned bathrooms. ②.

Hotel Los Linajes, c/Dr Velasco 9 ✆921/460475; fax 460479.
Good-value, atmospheric hotel in a quiet corner of the walled city, with a fine garden overlooking the river valley. ⑤.

EATING AND DRINKING

Segovia takes its cooking seriously, and culinary specialities include **roast suckling pig** (*cochinillo asado*) and **lamb** (*cordero*). There's a concentration of cheaper **bar-restaurants** on c/de la Infanta Isabel, off the Plaza Mayor, and

late-night bars on c/Escuderos and c/Judería Vieja, and along Avenida Fernández Ladreda.

Mesón El Campesino, c/Infanta Isabel 12.
One of the best budget restaurants in town, serving decent-value *menús* and *combinados* to a young crowd.

Bar-Mesón Cuevas de San Esteban, c/Valdeláguila 15, off the top end of Plaza San Esteban.
A cavern-restaurant and bar (serving draught beer), popular with locals. Excellent value.

Mesón de Cándido, Plaza Azoguejo 5 ©941/428103.
The city's most famous restaurant, reopened in 1992 by the founder's son and still the place for *cochinillo* and the like. The *menú* is a relatively modest 2500ptas.

La Cocina de San Millán, c/San Millán 3 ©921/436226.
A little out of the way, but the cooking is imaginative and prices are reasonable. Closed Sun eve & Jan 7–31.

Mesón José María, c/Cronista Lecea 11, just off Plaza Mayor ©921/461111.
Currently reckoned to be the city's best and most interesting restaurant, with modern variations on Castilian classics. The *menú* is a hefty 4000ptas, but there are dishes costing around 2000ptas.

EATING AND DRINKING

ÁVILA

Two things distinguish **ÁVILA** – its eleventh-century **walls**, two perfectly preserved kilometres of which surround the old town, and the mystic writer **Santa Teresa**, who was born here and whose shrines are a major focus of religious pilgrimage. Set on a high plain, with the peaks of the Sierra de Gredos behind, the town is quite a sight, especially if you time it right and approach with the evening sun highlighting the golden tone of the walls and the details of the 88 towers. There are also a number of fine **Romanesque churches** dotted in and about the old city.

From **Madrid** (Chamartín & Atocha) there are up to twelve **trains** a day to Ávila (daily 6.40am–8.30pm; 1hr 30min; 1640ptas return). **Buses** (Larrea from Estación Sur de Autobuses; Metro Méndez Alvaro) are less frequent (daily; 2hr; 1290ptas return). The main **Turismo** (Mon–Fri 9.30am–2pm & 5–8pm, Sat 9.30am–2.30pm & 4–7pm, Sun 9.30am–2.30pm & 4–6.30pm; ©920/211387) is in the Plaza de la Catedral.

SANTA TERESA IN ÁVILA

The obvious place to start a tour of Santa Teresa's Ávila is the **Convento de Santa Teresa** (daily 8.30am–1.30pm &

3.30–9pm; Oct–April till 9pm; free), built over the saint's birthplace just inside the south gate of the old town. Most of the convent remains *in clausura* but you can see the very spot where she was born. In a small reliquary (daily 9.30am–1.30pm & 3.30–7.30pm; free) there are memorials of Teresa's life, including her rosary beads and one of the fingers she used to count them with.

In the **Convento de la Encarnación** (daily: May–Sept 9.30am–1pm & 4–7pm; Oct–April 3.30–6pm; 100ptas), reached by leaving the old town through the *parador* gate and following c/de la Encarnación, each room is labelled with the act Teresa performed there, while everything she might have touched or looked at is on display. A small museum section also provides a reasonable introduction to the saint's life.

A third Teresan sight lies a couple of blocks east (away from the walls) of Plaza de Santa Teresa. The **Convento de San José** (daily 10am–1.30pm & 4–7pm; 50ptas) was the first monastery founded by the saint, in 1562. Its museum contains relics and memorabilia, including the coffin in which Teresa once slept, and assorted personal possessions. Lastly, you might want to make your way up to **Los Cuatro Postes**, a little four-posted shrine, 1500m along the Salamanca road west of town. It was here, aged seven, that the infant Teresa was recaptured by her uncle, running away with her brother to seek Christian martyrdom from the Moors.

THE CATHEDRAL AND OTHER SIGHTS

Ávila's **Catedral** (daily 10.30am–1pm & 3.30–6.30pm; 200ptas) was started in the twelfth century but has never been finished, as evidenced by the missing tower above the main entrance. The earliest Romanesque parts were as much fortress as church, and the apse actually forms an integral part of the city walls. Inside, the succeeding changes of style are immediately apparent; the Romanesque parts are made of a strange red-and-white mottled stone, then there's an abrupt break and the rest of the main structure is pure white stone and Gothic forms.

Although the proportions are exactly the same, this newer half of the cathedral seems infinitely more spacious. Here you can admire the carved stalls in the *Coro* and the treasury-museum with its monstrous silver *custodia* and ancient religious images, and the tomb of a fifteenth-century bishop known as *El Tostado* (the "toasted" or "swarthy").

Just outside the city walls, on the northeast corner, is the basilica of **San Vicente** (Tues–Sun 10am–2pm & 4–7.15pm; 50ptas) which, like the cathedral, is a mixture of architectural styles. Its twelfth-century doorways and the portico which protects them are magnificent examples of Romanesque art, while the church itself shows the influence of later trends. San Vicente was martyred on this site, and his tomb depicts a series of particularly gruesome deaths; in the crypt you can see the slab on which he and his sisters were executed by the Romans. The warm pink glow of the sandstone of the church is a characteristic aspect of Ávila, also notable in the church of **San Pedro**, on Plaza de Santa Teresa.

The **Monasterio de Santo Tomás** (daily 10am–1pm & 4-8pm; *Coro* & cloisters 50ptas; museum 11am–1pm & 4-7pm; 100ptas) is a Dominican monastery founded in 1482, but greatly expanded over the following decade by Fernando and Isabel, whose summer palace it became. Inside are three exceptional cloisters, the largest of which contains an **oriental collection**, a strangely incongruous display built up by the monks over centuries of missionary work in the Orient. Notice also the elaborate tombs and the thrones occupied by the king and queen during services. The notorious inquisitor **Torquemada** is buried in the sacristy here.

Ávila's small **Museo Provincial** is housed in the sixteenth-century Palacio de los Deanes (Tues–Sat 10.30am–2pm & 5–7.30pm, Sun 10.30am–2pm; Tues–Fri 200ptas, Sat & Sun free) which once housed the cathedral's deans. Today, its exhibits include collections of archeological remains, ceramics, carpets and furnishings from around the Ávila province.

One of the best things to do in Ávila is to walk along the **city walls** from Puerta del Alcázar to Puerta del Rastro; the view is stunning. Tickets (100ptas) are available from the green kiosk by the Puerta del Alcázar.

ACCOMMODATION

Hostal Bellas, c/Caballeros 19 ℗920/212910.
Friendly and fairly central, most rooms have showers and there are discounts out of season. ②.

Hostal Jardín, c/San Segundo 38 ℗920/211074.
Large *hostal* near Puerta de los Leales, which often has rooms when others are full. ②–③.

Hostal El Rastro, Plaza del Rastro 1 ℗920/211218; fax 251626.
A good mid-range option, this characterful old inn is set right against the walls, with a pleasant garden and popular restaurant. ③.

Palacio de Valderrábanos, Plaza de la Catedral 9 ℗920/211023; fax 251691.
This former bishop's palace beats the *parador* for ambiance. ⑥.

ACCOMMODATION

Parador Raimundo de Borgoña, c/Marqués de Canales y
Chozas 2 ©920/211340; fax 226166.
A converted fifteenth-century mansion set right next to the
city walls. The rooms in the tower are a little cramped, but it's
the cheapest of Avila's top hotels. ⑥.

EATING AND DRINKING

El Molino de la Losa, Bajada de la Losa 12.
Converted fifteenth-century mill, with a deserved reputation
and handy if you're with kids as there's a play area in the
garden. The *menú* is 3000ptas. Closed Mon & mid-Oct to
mid-March.

Mesón del Rastro, Plaza del Rastro 4.
Excellent bar, attached to the *hostal* of the same name, with a
range of tapas. Behind it is a modest-priced restaurant, an
old-fashioned place with solid, traditional food.

Bar El Rincón, Plaza Zurraquín 6.
To the north of Plaza de la Victoria, this bar serves a generous
three-course *menú*.

CONTEXTS

A brief history of Madrid

Although there is some evidence of small-scale prehistoric settlements on the banks of the Manzanares, of Roman villas around Carabanchel and a minor Visigoth settlement on the banks of a stream running down what is now Calle de Segovia, the city of Madrid was effectively founded by the **Muslims** in the ninth century. Even then it was more of a defensive outpost than a settlement in its own right. Arabic engineers soon saw the military potential of the escarpment, with its commanding views of the main routes stretching south from the Sierra Guadarrama, and used it as a way of shoring up the communications to the more prestigious city of **Toledo**. The area's other key attribute was its ready supply of water, hence its early name "mayrit" – place of many springs – successively modified to Magerit and then Madrid. Fragments of the old Arabic wall still remain on the Cuesta de la Vega beside the Almudena Cathedral.

In the late eleventh century, the city was taken by the Christians under **Alfonso VI**, although the Muslims did try to recapture it in an unsuccessful siege launched from below the Alcázar in the Campo del Moro in 1109. Nevertheless, many Muslims remained in the tangled web of streets and alleyways of **La Morería** making the most of their skills as builders and masons to help construct churches and residences; the distinctive *Mudéjar* towers of San Nicolás and San Pedro el Viejo still remain from this era. Despite being used as a royal stopover for the itinerant Castilian monarchy and the establishment in the city of several powerful religious centres such as the friary of San Francisco and the church of San Andrés, Madrid still remained a relatively insignificant backwater. The city was even given to Leo V of Armenia as a consolation prize for losing his kingdom to the Turks, although it later reverted to Castilian control.

Capital of the Empire

What changed Madrid's destiny from obscure provincial town into **capital** of the glittering Spanish empire was the caprice of one man, **Felipe II** (1556–98), who decided in 1561 permanently to locate the court here. His decision was prompted by the city's position in the centre of the recently unified Spain and his fear of giving undue influence to one of its overmighty regions. The population immediately surged with the arrival of the royal entourage and there was a boom in the building industry to house the courtiers and associated hangers-on. Much of this building was highly provisional as few thought Madrid would last very long as the capital. However, they had underestimated the determination of Felipe II who had also begun to construct the huge monastery complex-cum-mausoleum of **El Escorial** in the nearby mountains. Greater solidity and a touch of grandeur was added to the city with the appointment of **Juan Gómez de Mora** as city architect during the reign of Felipe III (1598–1621). He left his mark on the old city centre with characteristic buildings of red brick, slate roofs and needle spires which can still be seen in the Plaza Mayor and the Plaza de la Villa.

Between the mid-sixteenth and mid-seventeenth centuries, Madrid's population grew from 20,000 to over 150,000 and building continued with the foundation of a large number of **convents and monasteries** inside the city, including the Encarnación, Carboneras and Comendadoras which survive today. It was during this period also that the palace of **El Buen Retiro** was built, a royal village on the east side of the city to house and provide entertainment for the court.

However, the city was still very much one of outsiders and immigrants, a city of consumption rather than production. All was not well with the overstretched and beleaguered

Spanish empire and the increasingly inbred Habsburg dynastic line dried up with the chronically ill and malformed Carlos II. He died in 1700, his demise hastened no doubt by the succession of cures doled out to him by his doctors.

With the emergence of the **Bourbon dynasty**, a touch of French style was introduced into the capital. **Felipe V**, used to the luxuries of Versailles, was somewhat disappointed with the capital of his new inheritance, and proceeded to construct a grand country villa at **La Granja**. In the wake of the 1734 fire at the Alcázar, he took the opportunity to build an altogether more sumptuous affair in the shape of the **Palacio Real**. Baroque flourishes were added to the city with the buildings of **Pedro de Ribera**, including the Hospice (now the Museo Municipal) and the Cuartel del Conde Duque, while under **Carlos III** (1759–88), the "*Rey-Alcalde*" (King-Mayor), more thoroughgoing plans were made to make the city into a home worthy of the monarchy. The notoriously filthy streets were cleaned up, sewers and street lighting installed and work began on the creation of an intellectual showcase of museums and research centres along the **Paseo del Prado**. Madrid undoubtedly became a more pleasant place to live, but Carlos's foreign tastes didn't always meet with the approval of the *Madrileño* population. **Riots** broke out in 1766 protesting at increased food prices and the introduction of a ban on long capes and wide brimmed hats which the Italian minister Squillache had claimed were used by thieves to conceal their weapons.

Invasion and occupation

The improvements in Madrid lost momentum under the slothful **Carlos IV**, and the rise of the corrupt **Manuel Godoy** in the early years of the nineteenth century increasingly placed Spain under the influence of Napoleonic France. In March 1808, **French troops** entered the capital and many suspected that the royal family was preparing to flee. Tension mounted until it culminated in a rising against the French troops on **May 2, 1808**, with the heavily out-gunned *Madrileños* eventually having to admit defeat. The rising and the subsequent reprisals by the French entered Spanish folklore, especially after they were immortalized by Goya in his two magnificent canvases now hanging in the Prado. **Napoleon** installed his brother Joseph (nicknamed "*Pepe Botella*" because of his alleged susceptibility to a drink or two) on the throne and although highly unpopular he did begin a whole series of projects designed to create more open spaces in the cramped city; his legacy can be seen in the plazas Santa Ana and Oriente. Nevertheless there was also much **destruction**, with the plundering of the Prado and the virtual destruction of El Buen Retiro.

Division and instability

Once the French were removed by a combined Spanish and English army, the monarchy made a return under the myopic reactionary figure of **Fernando VII** in 1814, who soon annulled the liberal Cádiz Constitution of 1812. The lines were now drawn that were to scar Spanish society and politics for the next 150 years. One Spain (progressive, anti-clerical, constitutional) lined up against another (conservative, catholic and authoritarian). At first these divisions confined themselves to the emerging café society and *tertulias*, but with the disputed succession after Fernando's death, they soon exploded into a series of conflicts known as the **Carlist wars** and led to constant political instability, including a brief period as a republic until the monarchy under **Alfonso XII** was restored in 1875.

At the same time, Madrid was experiencing significant **social changes** with rapid growth of the population from 200,000 at the end of the eighteenth century to 300,000 by the 1860s and with the emergence of a genuine **working class** less tied to the established institutions of state. The Socialist party, the **PSOE**, was founded in 1879 in *Casa Labra* in the city. Madrid began to expand north with the construction of the working-class district of **Chamberí** and the development of the area that came to bear his name by the flamboyant speculator, the Marqués de **Salamanca**. The railway, improved water supply via the Canal Isabel II, the metro, electricity, trams and the construction of the Gran Vía all came to Madrid within the next 35 years. Despite these improvements many of the underlying divisions in Spanish society remained. Confidence was further undermined and the monarchy further discredited by the loss of Cuba and the Philippines in 1898, and this prompted a period of deep self-contemplation by intellectuals and politicians, sparking off the great work of writers such as Baroja and Antonio Machado known as the **"Generation of '98"**.

The Second Republic and the rise of Franco

Despite Spanish neutrality in **World War I**, the economy ran into problems in the 1920s and a hard-line military regime under the Captain-General of Barcelona, **Miguel Primo de Rivera** took control from 1923 to 1930 with King Alfonso XIII relegated to the background. When republican candidates unexpectedly swept the board in the 1931 municipal elections, the king decided to quit. The **Second Republic** was ushered in in a cloud of unrealistic expectations, but had to cope not only with the divided Spanish society, but also with the impact of the Great Depression. Political polarization continued, and when the

Popular Front won the 1936 elections the Right grew increasingly restless and called for the army to save the country. The ensuing **rising by the generals** in July 1936 was only partially successful and in Madrid the troops that barricaded themselves inside the Montaña barracks in Parque del Oeste were massacred by defenders of the Republic. Thus Madrid became a **Republican stronghold** with a revolutionary atmosphere prevailing in the city; many of the city's churches and religious institutions were torched by Anarchists. By late October, the city was **under attack** by **Franco's Nationalists**, with some of the fiercest fighting of the war occurring along the Carretera de la Coruña and in the Ciudad Universitaria. However, the arrival of the International Brigades, the firm resistance of the *Madrileño* population and the discovery of the Nationalist plans to attack the city, thwarted Franco's efforts and a long drawn-out **siege** began. The city was regularly shelled by the Nationalists camped out in Casa de Campo, where traces of trenches and bunkers can still be found. Shortages were terrible and meat and vegetables were hardly ever available. By 1939 divisions began to emerge between Republican groups prepared to negotiate with Franco and those who, together with the Communists, saw this as tantamount to political suicide. **Franco** and his victorious Nationalists eventually entered the city in March 1939. There was little sign of graciousness in victory from the general – mass reprisals took place and Republicans were executed, imprisoned, forced into hiding or had to flee the country. While *El Caudillo* installed himself in the country residence of **El Pardo**, just to the north of the city, Republican prisoners were put to work on the monstrous war memorial – later to house *El Caudillo*'s tomb – **El Valle de los Caídos**.

Spain had to endure yet more suffering during the postwar years – *los años de hambre* (the years of hunger) until the turn-around in **American policy** which rehabilitated Franco in a desperate search for anti-Communist Cold War allies. Madrid again experienced massive growth with the population trebling between 1930 and 1970 to reach three million. The **monumentalist architecture** of this period can be seen in the buildings of the Ministerio del Aire, Nuevos Ministerios and the Edificio de España. Waves of **immigrants** set up home on the outskirts of town, many in shanty town developments (*chabolas*). As the Spanish economy took off with mass tourism and the assistance of the IMF and World Bank, Madrid became more industrial with significant enterprises developing in the south and east of the city.

The return to democracy

By the early 1970s Franco was clearly ailing and the assassination of the man he was grooming to be his successor, **Admiral Carrero Blanco**, in a spectacular car bomb in c/Claudio Coello placed by the Basque terrorist organization, ETA, that catapulted his car over a nearby five-storey building, shook the regime to its foundations. The moribund Franco eventually died in November 1975. **King Juan Carlos**, chosen by the dictator to succeed him, eventually appointed **Adolfo Suarez** to take over the reins of government and he presided over the transition to democracy with the holding of the first democratic elections since 1936 and the drawing up of a new constitution. Much greater power was given to Spain's regions and Madrid became a *Comunidad Autónoma*, with its own elected regional government. The military, however, hadn't yet quite given up and in its last gasp attempt to re-establish itself, the Civil Guard commander, **Colonel Tejero**, stormed the Cortes in Madrid, firing his revolver and demanding everyone hit the floor. For a moment it looked as if the days of dictatorship were about to return, but lack of support from Juan Carlos in his TV broadcast and lack of commitment from a number of the army brigades saw it collapse. It was the Socialists under **Felipe González** who profited from the bungled coup attempt and proceeded to win the 1982 elections, remaining in power until 1996.

The new spirit: la movida and beyond

In Madrid, the freedom from the shackles of military dictatorship and the release of long pent-up creative forces helped to create **la movida**, an outpouring of hedonistic, highly innovative and creative forces that was embodied by the rise of **Pedro Almodóvar** and his internationally acclaimed films. The work of the city's Socialist mayor, **Enrique Tierno Galván**, also helped make Madrid the place to be in the late 1970s and early 1980s. He rejuvenated Madrid's old *fiestas* of San Isidro, poured money into cultural events and helped oversee the **modernization** of the city. The concentration on international prestige projects like the Olympics, Expo and the more downbeat nomination of Madrid as European Cultural Capital in 1992, placed Spain firmly on the international map once again.

However, the transition to democracy hasn't been quite as smooth as it may appear. The Socialists became increasingly discredited as they moved to the Right and were engulfed in a web of ever more incredible **scandals and corruption** until they lost control of Madrid in 1991 and the country in 1996 to the conservative Partido Popular under **José María Aznar**, the former tax collector and antithesis of charisma. Cuts in spending have replaced generous funding and the days of *la movida* have certainly passed, but the authorities are still committed to rehabilitating the centre of

Madrid and the city has developed a taste for enjoying itself that nothing can remove. Madrid has now made the transition from provincial backwater to major European capital, yet at the same time preserving its own stylish and quirky identity.

Books

The listings below represent a highly selective reading list on Spain in general and on Madrid itself. In the reviews, publishers are listed in the format UK/US, unless the title is published in one country only, in which case we've specified the country. If you have difficulty finding any titles, an excellent source for books about Spain – new, used and out of print – is Books on Spain, PO Box 207, Twickenham TW2 5BQ, UK ✆/fax 0181/898 7789.

The Best Introductions

Ian Gibson, *Fire in the Blood: The New Spain* (Faber/BBC, UK). Although not universally acclaimed in Spain itself, this is a splendid commentary on the Spanish people which accompanied the author's television series on Spain in 1992. Gibson is a passionate writer who makes a valiant attempt to describe and explain the complexity and contradictions of modern Spain and Spanish society.

John Hooper, *The New Spaniards* (Penguin UK & US). Revised, expanded and updated edition of Hooper's guide to contemporary Spain which first appeared as *The Spaniards*. It provides excellent and comprehensive coverage of all aspects of life in modern Spain, from the monarchy, the Church, the role of women, education, corruption, the regions and bullfighting. A perfect book for anyone wanting to scratch deeper.

History

J.H. Elliott. *Imperial Spain 1469–1716* (Penguin UK & US). The standard work on the Spanish Golden Age. It is elegantly written, highly readable and characterized by thorough research throughout.

Ronald Fraser, *Blood of Spain* (Pantheon, US). Subtitled "The Experience of Civil War, 1936–39", this is an impressive piece of research, constructed entirely of vivid oral accounts of these turbulent years.

Geoffrey Parker, *Philip II* (Hutchinson, UK o/p). Entertaining, accurate and revealing portrait of the most powerful man of his age, based upon Philip's personal papers and memoranda. Philip is brought to life in this compelling biography.

Paul Preston, *Franco* (HarperCollins, UK & US). On a par with Thomas's epic account of the Civil War, this monumental biography of the Caudillo is a truly enthralling read, tracing the genesis of Franco's dictatorship right through to his final few hours. Perceptive insights into Franco's background and upbringing and the evolution of his icy character.

Hugh Thomas, *Madrid, A Traveller's Companion* (Constable, UK) and *The Spanish Civil War* (Penguin, UK & US). The first is a varied anthology of travel writings on Madrid with a fine introduction to the city's history, while the latter gives a masterful account of the causes and course of the tragic history of the Spanish Civil War. An immense work of scholarship, this is the definitive account of the war. Initially difficult to wade through the complexities of the prewar era, but ultimately an extremely rewarding book.

Recent Travels

David Gilmour, *Cities of Spain* (Pimlico/Ivan R. Dee). Contains a well-written and evocative chapter on Madrid.

Michael Jacobs, *Madrid Observed* (Pallas Athene, UK).
Opinionated, witty and well observed, containing thoroughly
researched thematic walks around Madrid.

Art and Architecture

Jonathan Brown, *Velázquez: Painter and Courtier* (Yale, US). A
detailed study of the great painter.

J.H. Elliott and Jonathan Brown, *A Palace for a King: The
Buen Retiro and the Court of Philip IV* (Yale, US). Closely
researched account of the grandeur of the Habsburg Court.

Pierre Gassier, *Goya, A Witness of His Times* (Alpine, UK). A
comprehensive biography of the painter and the period in
which he lived .

Fiction

Miguel de Cervantes, *Don Quixote* (Penguin/Signet). No
apologies for including a classic sixteenth-century novel in a
reading list for contemporary Spain. The highly amusing
account of the adventures of the eccentric knight is a must if
you are to understand the Spanish character and outlook on
life, at least from the perspective of Castile La Mancha.

Benito Pérez Galdós, *Fortunata y Jacinta* (Penguin, UK & US).
Late nineteenth-century classic piece of detailed social
observation set against the backdrop of the political turmoil of
1860s Madrid.

Camilo José Cela, *The Family of Pascual Duarte* (Little Brown,
UK & US). The Nobel Prize-winner's portrayal of a family in the
aftermath of the Spanish Civil War. Another masterpiece, *The
Hive*, focuses on the comings and goings of a group of
characters frequenting a Madrid café in the postwar years.

Glossary of Spanish terms

Alcázar Moorish fortified palace.

Ayuntamiento Town hall.

Azulejo Glazed ceramic tilework.

Barrio Suburb or quarter.

Bodega Cellar, wine bar or warehouse.

Calle Street.

Capilla Mayor Chapel containing the high altar.

Capilla Real Royal chapel.

Castizo Traditional *Madrileño*.

Convento Monastery or convent.

Coro Central part of church built for the choir.

Correos Post office.

Corrida de toros bullfight.

Ermita Hermitage.

Iglesia Church.

Madrileño Inhabitant of Madrid or used to describe something pertaining to the city.

Mercado Market.

Mirador Viewing point.

Monasterio Monastery or convent.

Mudéjar Muslim Spaniard subject to medieval Christian rule, but retaining Islamic worship. Most commonly a term applied to architecture which includes buildings built by Moorish craftsmen for the Christian rulers and later designs inflluenced by the Moors.

Palacio Palace.

Parador State-run luxury hotel.

Paseo Promenade; also the evening stroll.

Patio Inner courtyard.

Plateresque Elaborately decorative Renaissance style. Named for its resemblance to silversmiths' work.

Plaza Square.

Plaza de toros Bullring.
Posada Old name for an inn.
Puerta Gateway.
Sacristía Sacristy or sanctuary of a church.
Terraza Outdoor bar or café annexe, often summer only.
Tertulia Semi-formalized discussion group.
Turismo Tourist office.
Zarzuela Madrid's own form of light opera.

INDEX

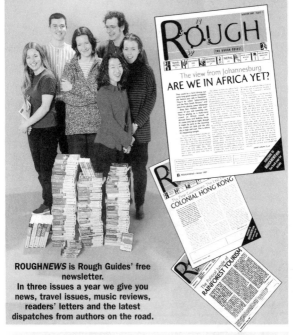

Stay in touch with us!

The view from Johannesburg
ARE WE IN AFRICA YET?

COLONIAL HONG KONG

RAINFOREST TOURISM

**ROUGH*NEWS* is Rough Guides' free
newsletter.
In three issues a year we give you
news, travel issues, music reviews,
readers' letters and the latest
dispatches from authors on the road.**

I would like to receive ROUGH*NEWS*: please put me on your free mailing list.

NAME . . . .

ADDRESS . . . .

Please clip or photocopy and send to: Rough Guides, 1 Mercer Street, London
WC2H 9QJ, England

or Rough Guides, 375 Hudson Street, New York, NY 10014, USA.

Backpacking through **Europe**?
Cruising across the **US** of **A**?
Clubbing in **London**?
Trekking through **Costa Rica**?

South Africa
THE ROUGH GUIDE

Barbara McCrea, Tony Pinchuck and Greg Mthembu-Salter
INCLUDES FULL-COLOUR WILDLIFE GUIDE

India
THE ROUGH GUIDE

David Abram, Devdan Sen,
Harriet Sharkey and Gareth John Williams

USA
THE ROUGH GUIDE

Samantha Cook, Jamie Jensen,
Tim Perry & Greg Ward

ROUGH
Travel Guides to more than
from Amsterdam...

AT GOOD BOOKSHOPS

Wherever you're headed, **Rough Guides** tell you
what's happening – the history, the people,
the politics, the best beaches, nightlife and
entertainment on your budget

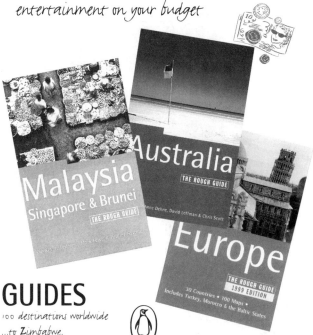

GUIDES
100 destinations worldwide
...to Zimbabwe.

DISTRIBUTED BY PENGUIN

CUESTA DE VEGA

Campo del Moro

Jardines de Sabatini

PL. MARINA ESPAÑOLA

CALLE DE BAILÉN

SAN VICENTE

CALLE DE BAILÉN

Palacio Real

PLAZA ARMERÍA

N

Catedral Ntra. Sra. de la Almudena

Parque Emir Mohammed I

CALLE

Capitanía General

Casa de la Villa

Casa de Cisneros

La Basílica de San Miguel

Convento de la Encarnación

Senado

Jardines Cabo Naval

PLAZA ENCARNACIÓN

PAVIA

CALLE TORIJA

CALLE LA BOLA

PLAZA DE ORIENTE

Jardines de Lepanto

CALLE REQUENA

C. NOBLEZAS

CALLE DE FACTOR

CALLE MAYOR

PLAZA DE LA VILLA

C. SACRAMENTO

C. NICOLÁS

San Nicolás de los Servitas

Torre de los Lujanes

CALLE MAYOR

CDE MIRANDA

INDEPENDENCIA

SANTIAGO

PLAZA SANTIAGO

Iglesia de Santiago

C. AMNISTÍA

RAMALES

C. SEÑORES LUZÓN

C. BARCA

FELIPE V

CARLOS III

CALLE DE VERGARA

PLAZA ISABEL II

M ÓPERA

Teatro Real

ESCALINATA

CALLE ARRIETA

CALLE SANTO DOMINGO

CTA. FOMENTO

M SANTO DOMINGO

PLAZA SANTO DOMINGO

VENERAS

JACOMETREZO

CALLE

Cine Callao

PLAZA CALLAO

M CALLAO

M CALLAO

GRAN VÍA

100 m

0

ROMANOS

CHINCHILLA

C. DE LA SALUD

MESONERO

CALLE DE ABADA

PL. DEL CARMEN

C. DEL CARMEN

TETUÁN

PL. CARMEN

SOL M

M

PLAZA PUERTA DEL SOL

CALLE DE LA PAZ

PLAZA JACINTO BENAVENTE

Casa de Correos

CALLE BOLSA

C DE ATOCHA

Palacio de Santa Cruz

PLAZA PROVINCIA

IMPERIAL

LECHUGA

C. ZARAGOZA

SAL

PLAZA PONTEJOS

CALLE PONTEJOS

ESPARTEROS

CALLE MAYOR

POSTAS

SOL M

ARENAL

San Ginés

CALLE

PLAZA DESCALZAS

DESCALZAS

CALLE CELENQUE

MAESTRO

VICTORIA

POST SAN MARTÍN

PLAZA SAN MARTÍN

TUDESCOS

Monasterio de las Descalzas Reales

PRECIADOS

CALLE DEL

Casa de Panadería

PLAZA MAYOR

CALLE DE TOLEDO

CAVA SAN MIGUEL

C. CUCHILLEROS

PLAZA S. MIGUEL

C. CIUDAD RODRIGO

CAVA DE SAN MIGUEL

C. HERRADORES

PRINCESA

C. BORDADORES

SAN MARTÍN

HILERAS

COSTANILLA DE LOS ÁNGELES

PL. SANTA CATALINA

CALLE FLORA

P. DONADOS

CAÑOS DEL PERAL

TRUJILLOS

CONCHAS

LOS ÁNGELES

FUENTES

BONETILLO

C. MORENAS

3

Campo del Moro

Casa de Correos
PLAZA PUERTA DEL SOL
PLAZA PONTE- JOS
CALLE DE LA PAZ
CALLE MAYOR
COSTAS
SAL M V
CALLE BOLSA
C DE ATOCHA
DOCTOR CORTEZO
PLAZA JACINTO BENAVENTE
M TIRSO DE MOLINA
PLAZA TIRSO DE MOLINA

Palacio de Santa Cruz
CONDE DE ROMANONES
JERÓNIMA
PLAZA PROVINCIA
CONCEPCION
CALLE JESUS Y MARIA
CALLE DEL AMPARO
CALLE ESPADA
PLAZA DE MOLINA
CALLE DEL MESON DE PAREDES

San Isidro
CALLE DE LA COLEGIATA
PLAZA DUQUE DE ALBA
CALLE DUQUE DE
ESTUDIOS
CALLE JUANELO
ENCOMIENDA
DOS HERMANAS
CALLE LOS ABADES
OSO
I
H
San Cayetano

Casa de Panadería
PLAZA MAYOR i
CALLE BORDADORES
IMPERIAL
LECHUGA
CALLE
CALLE DE TOLEDO
PLAZA SEGOVIA NUEVA
CALLE GRAFAL
CALLE DE TOLEDO
BRUNO
CALLE MILLAN
CALLE CASCORRO
C RIBERA DE CURTIDORES
SANTA ANA
G

PLAZA HERRADORES
PL C MORENAS
BONETILLO
TRV BRINGAS
C.S MIGUEL CUCHILLEROS
C. MORENAS
PLAZA SAN MIGUEL
PL C BARAJAS
PEPITA GERRADA
CAVA ALTA
CAVA BAJA
CALLE NUNCIO
LA LATINA M
PLAZA PUERTA CERRADA
LA LATINA
CALLE TOLEDO
RIDA
LUCIENTE
CALLE DE TOLEDO
F

Torre de los Lujanes
La Basílica de San Miguel
San Pedro el Viejo
BORDADO
CALLE MAYOR
CDE MIRANDA
PL CONDE MIRANDA
PLAZA DE LA VILLA
SAN JUSTO
PLAZA JUSTO
CALLE DE SEGOVIA
AMENDRO
Capilla del Obispo
Capilla de San Isidro
CALLE HUMILLADERO
Mercado de la Cebada
PLAZA HUMILLADERO
ORIENTE
CALLE HUMILLADERO
E

San Nicolás de los Servitas
Casa de la Villa
Casa de Cisneros
PLAZA RAMALES
PL SANTIAGO
C LEMOS
C SEÑORES LUZON
C BARCA
C NICOLAS
CALLE SACRAMENTO
PLAZA CORDON
PLAZA DE LA PAJA
San Andrés
PLAZA DE LOS CARROS
PL PTA DE MOROS
C DE CALATRAVA
D

Capitanía General
CALLE DE FACTOR
CALLE MAYOR
PRINCIPE ANGLONA
PLAZA DE LA MORERIA
CALLE ANGOSTA DE MANCEBOS
DON PEDRO
SAN ISIDRO
FRANCISCO
AGUAS
LABRADOR
CALLE PUERTA
San Francisco el Grande
PLAZA SAN FRANCISCO
C

Catedral Ntra. Sra. de la Almudena
PLAZA ARMERIA
CALLE DE BAILEN
CALLE MAYOR
Muralle Árabe
Parque Emr Mohammed I
CALLE DE SEGOVIA
CALLE REDONDILLA
CALLE DE BAILEN
CALLE SEGUE
B

CUESTA DE LA VEGA
CALLE DE SEGOVIA
Jardines de las Vistillas
CALLE BEATRIZ GALINDO
CALLE SAN BUENAVENTURA
CALLE YESERIE
N
A

1 2 3 4 5 6 7

0 100 m

4

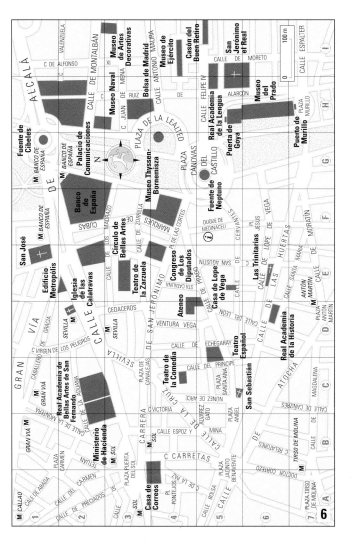

VALENZUELA

C DE ALFONSO

ALCALÁ

C DE MONTALBAN

Museo de Artes Decorativas

XI

CALLE DE MORETO

CALLE ESPALTER

0   100 m

Museo Naval

C JUAN DE MENA

Bolsa de Madrid

CALLE ANTONIO MAURA

Museo de Ejército

Cason del Buen Retiro

San Jerónimo el Real

C. RUIZ

DE

FELIPE IV

ALARCÓN

Museo del Prado

Fuente de Cibeles

DE

ESPAÑA

M BANCO DE ESPAÑA

Palacio de Comunicaciones

M BANCO DE ESPAÑA

PLAZA DE LA LEALTED

N

Real Academia de la Lengua

Puerta de Goya

PLAZA MURILLO

Puerto de Murillo

CUBAS

Banco de España

DE MADRAZO

Museo Thyssen-Bornemisza

MARQUES

PLAZA DEL CASTILLO

Fuente de Neptuno

CANOVAS

H

G

San José

Edificio Metropolis

Iglesia de las Calatravas

DE LOS

CALLE DE ZORRILLA

Circulo de Bellas Artes

Teatro de la Zarzuela

DE

PLAZA DE LAS CORTES

Congreso de Los Diputados

DE

DUQUE DE MEDINACELI

(i)

DE CERVANTES

PL VEGA

DE LOPE DE VEGA

JESUS

F

GRAN VIA GRACIA

M SEVILLA

CALLE

SEVILLA

CEDACEROS

SEVILLA

DE SAN JERÓNIMO

Ateneo

Casa de Lope de Vega

STA CATALINA

SAN AGUSTIN

CALLE DEL LEON

Las Trinitarias

CALLE DE LAS

HUERTAS

SANTA MARIA

MORATIN

DE

E

C VIRGEN DE LOS PELIGROS

VENTURA VEGA

CALLE DE

ECHEGARAY

LEON

Teatro Español

CALLE DE LAS

Real Academia de la Historia

ANTON MARTIN

M ANTON MARTIN

PLAZA

GRAN VIA

CABALLERO

PLAZA DE CANALEJAS

Teatro de la Comedia

CALLE DEL PRINCIPE

PLAZA SANTA ANA

NUÑEZ DE ARCE

San Sebastián

DE

ATOCHA

MAGDALENA

C

GRAN VIA M

GRAN VIA

Real Academia de Bellas Artes de San Fernando

CALLE DE LA ADUANA

C VICTORIA

CALLE DE LA CRUZ

ALVAREZ GATO

MINA

PLAZA ANGEL

CALLE

DE CAÑIZARES

B

CALLE DE ABADA

PLAZA CARMEN

CALLE DEL CARMEN

CALLE DE PRECIADOS

Ministerio de Hacienda

M SOL

CARRERA

CALLE ESPOZ Y

C CARRETAS

PLAZA PUERTA DEL SOL

M SOL

MINA

C CARRETAS

PLAZA JACINTO BENAVENTE

DE RELATORES

CALLE

DOCTOR CORTEZO

TIRSO DE MOLINA

M

A

CALLAO M

PLAZA PUERTA DEL SOL

M SOL

Casa de Correos

PL PONTEJOS

DE LA PAZ

CALLE BOLSA

PLAZA DE MOLINA

PLAZA TIRSO DE MOLINA

M

6

1   2   3   4   5   6   7

	A	B	C	D	E	F	G

CALLE DE ALCALÁ

1 Palacio de Linares

PLAZA INDEPENDENCIA

Puerta de Alcalá

RETIRO M

DE ALCALÁ

PUERTA MADRID

PLAZA COSTA RICA

Casita del Pescador

PUERTA AMERICA

PUERTA HERNANI

Quiosco de Música

PUERTA INDEPENDENCIA

PLAZA GALICIA

CALLE

2 Palacio de Comunicaciones

CALLE

AV. MEJICO

PO REPUBLICA DOMINICANA

Casa de Vacas

PASEO DE COLOMBIA

PUERTA REINA MERCEDES

PLAZA NICARAGUA

CALLE DE MONTALBAN

CALLE

PLAZA GUATEMALA

PO REPUBLICA PANAMÁ

Museo Naval

ALFONSO

3 C. RUIZ

JUAN DE MENA

C ANTONIO MAURA

Museo de Artes Decorativas

PUERTA ESPAÑA

PASEO DE ARGENTINA

SALÓN DEL ESTANQUE

Estanque

Monumento a Alfonso XII

PUERTA SAINZ DE BARANDA

GTA SARDANA

La Bolsa

DE ALARCON

CALLE MÉNDEZ NÚÑEZ

Museo del Ejército

PUERTA FELIPE IV

PO DE VENEZUELA

Jardines de Cecilio Rodríguez

4 CALLE FELIPE IV

Casón del Buen Retiro

PO PARAGUAY

PLAZA HONDURAS

Palacio de Velázquez

FERNÁN

C DE MORETO

San Jerónimo el Real

Real Academia de la Lengua

PO DE LA REPUBLICA

Lago

NÚÑEZ

5 **Museo del Prado**

ALFONSO

PASEO DE SAN PABLO

PUERTA MURILLO

Parque del Retiro

Palacio de Cristal

PLAZA MURILLO

CALLE ESPALTER

6 Los Jardines Botánicos

XII

LA CHOPERA

PO DE CUBA

GLORIETA PÉREZ GALDOS

GLORIETA ANGEL CAIDO

PO DE VENEZUELA

La Rosaleda

PUERTA ANGEL CALDO

PO DUQUE DE FERNÁN NÚÑEZ

PO DUQUE DE FERNÁN

7 CLAUDIO MOYANO

Ministerio de Agricultura

VIVEROS MUNICIPALES

N

M ATOCHA

ATOCHA M

DUQUE VELAZCO

Museo de Etnología

Observatorio Astronómico

CALLE

PLAZA MARIANO DE CAVIA

8 ATOCHA M

ATOCHA RENFE

M ATOCHA RENFE

PO INFANTA ISABEL

CRISTINA

JULIAN GAYARRE

PO REINA

9 ATOCHA RENFE M

Estación de Atocha

0   100 m

Panteón Hombres Illustres

FUENTERRABIA

Real Fabrica de Tapices

8

MADRID METRO